the canals of mars

A MEMOIR

GARY FINCKE

MICHIGAN STATE UNIVERSITY PRESS EAST LANSING

Copyright © 2010 by Gary Fincke

☉ The paper used in this publication meets the minimum requirements of ANSI/NISO Z39.48-1992 (R 1997) (Permanence of Paper).

 Michigan State University Press
East Lansing, Michigan 48823-5245

Printed and bound in the United States of America.

16 15 14 13 12 11 10   1 2 3 4 5 6 7 8 9 10

LIBRARY OF CONGRESS CATALOGING-IN-PUBLICATION DATA
Fincke, Gary.
The canals of mars / Gary Fincke.
p. cm.
ISBN 978-0-87013-880-5 (pbk.: alk. paper) 1. Fincke, Gary—Childhood and youth.
2. Authors, American—20th century—Biography. I. Title.
PS3556.I457Z46 2010
813'.54—dc22
[B]
2009045078

Cover and book design by Charlie Sharp, Sharp Des!gns, Lansing, Michigan

g green press initiative Michigan State University Press is a member of the Green Press Initiative and is committed to developing and encouraging ecologically responsible publishing practices. For more information about the Green Press Initiative and the use of recycled paper in book publishing, please visit *www.greenpressinitiative.org.*

Visit Michigan State University Press on the World Wide Web at *www.msupress.msu.edu*

As always, for Liz, and in memory of my parents.

Contents

Endings

the canals of mars

The names of relatives and people I know very well are real.
The names of those I've lost contact with have been changed.

Beginnings

"I want to find the farm where The Prince fell off the silo," I tell my father as we cross Route 8 and head into territory I haven't visited in nearly thirty years.

"A farm like that won't be there after all this time," he says.

Passing another new housing development, I see the sense of his caution, but I say, "Let's find out."

We drive for almost an hour, taking each of the through roads, looking for where The Prince, my grandfather, lived for nearly fifteen years in a sort of halfway house between a dissolved marriage and the charity home where he spent the last two decades of his life. We cross and then recross the Pennsylvania Turnpike, so I know we're close because I remember my father pointing and saying how that road, just completed, was the first of its kind in the United States. The third time we pass over the turnpike, I remember the mink farm we drove by just before we arrived. I never saw those minks, but each time my father would announce it—"There's the mink farm"—and I'd stare at the long, low buildings, expecting to see women in brand new luxurious coats saunter out the doors.

The Ass-End of Everything

"Turn up here," my father suddenly says. "This is it, right across from what's left of that orchard. That's where Huggins' Farm was." The sign, when I crest the hill, says Treesdale, which turns out to be a luxury golf course and expensive houses. "My guess is out there somewhere is Huggins' Farm. Maybe a half dozen of those holes and some of those mansions."

The golf course looks perfect, as if nobody plays on it. As if it were there for scenery from the windows and decks of the half-million-dollar houses set back to shank distance from the fairways. Were he alive, The Prince, skillful with a knife, could have carved miniature sets of clubs from balsa wood or, more profitably, from soap. Those wealthy enough to belong to this club would refuse the wood, but they would buy soap shaped like the head of an oversized driver or the grooved face of a sand wedge.

I slow down, but we keep moving, leaving the fairways behind. "I thought it was Rabold's Farm," I say. "I never heard of Huggins' Farm."

"The Prince lived at Huggins'."

"But we visited Rabold's?"

"Yes. Your mother walked to Huggins'. It was almost next door. The rest of us didn't visit The Prince. I worked for Rabold when I first started in the bakery."

"They had a retarded kid who scared me."

"Down Syndrome," my father says. "So did the Huggins."

Walking distance. Less than a mile apart, then, those farm houses, and two Down Syndrome boys of nearly the same age. Coincidence? Something in the water? When I ask my father, he says, "Nobody talked about such things in 1950." But it's no wonder I was confused. The Down Syndrome double play is the sort of detail that makes a story implausible. In fiction, I would strike one of those retarded boys. And I would make The Prince worse.

"So I just think we were visiting The Prince. We really weren't?"

"Oh no. Never."

"But he was within walking distance?"

"Well, call it what you want."

It was absurd, of course, that my father, my sister, and I visited one farm so my mother could visit with her father at another. And it was miraculous that The Prince tumbled off the top of a silo and not only lived, but walked away unharmed—relaxed as a cat, according to Aunt Margaret, my mother's oldest sister, by alcohol. "He looked like Little Boy Blue in that haystack," Aunt Margaret would say every time she told that story. "The s o b. Only an old stew would live through a fall like that."

He fell in 1950, the same summer my parents took my sister and me with them to visit Bethesda Children's Home, the orphanage overseen by a friend of my parents. We took a tour around the spacious grounds and ended up entering the dining hall when hundreds of children of all ages were sitting down to Sunday dinner. "Children," the director said, "I have someone to introduce to you. These are the Finckes, Judy and Gary. Welcome them to Bethesda."

The children clapped, but I had just turned five years old and became terrified by the last sentence. *My sister and I were staying!* She waved and smiled like an idiot who was happy to move into Bethesda, and I began to cry, convinced I was about to be led to a seat along the benches.

I took a step forward and turned to plead with the director just as he extended his hands. "Aren't you feeling well?" he said, leading me up the stairs into daylight.

My parents were sitting in chairs talking with the director's parents. "Did you fall?" my mother said.

"No."

"What's wrong then?"

"Nothing," I said, and I smiled so broadly I could have blossomed into my own version of Down Syndrome, goofy and congenial. I had another year before I started first grade. By that time, The Prince was taken in by the St. Barnabas Home, where at first he worked for room and board, before becoming, like all the other residents, an outright charity case.

My father, earlier in the afternoon, handed me the hospital bill for my birth. "You might want this," he said, and I followed the numbers down the column to the total: $95.96. After deductions for his "subscriber savings," my birth cost him and my mother $15.80.

Remarkable, considering my mother and I both stayed in the hospital for ten days in July, 1945: $6.00 a day for my mother, $1.00 per day for me.

So I came cheaply into this world, but I'd been asking my father for information, not about my mother's son, but about her father, and he finally handed me a handwritten letter from July 1920. The volunteer fire company had passed a resolution congratulating my grandfather on the birth of his daughter Ruth and wished to thank him for "the box of cigars presented to the company."

Now I was getting somewhere. Soon I had pictures, newspaper clippings, and a series of anecdotes my father was willing to tell, nearly all of them preceded by the qualification, "I never told your mother this, but . . . ."

Because all of the stories had alcohol in them. Because all of the stories featured waste of some kind—money, jobs, friends, family, respect.

"He made some sort of mistake with the furnace," my father said, explaining how my grandfather lost his job as the high school janitor. "A dangerous one."

I understood the mistake to have arisen from alcohol. I understood that without a job, sixteen years after the firemen had congratulated him, my grandfather was lost, eventually becoming a farm hand for room and board, and then, at last, becoming a destitute resident of a charity home. There was no divorce, an action unthinkable to my grandmother, but my mother's family had locked him out of his house for good.

Tracing a family tree is often a leisure-time activity, like collecting stamps or coins or all the commemorative plates replicating *Gone with the Wind* characters,

advertised in the Sunday paper. Often it's a matter of "roots," trying to get at the place and culture of family origin.

Because it's not a matter of all the "begats" of family history, where my ancestors lived, what church they went to, their politics or ethnicity. It's a matter of behavior. It's a matter of values. It's the passing down of fears and ambitions and weaknesses.

A student in one of my writing workshops had told me, the week before, how she'd found a bottle of vodka in every drawer in her father's bedroom. Among underwear, between shirts, under sweaters, even beneath a sheaf of bills saved for income-tax deductions.

Another student had begun his memoir with this sentence: "'Matt, make me another fucking drink,' my father said every time we were home together at night during my senior year in high school." My grandfather, however, never drank in his house. Which is why, my father says, as we drive back to Etna, he lasted as long as he did.

I knew about the private club most often frequented by my grandfather. I knew the DOH ("Doors of Hell," according to my Aunt Margaret) and its bar had survived the sixty years since my grandfather had leaned on it. I'd met a few of the old-timers who still talked over beer and bratwurst there, but nobody was ancient enough to remember specific stories about The Prince firsthand. The best I'd gotten was, "I heard he was a real character." If I wanted to know firsthand what was behind the "doors of hell," I needed, sooner or later, to enter the DOH.

I take us through Etna to the Circle Bar (you could see it from my grandmother's porch), but now it's somebody or other's sports bar, one of those places with two pool tables, a dart board, and dual televisions tuned in to ESPN and ESPN2 below a display of Pittsburgh sports memorabilia and a sign advertising fifteen-cent wings during Monday Night Football. Late afternoon on a weekday, it's deserted, except for two men simultaneously watching an equestrian competition and a dog show. "You're too late for all this," my father says. "You should have been this interested when your mother was alive."

I look up the street and see Ogrodnik's, the funeral home where my grand-mother was laid out more than forty years ago. Nothing else looks familiar, but I let the car idle until my father says, "You want to see what you don't remember?"

I nod, and he tells me to drive down an alley, and there, in the town a few

miles north of Pittsburgh where I grew up, is an entire neighborhood I never knew existed. "What's all this?" I say.

"The Prince was a regular at Tomashek's," my father says. "It's down this way."

I remember the name. "Hell itself," Aunt Margaret called it.

"I never told Ruthy this," my father finally says. "After a softball game—The Prince was sitting on the curb outside Tomashek's. My friends asked him to sing. You know, because he was feeling good.

"He was a character by then. I started dating your mother just after that. I never went back to Tomashek's."

I understand this story illustrates public humiliation, but my father simply relates it and then tells me to turn into an alley of decrepit houses. He shows me three houses from his Meals-on-Wheels route, one where a man has just lost a leg to diabetes. When we turn into the last street, the freeway bypass looms over our heads.

Miraculously, the field my father played semipro football on is still here, level and hard packed. "Millvale, Arsenal—the fields were used so much and baked so hard that the grass only grew over by the sidelines," my father says. "You knew you'd played a game when you came off a field like that."

I stop and get out. My father sits in the car. Well past eighty years old, he's grown as small as The Prince sitting on his bed in the St. Barnabas charity home.

"You go on," he says, meaning for me to believe he isn't going to follow. I walk, listening for the click of the car-door latch, and when I hear it, I make myself keep walking so he can get out in his own good time.

I don't have to look back to know how he puts his hands to both sides, how he swings both legs outside and then pushes off slowly with his arms, gritting his teeth until the short, tight lift of his head means the pain is running through the bone-on-bone contact in his knees.

It's level here. After a few breaths to settle things down, he's able to shuffle. I give him a minute, and he manages twenty feet or so—far enough that when I turn, he can stop as if he's decided that patch of packed earth is the perfect spot, right there, along the near sideline. He can look around as well from there as I can from the end zone to our left.

I stare up at the bypass from underneath, remembering when traffic backed up the entire six miles to Pittsburgh during rush hour because tens of thousands of people who worked in the city had moved to its northern suburbs after World War II. By the time this bypass had been built, Etna, a small steel-mill town, was

a bottleneck. A year after the new highway was opened, Etna was a town without a steel mill that people passed rather than visited.

Tomashek's, when we finally reach it, is closed, its beer and whiskey signs replaced by boarded windows and a padlocked door. The building is three times larger than the ones that house the other local bars. That size would doom any sort of reopening in this decaying neighborhood.

"My football coach got himself killed in there," my father says. "Drinking and money."

I look again at the shut-down building and the deserted street. "Fats Skertich. He made a bet and there were words spoken about paying. Fats slapped a man, and that man went home, got a gun, came back, and killed him right there in Tomashek's." My father stares at the door as if he expects to see Fats Skertich walk out with his arm over the shoulders of The Prince. "A baseball bet. It was summer."

"Fats Skertich was a man you listened to," my father says, and then he adds, "You know, I always thought there were reasons The Prince had problems. A man gets married and moves into his wife's house. It's a hard thing. He and your grandmother sleeping in a room between her parents and her brothers, all four of them still there when they were starting out."

I remember the layout of the rooms in that house, how there were doors that connected those bedrooms, how you'd have to lock them if you wanted privacy. Or leave them unlocked as a sign of trust.

"The Prince fixed things around the house. All those men lived there, and none of them could fix anything but The Prince. Right up to the end, there were still two brothers and the father plus his own five children, all old enough to have a mind of their own. The house was never his."

I drive us through Etna, past the long-closed steel mill, across the railroad tracks. "The Prince went out to Huggins' Farm before the war," my father says as we reach the block where his bakery had stood. He stares at each building as if he expects to see someone he knows standing in a doorway. "You might want to know this, too," he says. "When the war started, I didn't want to go in the service. I had deferments for a year—married, a baker—and then they just needed too many to not call me up."

I turn down the alley that I remember curling behind the bakery. Large patches of its bricks are missing; a chunk of concrete, displaced from an abandoned garage, sits so far into the alley I have to squeeze by it. Weeds that have grown door-handle high scrape against the car as I creep past them. When a section

of newspaper, caught among a patch of thistle, flutters open, I expect to see headlines about Kennedy's assassination.

"I went down there with Al Kopniski, who played football with me," my father keeps on. "He went through the line and passed. I got taken aside because of this bum ear. We didn't talk about it. Al went and I didn't. And then he didn't make it back. So neither would've I. And then where would we be?"

It's been a mistake to drive my father here, I think. It's like his high school reunion gone bad—classmates unchanged, just older and uglier and bunching up in the same way they had nearly seventy years ago.

Behind where the bakery had stood, I stop and let the car idle. "It's the same," my father says, "only worse."

He's right, I think. Except for the bakery being leveled, the area looks untouched by the last thirty years. "You can see the ass-end of everything from here, that's for sure," my father says. "Your mother hated to even park back here."

The shale hillside seems dotted with the same sparse sumac and burdock that grew there when I was a child. What I remember is the summer before second grade and the first time I left the sidewalk in front of the bakery where I was supposed to stay "no matter what" while my mother worked inside. I'd been trying to sell paper for a penny a sheet from my Rainbow Pad tablet in front of Miller's Tavern. For fifteen minutes, nobody passing by gave in to my simple sales pitch of "One-cent paper here." Then, instead of walking back to the bakery along the sidewalk, I took the path over the hill beside Miller's, ending up where the back door opened into the alley beside the railroad tracks.

From the rear, the six buildings between Miller's and the bakery appeared to be in danger of tumbling backwards down the hill. A train heading toward Pittsburgh looked enormous hurtling on the downgrade, arm's length from where I stood staring at it. As soon as it passed, I noticed the dogs, two of them emerging from under the loading dock behind Hoburg's Hardware.

I started to backpedal toward the bakery, and when they snarled and began trotting toward me, I clutched my tablet, turned, and ran—one of those dogs catching the cuff of my pants, tugging me sideways toward the tracks until my mother, who hated pets of any kind, swept down the shale hillside with the stiff-bristled brush she'd been using on baking pans. "Go to hell," she screamed, and those dogs retreated to the tracks where I thought hell would find them if they didn't watch out. And then I closed my eyes, waiting for my mother to use that brush on me because I wasn't allowed where you could see the ass-end of everything.

"This isn't about The Prince anymore," I say, "but that's OK."

My father shakes his head. "The Prince always came up this way," my father says. "Afterwards, you know. When he hitched a ride to town from the farm. He'd slip out the back door of Miller's down there at the end of the block so nobody would see he'd been having a few, and then he'd come down the alley here and up between the bakery and the beauty parlor."

I nod, remembering the narrow passage between the buildings, just wide enough to walk through without turning my shoulders. "The Prince would slip through there, then turn the corner fast and open the bake-shop door to get inside. He thought he was fooling somebody."

I back up and work the car slowly down the alley toward what's now Huntz' Tavern. Though Hoburg's is long gone, the loading dock, rusted and cracked, still stands, and I look in the shadows beneath it for the descendants of those snarling dogs. My mother had simply told me not to cry. She'd sat me on a folding chair and told me to settle down while she finished scrubbing. After a few minutes, she said, "Did you learn something just now?"

After I pull out onto the highway that takes us back to his house, my father says, "Like I was telling you, The Prince was handy with his hands. Let me see if I can find what I'm thinking of when we get to the house, and I'll show you something. It should only take me a second."

I sit in the living room while he's gone for a second and then a hundred more. I hear him rooting through the closet in my sister's old bedroom. When he reappears, he carries an old Gimbel's box. "Look at these," he says, and he dumps a dozen pairs of wooden pliers on the table, each set slightly larger than the next until one sits full-size. I open and shut three of them. Each works as if oiled, and I try to figure the method my grandfather used to create a hinge in one piece of wood.

"I've never taken a drink," my father says. "You know that." I pinch one of the smaller sets between the claws of the largest, lifting it, waiting. "I was afraid," he goes on, "I wouldn't be able to stop."

"The Prince wasn't your father," I say. I lay the small set of pliers back on the table before I open the claws.

"Take one if you want it," my father says. As soon as I pick up one of the smaller ones, he gathers the rest, returns them to the box, and closes the lid. "Good," he says, carrying the box down the hall, closing the door to my sister's room, returning that box to wherever he wants it to sit until he dies.

"Party food" was a plate of "blind robins," dried fish so heavily salted I thought I was swallowing ocean water. It was pig's feet and liverwurst, olive loaf and summer sausage, three-bean salad and deviled eggs—all of it, even at ten o'clock on a Saturday night, preceded by a prayer that blessed our food and the wisdom of God that "passes all understanding."

Always.

The earliest Saturday night get-together with relatives that I remember comes back to me because of something besides the food. My father scattered twenty of his records on the carpet of our living room and called me over to demonstrate how I was a four-year-old who could read, because I could correctly choose each requested 78. My relatives must have known I was performing so well because I'd attached the color of labels to the shape of titles, selecting, by memory, the tunes they wanted to hear, but they did nothing but marvel and applaud as I handed up one and then another, appearing to be the world's youngest DJ. For that night, at least, I was so perfect I could have possessed the wisdom of God, passing all understanding in one of the three upstairs rooms we rented in Etna, in 1950.

The Plagues

Everyone clapped when I finished. As if it took brilliance to remember the shape and color of "Tennessee Waltz" and "Slow Boat to China." As if I could sort and choose among an eternity of records if someone would supply them. I couldn't wait to go to school, where I would get a chance to be rewarded for being perfect.

A year and a half later, although I didn't know it, the day I carried my first report card home from Wilson Street Elementary School, dogs had been fitted into specially designed slings at the Yucca Flats atom-bomb test site in Nevada.

I had to walk four blocks altogether, two of them through an alley I used as a short cut before I had to cross Grant Avenue, the main street that ran through Etna on its way to Pittsburgh, six miles away. In early November, in 1951, there weren't any crossing guards. I'd been taught to look both ways by my parents. During the first two weeks of school, I'd been led across the street by a policeman

who stopped traffic before we stepped off the curb. After that, the policeman had something better to do than watch over children who should have learned by then. I knew it was up to me, not some adult, to make certain I didn't get hit by a car.

Those dogs, I learned later, hung upside down, spaced at intervals of a thousand feet in an imaginary spoke of radius beginning at ground zero. They wore different kinds of material—cotton, rayon, wool—and they were as fit as their handlers could make them after weeks of training.

I had all A's—reading, spelling, arithmetic, art, music, penmanship, and citizenship. First grade, so far, had been a success, and I'd been looking forward to report-card day and my chance to collect quarters from my grandmother and my Aunt Margaret, the way my sister had for the past two years.

After the atomic test blast, men inspected the effects on those dogs, moving within four blocks of ground zero to check. Mostly, those dogs were dead, torn apart and roasted. Numbers five and nine, though not the farthest away, were still alive. And one of the dead dogs, it was reported, was warmer than the others, so it seemed that it had at least survived the initial blast and shock.

Interesting news for those who thought it important to study such things to see how close you could be to a nuclear explosion and live, and to see if it mattered what you were wearing when the bomb went off—but nobody else in my family knew about those dogs either. We didn't own a television. We didn't buy newspapers. Those were things for people who had time and money. The news in the three upstairs rooms my parents rented was my straight A's and the straight A's of my sister, who was in third grade.

Perfect, my mother said. And so was our attendance—neither of us, so far, missing a day of school. When my father woke up for dinner and the few hours he spent at home before he walked to the bakery at 10:30 to work until 9:00 the following morning, my mother had both report cards and, because it was one of the few meals my sister and I liked in common, a casserole of macaroni and cheese on the table.

"This will happen again," my mother said. "In January, and then in April and June."

My sister, who now had nine consecutive straight-A report cards with perfect attendance, smiled like she was measuring the distances between her and those successes.

Before I returned that report card with my mother's signature on it to my teacher, Mrs. Spangler, my cousin died. Leukemia, I heard my mother repeat, and the word sounded like it was in a foreign language, like listening to the German my Aunt Margaret and my grandmother spoke when they were angry. I thought it stood for something I might recognize, something I might get because it was common, but all I remembered about Craig was how pale he always looked the summer before and how he didn't come outside to play with us.

Twice, since school had started, I'd sat with my sister in the waiting room of St. Francis Hospital in Pittsburgh. I looked at the two magazines that had the most pictures—*Life* and *National Geographic*—while my parents visited. Children weren't allowed in the rooms. We were told to stay in our chairs, and so we did.

At McIntyre's funeral home, Myrtle, Craig's mother, talked about "all this poison in the air now," and my relatives nodded as if they knew what she meant. Wearing a white shirt and a clip-on tie, I'd left Mrs. Spangler's room an hour early, the first minutes of school I had ever missed. "They had the atomic snow all the way up to New England last winter," she said to my mother as my sister and I stood beside her. "You best watch your own. You keep your eyes peeled for the first signs of anything." Nobody spoke German here like they did on my mother's side of the family, so when leukemia was murmured again and again, I knew this was something I would ask Mrs. Spangler about when I went back to school the next day.

I learned what *pallbearer* meant when I became one after the service ended. I and my other male cousins on my father's side, all of them older than I was, were told to "help Craig along on his journey." The four of us gripped the handles while three uncles, two for the sides and one in the back, helped us carry Craig's casket. My father, awake for once in the middle of the afternoon, patted me on the back when we left the gravesite. "God works in mysterious ways," my mother said in rhythm with the palm of his hand.

The following week, the primary Sunday School classes put on a play based on the story in Exodus of the Israelites leaving Egypt. The third graders like my

sister had speaking parts—Moses, the Pharaoh, an assortment of Israelites and Egyptians. Our minister stood in the darkened choir loft to speak the words of God each time Moses needed to hear them. The first and second graders were the plagues in order.

Under two red bedspreads, the six second graders were a river turned to blood. Masked and hopping, the five first graders, me included, were frogs. The second graders were lice and then flies, and I could hear the murmurs of the adults from the shadowed pews we could barely see.

Next, I was part of a herd of cattle, going on all fours and lowing like our teacher had taught us. The Pharaoh hardened his heart again while we milled around in our black and white outfits until we buckled and fell onto our sides because God had killed us.

All of us wore white hoods circled by the red of boils, and all of us flung brown rice as hail before we chattered like locusts. Finally, the eleven of us put on our black sheets and waited until all the lights but the ones at the base of the chancel went out. On that cue, we walked around slowly, making that church seem even darker, until the first-born among us dropped and died. The rest of us with older brothers and sisters, though we had escaped because of the lottery of our birth, gradually stepped back and back until only the four who were first-born were lying there in the dark.

I stood to the side, still dressed in black, while the third-grade Israelites walked between two pieces of plywood painted like waves. When the rest of the third graders, playing Egyptians, stepped between them, the plywood tumbled over to applause.

Even weeks later, when we visited my grandmother and my Aunt Margaret, the plagues were still being talked about. "What would they be if we were trying to get out of Pittsburgh?" I said.

"A flood, for sure," my father said. "A blizzard. Freezing rain."

"The A-bomb," my mother said. "With all the steel mills here, we're ground zero for the Russians."

My grandmother shook her head and made the *tsk* sound with her tongue she always used when she was displeased.

"The first-born would get polio," my mother went on. "They'd have to live in iron lungs." *Tsk*, I heard my grandmother say.

Aunt Margaret said, "Smallpox," and I smiled, rolling up my sleeve to show off the vaccination mark on my shoulder.

"I'm safe," I said. "All of us are safe." I'd seen the scars on the arms of my sister and my parents. My mother's mark was twice the size of mine, as big as a quarter.

Aunt Margaret began to lift the hem of her housecoat, bringing another *tsk* from my grandmother. Suddenly, on the outside of her thigh, a scar the size of a silver dollar appeared. It was milky and concave, not like mine, and I thought it was something other than a vaccination mark. "I'm twelve years older than your mother," she said, "and we still went to that horse doctor who did this to me."

Aunt Margaret pulled her housecoat back down, but I could still see that white circle. "I have one more," I said. "Leukemia."

"That's enough for one night," my grandmother said. "That's enough about the plagues."

Shortly after Craig's funeral, my mother started browsing the newspaper to look for disasters that happened to people she might know, skipping to the section with the heading "LOCAL." Monday, Wednesday, and Friday, she had begun to buy the *Pittsburgh Press*, because, she explained, those were the days the paper was the biggest—except for Sunday, which cost more and was full of advertisements, not news.

She kept us up-to-date on any news that took place in Etna, which wasn't often, but at the end of January, right after my sister and I had brought home another pair of perfect report cards, she found an item about an Etna boy my age who had been killed when his sled had gone under the wheels of a truck. "Thank the Lord he's nobody we know," my mother said after she read a name I'd never heard.

My mother reminded me again about where I was permitted to take my sled, and I listened like I was going to be tested by Mrs. Spangler. The boy was six, like I was, but he went to the Locust Street Elementary School because he lived in lower Etna, which started at Spang-Chalfant, the steel mill that stretched for more than a quarter mile along the railroad tracks from the A&P to the Sparkle Market, the other grocery store in Etna.

He didn't go to our church either. He was Catholic, my mother said, which meant he went to All Saints, the church beside the Wilson Street School. At recess, two days later, I could see the cars parked along Dewey Street, which ran

behind the school. There was a hearse that looked exactly like the one that had carried Craig's casket, but I couldn't tell if it was from McIntyre's.

In April, a man was struck and killed by a train in Etna. My mother read us the story from the newspaper, but her caution about the railroad tracks didn't seem important, because Aunt Margaret, who was visiting, called the victim "that old stew," a phrase she used to describe anyone who took a drink.

Two days later my sister and I received straight A's again, but the next week my mother became so sick with the flu she stayed in bed, and Aunt Margaret stayed overnight to take care of her and get us off to school.

It was the first warm weather of the year. On the day Aunt Margaret arrived, instead of cutting through the alley after school, I walked to the candy store at the corner of Wilson Street and asked for a glass of ice water. The man behind the counter smiled and poured water into a paper cup. "Thanks," I said, and handed him back the cup when I was finished.

The next afternoon, an even warmer day, I walked into the store and asked for ice water. This time the man didn't smile. "It's for people who buy something," he said.

Outside, I remembered that the A&P had a refrigerated fountain beside the meat counter. The water from that fountain was as ice-cold as anything poured into a cup at the candy store. It would only take five minutes to walk past the football field and the car dealer.

Inside the A&P, I took a long drink, losing my breath twice, the way I did when I quickly swallowed something cold. By the time I was leaving the store, making the door open and shut by putting my arm through the electric eye, I wanted another drink and went back to that ice-cold water for seconds. I stared at the steaks and chickens and rib roasts. I read the labels on twenty kinds of candy bars and made imaginary selections of ice-cream flavors, potato chips, and cookies before I returned for a third drink.

When I finally came out of the A&P, I decided to cross the street and go home by walking the railroad tracks. I knew where they passed three blocks behind where we lived. All I had to do was cut through a backyard and follow Angle Alley to the house with our three upstairs rooms.

I stepped from tie to tie, beginning to count because I thought it might be a thousand ties before I reached Angle Alley. I stopped to toss stones across Pine Creek. I looked back to watch a load of molten slag being dumped onto the pile

behind the mill. I was only at 180 when I heard the crossing alarm near the mill begin to sound. Coming uphill from Pittsburgh, the train was moving slowly, but I stepped to the side and waited because I didn't want to lose count.

After it passed, I counted another 120 ties before I reached the crossing where the policeman had stood for the first two weeks of school. I changed my guess to 900 and started to count again. At 430, when I was on the other side of the street, a man walked up beside me and started to talk.

"Are you lost?" he said.

I laughed. "No. I'm taking the back way home."

"Is it far?" he said.

"Pretty far," I said, but I didn't want to tell him about my counting because it sounded, with him walking alongside, like something a little boy who might be lost would do.

The tracks curved behind a row of houses that faced away from any trains that might pass. On the other side, once we passed a factory parking lot, was Pine Creek. The man didn't say anything else, but he walked in the cinders beside the tracks, his shoes crunching so loudly I lost count and started walking faster, leaving him, by the sound of it, behind. The houses stopped and were replaced by a row of empty garages. "Is it far?" the man suddenly said again, surprising me by closing up from the Pine Creek side.

He was scanning the garages, and so was I, and then I saw Mike Nicolazzo and Dave Metzger, who lived on the street next to ours and were in my sister's class, bouncing a rubber ball off the garage at the end of Angle Alley.

"Hey," I shouted, not looking at the man, and I hopped off the tracks and ran toward them as if I was just in time to join their game. The man didn't follow. When I looked behind me, he'd turned around and was heading back toward the crossing. Mike Nicolazzo acted like he was going to throw the ball to me, but I kept running until I reached the Grant Avenue end of Angle Alley, slowing down then to catch my breath before I climbed the stairs to our three rooms.

Aunt Margaret opened the door and stood with her hands on her hips. "If you were mine," she said, "I'd take the strap to you."

I looked at the clock. I was nearly an hour and a half late. "Your father is out looking for you. Your mother's in her sick bed worrying herself to death." Aunt Margaret gripped my arm, twisting just enough to let me know this was unforgivable. "An hour she gave you," she said. "Your mother thinks you're dead."

"I watch for cars," I said. "I know when a train is coming."

"There's more to watch out for than a set of wheels," Aunt Margaret said,

but I knew it was time to shut up, to say nothing about not having leukemia or polio or smallpox. And for sure, I kept it to myself that the Communists hadn't dropped the bomb on Pittsburgh.

When I tried to think of another reason I could be dead, one that I could say out loud, all I could think of was the man who had walked beside me; but he was something else to keep secret, because my mother had drilled me on strangers before first grade began. Aunt Margaret said she was through with talking. My mother, when I walked into the bedroom, began to cry. My father, seeing me sitting on the bed fifteen minutes later, said, "You don't know how lucky you are." My sister sat on the pull-out bed in the living room where my father had been sleeping until Aunt Margaret had woken him forty-five minutes earlier. She didn't move or say a word until my father, walking by, said, "You can get up from there now."

While she was sick, my mother started reading the newspapers from front to back. "I'm getting my money's worth," she said, and that's why she started learning about the atomic tests. "Myrtle might be right," she said. "They started these tests in January of last year, and by the beginning of the summer, Craig had his problems. Eleven bombs they set off last year, and more where those came from. Think of that. And now think how long it's been that the air's been blowing over us."

Although the only thing my father read was the sports, he was skeptical. "We're thousands of miles from there," he said. "There's some children that are just weak. There's some that gets anything that's catching."

"Leukemia isn't catching. It's not the chickenpox," my mother said, "and there's talk of people complaining out there in Utah and Nevada."

"Communists?" my father said.

"Mormons."

My father nodded as if that made the complaints have more weight. "It's a hard thing to prove," he said.

My mother told me about the pink clouds that signaled fallout. She explained about the bright flash and the mushroom cloud and what the half-life of an element was, though it would be forty years before I read for myself about the dogs in the slings on that first report-card day. If my mother had purchased a newspaper at the beginning of November 1951, she would have learned that the bomb test was called Shot Dog, that it was twenty-one kilotons, that the army

stationed more than a thousand of its troops six miles away (farther away than those dogs) to see how things would work out with them.

My mother told us all, eventually, about the May Day atomic bomb test. "It was another big one," she said. "They had the Marines watching this one from only three miles away. They marched right down to ground zero to show they could take it."

"See?" my father said.

My mother tapped her fork on the edge of her plate, but he didn't elaborate. Finally, she stopped tapping and said, "How can any good come from something like that? They should use animals if they want to experiment."

In June, at the end of the school year, I carried home my report card, a folder full of my art projects, and a box of twenty-four Mr. Goodbars. Mrs. Spangler had presented them to me because I'd had perfect attendance. I had all A's for the year, and so did my sister, but when my mother propped our report cards on the kitchen table for my father to see, my sister cried. Instead of all 0's where it said "Times Absent" and "Times Tardy," my sister had a 3 for the last marking period because right after my mother had been sick, she had missed three days of school. Now I was the only one in our family, my mother said, who could still be perfect in school.

While we ate macaroni and cheese, nobody said anything else about perfection. Neither my father nor my mother mentioned the atomic bomb or radiation. But since it was Friday, my mother had been reading the *Pittsburgh Press*, and now she was worried because there had been an article about the approach of polio season.

Nobody in my class or my sister's class had polio, she said, so it was overdue. "You make sure you wash your hands any time you touch something dirty," she said. "You make sure you keep the flies off you, because you never know where they've been."

The article she'd been reading told the story of a man who'd built a sandbox for his daughter, and when she got polio, it seemed, after playing in it, he'd taken it apart, burned the wood, and shoveled all the sand into wheelbarrow loads and dumped it in the woods near his house. "Think of that," she said. "Anything at all can be dangerous."

"You look like something the cat dragged in," my mother would say, meaning the parts of me that were easily repaired—a wrinkled shirt, dirty fingernails, uncombed hair. "You look a little peaked," she would say when my problems were difficult enough for the solutions of home remedies, her pick-me-up nostrums for paleness, listlessness, apathy, and the telltale look of down-in-the-dumps.

She had faith in what she prepared herself, tangible things to gargle or swallow or lay upon the skin, and when I complained, asking how they could work better than drugstore remedies, she said, "These things come from the old country. They've always worked." I swallowed and gargled, but I had my doubts.

Boric acid in hot water was a frequent remedy, the potency of the solution I bathed my arms or legs in decided by my father's diagnosis of the severity of my latest skin problem. Most frequent and much worse was baking soda in warm water, mouthfuls poured down my throat by my mother until I vomited whatever seemed to be causing my current stomach distress. The worst was a razor blade held to the flames of the gas stove or a lit match by my father until my mother said it was sterilized, both of them working to open up my occasional abscess.

Home Remedies

I could whimper, whine, and cry, my father explained, or I could take my medicine—because if I didn't, I would be a pantywaist, a sissy, a Little Lord Fauntleroy who would surely accept being effeminate for life. Everyone, my parents said in unison while administering these treatments, could be better in some way, and this was one, letting them draw out the poisons without complaint.

After all, they insisted, their home treatments worked as well as store-bought. We didn't need doctors, who cost money, when most things could be helped with simple solutions. And likewise, self-improvement came to those who tried their best, not boys who cried and merely thought they had struggled. "Just you wait," they said. "You'll find out that bearing pain strengthens spirit."

"You're big enough to stop all this complaining," they quoted

from the hand-me-down advice of their own parents. And anyway, what did a boy just starting school think? That my failures could go untreated? That if I shut my eyes, those failures would leave?

We moved in early December. I took my place in what the teacher, Mrs. Leggett, called "the new boy's seat," the last desk in the last row. None of the other second graders said anything about the empty desk, third row, second seat, which, for all I knew, could have been "the new girl's seat" in case she joined the class. Not even Mrs. Leggett mentioned Harvey Walker until two weeks later, a few days before Christmas vacation, when we were instructed to make get-well cards by the art teacher who visited each Friday.

Now I knew that desk belonged to Harvey Walker, who had whooping cough and had been absent for two weeks before I arrived; but I didn't know what kind of design would please him. I tried lightning bolts and flaming arrows speeding through *Get Well Harvey*. I printed my name and then added "I'm new," so he wouldn't think a card meant for another Harvey had been mixed in with his.

Harvey Walker showed up on Groundhog Day. He was short and skinny and sat down as quietly as a new boy. By then, Roy Kelman was out with scarlet fever. We didn't make cards for him. If he had stayed absent until Easter, maybe we would have sent him a batch, but the week before he came back, apparently unharmed, a boy who'd had polio the summer before hobbled back into first grade. "Robert Hutchings," somebody whispered to me, even though Mrs. Leggett wasn't in the room. "He was with us last year."

"Thank God for His favors," my mother said when I told her about the partial recovery of Robert Hutchings.

"Dear God, please make my eyes better again," I repeated every night after the Lord's Prayer, which wasn't special enough to make an impact on a specific handicap like nearsightedness. I ate the raw carrots my mother forced on me, and by the end of second grade I'd had my seat moved up to the third row so I could see the blackboard. Now I sat right behind Harvey Walker, who, I thought, would fail second grade, because we passed our math and spelling tests one seat behind us to be graded while Mrs. Leggett called out the answers. I marked twelve wrong out of twenty for Harvey's spelling; I marked seven wrong out of ten for Harvey's subtraction. He didn't know how to take a larger number away from a smaller number; he didn't know how to spell words like *table* and *purple*.

After Roy Kelman returned, Mrs. Leggett asked me to listen to him and Harvey read from a book I'd finished the year before. I sat in the cloakroom, told them how to pronounce words, and thought I was curing them with my

teacher's home remedy for failure. Robert Hutchings, the polio victim, lurched through the playground and hunched over his crutches beside the kickball field, but none of his former classmates ran over to talk to him.

Roy Kelman passed. Harvey Walker moved during the summer before third grade. Nobody knew if he had failed or not, and after two days of school, nobody said another word about Harvey Walker or whooping cough or the woes of subtraction. There had been, we understood, a great polio scare that summer, but everybody in the school was still walking except Robert Hutchings, who still wore braces and used crutches and had been promoted to Mrs. Leggett's class.

Two years later, children everywhere were lining up for Salk's miracle shots—one cure that worked—but all through third and fourth grade, I was miserable with carrots, prayer, and failing to recognize classmates across the room. I didn't have faith, my mother said, or I would be able to see just fine. And she was right. I hadn't lasted a year on that home remedy, and during the day, outside of the house, I saw everything blurry and wished myopia on the rest of my class, because I knew I had a better chance of seeing that wish come true.

For a while, I kept my nearsightedness as secret as my afternoon on the railroad tracks. With a minute to memorize before the twice-a-year eye exam, I slipped to the back of the line and stood closer than the marker taped to the cement floor. For those few minutes I repeated F G T E D M and D B O E V to myself, getting ready for the patch to each eye and reciting for the school nurse who said, every time, "Start with the smallest letters you can see."

I earned 20/30 vision that way, improving myself without giving in to the weakness glasses declared. The world turned to haze, populated by people I didn't recognize until they said, "Aren't you going to say hello?" When a car driven by an older cousin stopped to pick me up as I waited outside my father's bakery, I didn't approach it until she opened the door and called my name. "It's good that you make sure who's in the car before you get in," she said, drawing that conclusion instead of one that decided I was half blind.

One morning, when I stepped up to the taped line, the nurse said, "Start at the top and read what you see," and I stuttered after the E and the O T, seeing nothing but two blotted lines between those letters and the lines I'd memorized. That white-winged woman clucked and marked her black book with the small fraction of my imperfection, teaching me failure.

Of course, you could join the sick and the lame through accident. That winter, I took my best speed skater's stance at the high end of the playground, pushed off into a splayed-step spring through the snow, and hunched, turned sideways,

for the thirty-foot slide down the packed ice to where four catchers linked arms at the brink of the steep drop to the culvert and cyclone fence.

It was the foolproof safety system of the nine-year-old. None of us carried much bulk. Our legendary speeds weren't fast enough to draw our teachers outside to throw ashes on our slides. But when Billy Shaner was sufficiently silly to kneel and catch me below the knees, I upended in the great tradition of the banana peel and hit head first, unconscious, then conscious again, doing a slow slither down the incline in a poetic sprawl.

I was hoping Nancy Housel or Sharon Daniels was watching my heroic trek across the playground on the arms of two boys who promised they'd get that stupid jerk for me. Billy Shaner had already run for it. He'd got himself a head start into the cloakroom, out of his coat and gloves, and into the doorway where Mrs. Anderson could see he was early for spelling.

I didn't explain that I shouldn't be moved or protest I was fine. I grinned stupidly at everyone, especially Nancy Housel, who was standing at the base of the stairs like a wife watching planes return from a bombing run.

I had a real goose egg, according to Mrs. Anderson. I should spend the rest of the day at home. What a life—four hours of comic books and board games while Billy Shaner suffered the pushes and shoves and name-calling of fourth-grade justice, plus the humiliation of being barred from the slide until the next thaw turned everyone away.

I returned the following day, giddy with a recovery accomplished through the folk medicine of a good night's sleep and my mother laying her hands to my head, saying a prayer of her own. "You'll get better," she said. "You're not so bad off you need Kathryn Kuhlman."

I knew who that was. During the summer, fascinated, I'd listened along with my mother and grandmother to Kathryn Kuhlman's daily broadcasts from Pittsburgh. A self-proclaimed faith healer, Kathryn Kuhlman exhorted all sorts of crippled and diseased worshippers to come forward with their afflictions.

She laid her hands on deaf ears and mute tongues to produce hearing and speech. She touched paralyzed limbs and encouraged movement. I don't remember whether or not she claimed universal success, but a fair number of these handicapped people professed to be healed, and her assistants guided them right up to the microphone that took their testimony to our radio.

I could hear the evidence when they answered questions, speaking for the first time in years; I could hear Kathryn Kuhlman say, "Drop those crutches and walk," and then listen for the great hallelujahs of success disappearing back the aisle.

"Who would doubt such proof?" my mother asked. And so did my father, both of them believing that tumors could shrink from the power of Jesus, that Parkinson's disease could be reversed by faith.

On Sunday nights, if we were visiting my grandmother—who, unlike us, had a television—Bishop Fulton Sheen was must viewing. Even then, when I was in elementary school, he seemed ludicrous to me in his exotic religious garb, as if he was portraying a medieval bishop in a costume drama.

And boring? Most of the time he used a blackboard as a visual aid. No child wanted to see an adult writing on a blackboard during the weekend. And surely nobody I knew who was my age and attended church regularly wanted to hear, for the second time in one day, something that sounded like a sermon.

"Life is worth living," Bishop Sheen reminded us. A murmur of approval rippled between my parents, and I knew to keep silent. Each week, Sheen gave out prescriptions like Christ, flourishing his robed arms into a brief drama of blessing.

The Power of Positive Thinking, a book by Norman Vincent Peale, had been published to enormous popularity in 1952. I never saw it in our house, but he was referenced as often as Christ. Those who took to heart his homilies about daily life were preparing themselves for eternal success, influencing God with their self-imposed positive behavior.

Self-improvement—that's what Sheen and Peale stood for—just the opposite of what my long-banished grandfather represented. When he lived with my grandmother before I was born, he didn't take care of himself—meaning he expected others, including his children, to do his work. The Prince lived like his namesake—drinking, staying out late, avoiding responsibility. And when it came time to improve himself or be tossed out, my mother said, "He ran like nobody's business."

Of course, I wasn't to repeat any of this to anybody at any time. This was family business, and so were my thoughts about the stupid and the fat, the crippled and the old. "You keep those things to yourself," my mother said. My father, tired of me not heeding that instruction, slapped my face during dinner one evening just as I finished punctuating my description of a fat girl in my fifth-grade class with a series of oinks. "That's the end of that," he said, and returned to cutting the beef liver we ate every Tuesday. I zipped my lips. Like the best in the Bible, I kept my tiny troubles to myself because it was a free and simple way to self-improvement.

In the company of others, I kept the silence of martyrs. Throughout elementary school, I was a little angel who never peeked where nobody wanted me to see.

You don't say a word about The Prince, I was told, and I kept that promise easily because he was a character in a story, somebody I never saw.

I had other problems that needed to be remedied and improved. During fourth grade, the first thing I did to straighten my teeth was push them with my fingers—ten minutes of pressing each morning and night. My mother maintained that as long as I was faithful to that schedule, my hands could do the work of braces—that my teeth, although fighting for space, would line up like soldiers if I made regular time for pushing. There were so many things I did that left one hand free to press, she explained—watching the television my parents had just bought, reading a book. "Those two in the front," my mother said, "you just keep at it, and they'll be good as new"—an odd way of expressing it, I thought, since they'd arrived in the overbite position.

I was ten years old by now, grown up enough to know skepticism. At school, braces were sparkling in the mouths of the fifth and sixth graders, but not mine. When, despite carrots and prayer, I still couldn't make out what was written on the blackboard in school or clearly see a baseball during Little League games, she prescribed eye exercises, proper rest, and giving up comic books. She taught me how to squint to see something besides fog. "Make those muscles believe they're strong," she told me, so I rolled my eyes, pressed my teeth, and prayed, keeping her commandments.

And every time I misbehaved, I knew The Prince would come up. Every time I didn't finish a job and asked for help, I knew The Prince would be mentioned. The St. Barnabas Home, where he lived, was another name for the poorhouse, which was where the unfortunate and the unfit—we all knew which category he was in—ended up. "You see what becomes of waste and bad habits?" my mother said. "You see where weakness and depending on others leads?" The Prince couldn't take care of himself, and neither could I unless I improved myself. "We don't ask for help in this family," my father repeated, and I understood that he meant that statement as an absolute.

Work wasn't supposed to be easy. Wasn't my grandfather, who took the easy way, sitting alone in a tiny charity-home room because of God's judgment? Salvation required discomfort. Silence, for instance. Quite often, pain. I learned about the flagellants and the celibates, those who wore coarse clothes—sackcloth and ashes, according to the Bible. Each Sunday I heard the advantages of death for the good while I scouted the short front row of the hunchbacked widows, the back pews stocked with the coughers and the tremblers. Weren't fever and fatigue the early warning systems of God tracking us like radar? Don't our bodies

lead us to redemption with leukemia that made me pray and check my body for bruises that healed as slowly as the ones on my dead cousin?

Before I finished fourth grade, my father's mother died. "She worked so hard, she just wore out," my father said, his explanation bringing up worry about both of my parents' chances of living long lives. This time I knew what a pallbearer was. The same cousins who had helped to carry Craig carried her. I gripped her coffin right-handed, still taking so little of the weight that it would have required twenty of me to carry it. This time, McIntyre, the funeral director, and his son lifted on both ends to keep everything steady.

I was nine. The oldest of my cousins was fifteen. My mother had clipped on my tie and straightened the sport coat one of those older cousins had worn until the month before, and I'd been smart enough to choose the side that let me use my right hand and arm. I knew enough about my body to understand my left hand would pull the weight of a five-year-old. We slid that coffin along a set of rails into a hearse, and then we were directed by McIntyre's glance to the leather couches of an enormous car. On the inside of the fingers of my right hand, a white groove darkened to red, then vanished, while silence shouldered among us.

The last time I'd seen my grandmother, she'd looked pale as an angel. She'd held both her hands against her head as if she was listening closely for the shallow breath of God, but that morning, among my cousins in that limousine, I became a boy who believed he was the only one in the whole world who was nine years old and understood he was alone.

The suited driver watched us in the mirror. I tried, each time his eyes flicked over and up, to stare what I'd learned into his memory. There was a war not won recently ended in Korea. The Communists whispered darkness while we slept. No one talked about the inconceivable while I'd been learning a list of in-words: incomplete, incurable, inconsolable, incensed. As if I'd stolen them from my mother's black handbag, I kept those words to myself, afraid to spend them.

During the weeks that followed, it didn't take long to learn that "one foot in front of the other" wasn't my father's fresh advice. He borrowed from the public domain of mottoes. He stood on his feet ten hours each night in the bakery and brought home the platitudes of handwork.

One early Friday evening, my father showed me how to roll sandwich buns. We had time while my mother sliced apples for coffee cakes, after she'd driven him to the bakery at seven o'clock for his weekend, twelve-hour shift.

After my father cupped pieces of dough, after he rolled them in small circles, creating spheres and cupping the next pair as if he was teaching the shell game,

I set fresh bits beneath my hands and pressed my way to embarrassment, rolling one lopsided ball and a thing that suggested turd. As if one side of my body was crippled, I couldn't make circles—the left hand refusing, the way it had begun to do for basketball and piano practices.

My father's hands cupped and circled, cupped and circled without one word of advice about the way to bloom sandwich buns for families who were willing to pay for his handwork. "In a couple of years you can help out here," he said. "Idle hands make mischief," he added. But already I was beginning to tell myself a story about the uselessness of handwork, what I was learning to do when I felt failure fill my throat like a short cough or a comma, where I paused and chose a future that relied on something other than how well I could use my hands.

In fourth grade, when I finally stayed home sick, missing my first day of school, my father said, "Well, now you can't be perfect either. You missed."

I croaked out, "Sorry," my throat still raw despite a day of saltwater gargles. "It hurts."

"You think you have it bad?" my father said. "Just you wait. You don't know what pain is." He had perfect-attendance pins for Sunday School dating back to high school. Even when we traveled, we went to Sunday School and church in strange towns, getting a visitor's card from whoever taught me, my sister, and my parents. And those trips were always less than two days long because he never shut the bakery down, keeping perfect attendance there as well.

Still, there were other prescriptions. Memorizing Bible verses to earn eternal life, reciting them on Children's Day to the applause of the congregation. Each verse was a rung on Jacob's Ladder, which had exactly one hundred rungs. And there, at the very top, was an open gate, which glowed in the golden rays from the strangely blurry face of God. He looked, on my wall chart, as if he'd been drawn from the third row by an artist who carried his glasses in his pocket because he was too vain to wear them.

The glasses my mother had finally bought for me were inside my fifth-grade desk so I could put them on to see the board when Mr. Lodge had a quiz hidden behind the map of the United States he scrolled up at 9:45, giving us exactly fifteen minutes to complete it.

I told myself my motive wasn't vanity. I thought, because my father told me, that wearing my glasses would weaken my eyes more; that my vision would keep getting worse if I wore them; that, most important, I could never play baseball or football if I wore glasses, because "athletes don't wear glasses."

He was right. Nobody on the Pittsburgh Pirates wore glasses, although I had

no way to confirm that except from listening to the radio, checking my Topps bubble-gum cards, or squinting from the left-field bleachers at Forbes Field toward the players so distant they could all have been wearing the Lone Ranger's mask without me knowing.

And so I played Little League in the summer without wearing the second pair of glasses I'd had to get because the old prescription had been superseded within eighteen months by the demands of my personal fog. One Monday, at twilight, the game in extra innings, I covered third base after a short passed ball, saw the catcher cock his arm and fling an invisible ball that resubstantiated ten feet from my left shoulder, which in turn twitched a couple of inches before it substituted for a glove.

"Are you blind?" the shortstop screamed, retrieving the ball while the happy base runner scored the winning run.

"No," I said, preferring the disgrace of an error to the irrevocability of a physical flaw.

A few minutes passed as we packed the bats and helmets and catching gear. By the time I picked up the last loose baseball behind the bench, I thought it was dark enough to fling it sixty feet at any of my teammates and blacken one of their unblinking eyes.

"Hey!" I said, firing the scuffed ball at the shortstop, who was near the batter's box. He gloved the ball and dropped it into the bag.

"What?" he said. And then again, when I didn't answer: "What?"

And I could have told him why I couldn't see—that I sat closer than ten feet to the screen when I watched television, that I still read comic books, that I'd started flushing those carrots down the toilet, and I'd stopped praying before sleep, let alone adding a plea for better eyesight.

I had my own solutions. I'd started to play basketball, where players were closer and the ball larger. So what if I couldn't read the scoreboard. I kept the score in my head and checked the minutes and seconds whenever somebody was shooting free throws, squinting just like my mother had suggested while I waited for home remedies to cure me.

W hen Mrs. Sowers, during the first week of sixth grade, showed us the canals of Mars, she traced the straight lines of them with the rubber tip of a wooden pointer. "Think of the Erie Canal," she said, holding the stick against the poster-sized map of Mars. "Better yet, think of the Panama and the Suez," she added, starting a list we were to memorize for one week's worth of geography.

"It's very likely," she said, "there were countries on Mars that fought over their technological marvels," and then she named, for our current-events lesson, the nations threatening war for the Suez Canal, hissing out the names Nasser and the USSR, explaining the possible domino effect to the A-bomb.

The map, Mrs. Sowers went on to explain, had been drawn by Percival Lowell, a respected astronomer who had calculated the locations of Martian infrastructure. I believed her because up to that point, I'd been relying for my information about Mars on a handful of science-fiction movies I'd seen and a comic book Dave Tolley had brought to school the year before.

The Canals of Mars

Through early September, before she brought us up to date on the Suez crisis, Mrs. Sowers ran a series of experiments for science. She demonstrated the water cycle; she wowed us with magnets and electric current that stood our hair on end.

Nature lessons were another matter. We fidgeted through two weeks on Pennsylvania plants. None of us liked the taste of the sassafras tea she brewed from a small tree on the hillside behind our school. It was like drinking the chewing gum our parents preferred to the sweet pleasures of Double Bubble and Bazooka.

What my friends and I wanted to know about were killer plants. Venus flytraps, for instance, or pitcher plants—or most of all, the whereabouts of those wonderfully gigantic man-eaters from the double features we watched on weekends at the Etna Theater.

All those enormous leaves. The suffocating, hair-trigger, relentless vines. Those plants were as dangerous as the giant squids created by atomic tests leaving excess radiation in the ocean. If even

one of their million fine-threaded leaves were brushed by careless explorers or women who wandered off from jungle camps against the advice of the guide, the horrible gulping would begin.

After one of those movies—a new Tarzan, with Lex Barker—Charles Trout, the smallest boy in our class, was tossed into brambles behind the Etna theater by boys we didn't know because our parents had saved enough money to make down payments on houses rather than stay in Etna, where the steel mill and railroad yard were showing signs of shutting down for good. "See?" my father would say, running his finger over his newly painted bakery. "See what Etna does to white?" And I nodded, thinking I could write my name and the names of all my friends with my finger through the soot.

Charles Trout laughed it off. None of us lived in Etna anymore. We never saw those boys on the streets where we lived. And no matter, we couldn't get enough of those movies. We looked for plants in the neighborhood that might thrive on blood, dropped ants by the hundreds into any flower that grew wild, but never once did one close on the insects. It was as hard to find a carnivorous plant as it was to find quicksand. Apparently, we thought, you had to live in some steamy, forbidding place to watch anything being eaten by flowers.

Mrs. Sowers told us plants couldn't possibly get that large. She said we didn't study the Venus flytrap because there weren't any in Pennsylvania. Worse, she insisted there weren't any within hundreds of miles of us. We were right, though, about one thing—they lived in bogs where other flowers seldom live.

That weekend, Dave Tolley and I hiked to every marshy place we could find. It was late September—the weather, we thought, still warm enough for those traps to be working. Now that we had an important clue, we wanted to prove Mrs. Sowers wrong.

Meanwhile, we were glued to *You Asked for It*, where every Sunday on television we could see the impossible come true. Sooner or later, we thought, somebody would write in and ask to see a man-eating plant, but later that fall we settled for a man who could catch a bullet in his teeth.

While Dave Tolley and I watched, a bullet was marked by a witness from the audience so the rest of us would know it had really been fired. The camera, while the bullet was loaded, showed us the audience, all of the studio guests sitting up straight. They looked as if they were holding their breath. Every man was wearing a coat and tie, every woman a dress, and all of them were as old as our parents or older.

Even the man who could catch a bullet in his teeth was wearing a coat and

tie as if he were going to church to pray for perfect timing. He furrowed his brow. He squinted. He concentrated. The marksman aimed carefully and fired. Across the studio stage, the man was still standing. The camera panned in to show us it was the marked bullet he pulled from between his teeth, and we immediately set out to attempt a sort of beginners' lesson for bullet catching.

In Dave Tolley's refrigerator were bunches of green seedless grapes. His parents played Canasta on Sundays; they wouldn't be home for hours, and we threw those grapes across the living room at each other, never once catching even a lob toss between our teeth.

There were over a hundred grapes on the carpet. "Either he's a fake," Dave Tolley said, "or we're spastic." I shrugged. We had to pick all those grapes up and wash them, eating enough to make it look as if we were helping his parents rather than using their grapes as ammunition. Twenty grapes into that bowl, we decided to try one more time, and when Dave Tolley, a few minutes later, caught one of my tosses between his teeth, we shut up about impossible and decided that if somebody practiced longer than the ten minutes we'd just spent, maybe it could be done.

After all, Richard Turner, another boy in our class, could already juggle three balls. He'd learned to do it in one afternoon from his father. We thought of four balls, then five; we thought of swords and flaming sticks; we thought of increasing the speed of grapes until we could take on a bullet, how we could perform a feat so incredible nobody would believe it.

Mrs. Sowers, of course, was no help. On Monday morning, when we told her, she said it was a silly thing to try. "Oh, that's just impossible," she said, even though we described the careful ways the program had made sure the whole thing was genuine. She shook her head and started current events, beginning with the Soviets invading Hungary. "For a few days there, the Hungarians thought they were free. Nothing's the way it looks," she said, "when it comes to Communism."

She went on and on about misuse of power, how France and England had invaded Egypt. They equated power with authority, she explained, and everybody in our class wrote it down.

Dave Tolley and I had some authority. We were patrol boys. We directed traffic for a few minutes in the morning and the afternoon. I loved wearing that belt and the crossed white strap that sported the patrol badge. It showed Mrs. Sowers approved, that I was responsible and trustworthy, that even the low-readers from the Locust Grove trailer court had to wait for my signal to cross. The badges

we wore were like magic that warded off danger. None of those thuggish boys had ever threatened us.

The Invasion of the Body Snatchers arrived at the Etna Theater. We'd been waiting so long, every boy in our sixth-grade class but Jimmy Mason, who was thirteen and lived in the trailer court, watched it on Saturday afternoon. The Body Snatchers, it seemed, were plants. None of us could figure out how they'd changed the first human victims, but after that, people carried the big seed pods for them, placing the pods near the sleeping, who woke up transformed into aliens. Sure enough, all the people in the movie who changed acted like plants. They didn't have emotions. They did anything they were told.

Just like in the Tarzan movies, it seemed scarier to be threatened by plants. You could recognize which animals were threatening. You stayed away from them. But plants? Except for poison ivy and the thorns on berry bushes and roses, there wasn't anything to be afraid of. Trees, bushes, flowers, weeds—if some of them could attack, we'd be out of luck, because we were surrounded.

In the middle of November, Mrs. Sowers took Dave Tolley and me aside. "Listen, boys," she said, "I've come across a story you might enjoy. In England, a man came across a large meadow completely covered by sundews."

She looked at us for a moment. "Sundews are carnivorous plants," she said, and both of us started paying attention.

"There were a million plants," Mrs. Sowers said, "and all of them, as far as the man could see, had just swallowed butterflies. An enormous flock of them had decided to settle on those flowers, and they had paid for their mistake, millions of them simultaneously eaten in minutes."

Dave Tolley and I nodded like carnival dolls. "Imagine," she said, "a whole field of insect-eating plants." We did, but like everything we wanted to see, the butterfly eaters seemed as far away as Mars.

"And as for *The Invasion of the Body Snatchers*," she said, "and all that big seed pod business, that's the Communists. Did either of you see *The Thing* a few years back? The alien in that movie was a vegetable that drank blood—it was a Communist, too. Korea and Red China—that's what all the to-do was about then. This thing in Egypt might be over for now, and all the Communists have to show for it is a canal nobody can use because it's full of sunken ships and broken bridges."

The last day before Christmas vacation, beginning at lunch, was our party—the gift exchange, games with candy bars as prizes, mothers bringing cookies and

potato chips and Coke—but first, Mrs. Sowers said, she had a surprise, flinging her arm toward a man in a dark suit who had materialized in the doorway.

"Who can remember their canals?" Mrs. Sowers asked. The stranger smiled while we chorused Panama and Suez, and then pieced together the canals of Pennsylvania, pleasing Mrs. Sowers by conjuring Main Line, Schuylkill, Delaware, Lehigh, and Morris.

The man in the suit, Mrs. Sowers said, had helped build the Pennsylvania Turnpike. That road had been completed, a wonderful success, nothing like that old dream we had studied in September, the Chesapeake and Ohio Canal, which was supposed to come right from the bay to Pittsburgh and the beginning of the river, seven miles from where we were sitting.

It turned out, after we had passed her retest, showing we remembered the long-closed canals of Pennsylvania and the still-open canals of the world, Mrs. Sowers was having that engineer show us a film on the first turnpike in America because part of that road ran through our county. And when Charles Trout, looking at the map of the turnpike, everything else in Pennsylvania blacked out, said it reminded him of the canals of Mars, the engineer told our class those lines on Mars weren't canals at all. Nobody said anything. Nobody looked at Mrs. Sowers. The engineer kept going, telling us those lines were just Martian forests that flourished on either side of the canals, how irrigation would show itself to approaching spacecraft, how growth along our own lengthening turnpike system would tell the monsters coming our way we could think.

So that settled that, we thought. Mrs. Sowers wasn't wrong, but she wasn't infallible. If we knew who to ask, he'd lead us to carnivorous plants; if we talked to an expert, we'd learn to face a one-man firing squad and live to hear the applause. But when she told us, just before the gift exchange, that the troops were withdrawing in the Middle East, we all smiled because the inevitable atomic war had been postponed a while longer.

I gave her a gift-wrapped box my mother said contained a pair of stockings. "Thank you," Mrs. Sowers said, and I nodded, embarrassed, because I hadn't even seen the stockings before my mother wrapped them. Anything could have been in that box, as long as it lay flat, was light, and was less than ten inches long and six inches wide.

Because it was Friday, I got off the bus two miles from my house where a path between the Atlantic station and a car dealership made a shortcut to the Locust Grove trailer court. I walked, on Fridays, from the Atlantic station to my father's bakery in Etna. It was a mile, maybe, from that bus stop to the bakery,

all of it along heavily traveled Route 8, but there was a sidewalk most of the way, or parking lots to cut across, and I'd been walking that route once a week since fourth grade, during all that time talking to nobody who got off the bus there except Jimmy Mason after he flunked sixth grade and ended up in my class instead of the junior high school.

My mother worked until six o'clock on Fridays, but on that first official day of winter, it was cold and gloomy and already nearly dark at four P.M. Instead of going up the path like he always did, Jimmy Mason fell in beside two older boys I'd never seen. All three of them caught up to me as soon as I crossed the Route 8 bridge where Pine Creek ran under the highway.

Jimmy Mason said the three of them had a job selling Christmas trees in Etna. He cut in front of me and walked backwards, slowing us down. If I had any money, he said, I should buy a tree from them, or better yet, just give the money to them and they wouldn't bother me any more.

"I don't have any money," I said, telling the truth.

"Not on you," Jimmy Mason said, but the other two boys bumped against me from either side.

"What's that badge for?" the biggest said. "You play cops and robbers at your school?"

"Safety patrol," I said. He turned and put his forearm against my chest, resting it across the badge. I noticed he had a mustache.

"You keep the babies safe?"

I didn't say anything. I already wished I hadn't said a word or had the stupidity to wear that patrol gear outside my winter coat. "Patrol boy," he said. "I want to cross here. Why don't you step out and stop those trucks?"

I cut to the inside, afraid he'd push me into the highway. I kept walking, down to the last section of my trip, a quarter mile of crushed-cinders sidewalk, Pine Creek ten feet below us on one side, a hundred-foot cliff running down to the highway on the other.

All three lanes were patch-iced, the traffic one step from where he waved his arms. I could see the stoplight where businesses, including my father's, began. My mother would be wrapping bread and sandwich buns. In a few minutes, she'd start looking out the window to see if I was coming.

He snapped the white straps crossed over my red jacket. "Safety patrol," he said. "Pussy." The badge blinked from the early sets of headlights. He pulled on a pair of black leather gloves. "Give me that badge," the boy said, "or I'll beat the shit out of you, patrol boy."

He shoved me toward the guardrail, and I looked down the hillside at the creek I could see moving beneath the thin ice. "Don't move," he said, sticking a blue pen in my face. "Patrol boy, you write this down: 'I died here, December 21'"—and then he shoved my arm toward the guardrail that made that pen skip along the metal's white and rust until I stopped where a string of *fuck you*'s began.

"More darker," he said, and I went over and over the letters. "So the police," he said, "can read it when your body's found—now walk."

All four of us skidded down a path through the trees that lined the creek bank. Anybody driving a car along Route 8 couldn't see us anymore. On the other side of the creek, an identical thick set of scrub trees covered a bank that sloped up and stopped where the leveled slag of the parking lot for National Valve began. Anybody in that factory, even if he was taking the time to stare out a window instead of shaping and cutting pipe, couldn't see us. Only someone overhead in a helicopter or a hot air balloon could have watched what was happening.

"You ever seen it hard, patrol boy?" he said. "You can fight back right now or else you can kneel and suck it." I checked the bank on the other side of Pine Creek for an opening among the trees. For all I knew, nobody worked at National Valve after four o'clock. When he cocked his fist, I stepped into water that ran over my shoes. "Cold?" he asked. "Wet?"

I watched his hands as I backpedaled to knee-high, the ice collapsing under me, and then I turned and slogged to the other side, eleven years old and dying at 4:15, December 21, in Pine Creek, all three of those boys screaming "Safety Patrol" across that ditch of factory runoff as I scrambled to the almost empty lot where two cars were parked so near the edge, so close together, I thought, before I began to run toward the bakery, one driver was kneeling for another or both of them were waiting to kill me.

The next spring, a boy named Jimmy Scharf dropped a pop-up lofted in an easy arc between first and second base during a recess softball game. "Butterfingers," Charles Trout burbled, happy to be standing safely on first base instead of trudging back toward teammates who were anxiously listening, down two runs, for the bell that would say they'd lost.

Charles Trout didn't say anything else, but Jimmy Scharf picked up the ball, got a running start, and threw it as hard as he could, from ten feet away, at Charles Trout, slamming him in the stomach.

Not one of us asked Charles Trout if he was OK or bent down to help him as he sat in the infield between home plate and first base. Jimmy Scharf had started running, and we all chased him—twelve other sixth-grade boys trying to make up the fifty-foot head start he had.

Look Both Ways

Jimmy Scharf wasn't the fastest runner, but he had the endurance of the truly frightened. All twelve of us fanned out like cavalry, but he wasn't slowing down for the pain in the side or the struggle for breath, and Jimmy Scharf reached the woods beyond center field and darted among the trees like he'd been raised by wolves. Pretty soon our posse trickled out into the sunshine and walked back toward Charles Trout, who was up and sitting on the bench near the backstop.

We were late for class, and Charles Trout was waiting for us so we could all walk in together, thirteen boys filing in without Jimmy Scharf. We sat at our desks while Mrs. Sowers asked for explanations. When nobody volunteered a word, she started in with moralizing and judgment, and we were safe in collective guilt.

Until we heard, from a girl in the back, that Jimmy Scharf was sitting on the railroad tracks that ran along the highway by the school. All of the girls, the two boys who didn't play softball, and the teacher went to the window; the rest of us sat at our desks. We were finished with Jimmy Scharf. If he let himself be run over by a train, it didn't have anything to do with us. Charles Trout wasn't hurt; we weren't chasing him anymore—yet there he was trying to

make the story a morality tale, creating a lie. The truth was that none of us, not even Charles Trout, cared anymore. We'd reacted; he'd seen us react. Anything else was fabricated.

Eventually, without any of us getting out of our desks, Jimmy Scharf came back to class. It was two days later, but we knew he'd gotten off the tracks as soon as he heard the whistle that meant the train was a half mile away. He'd been standing on the other side of the crossing after the train had passed, Mrs. Sowers facing him across the emptied double set of tracks.

He just sat down two rows from me and got out his spelling book. Twice a week, first thing after the Lord's Prayer, "The Star-Spangled Banner," and the Pledge of Allegiance, we copied twenty words. Jimmy Scharf knew the routine.

Jimmy Scharf took his turn at bat at recess. He caught a fly ball that Charles Trout lofted into right field, and he moved to Indiana three months later, six years before we graduated from high school and twelve years before I was told that Charles Trout was dead, with no other details. But by that time neither one of them was somebody I knew, and all I could say, when I heard about Charles Trout, was "Oh," and "Christ," and "Damn," like anybody would who was even half listening.

That same week, my mother, after the last PTA meeting she would ever attend, announced, "Mr. Bell has cancer of the spine." In six weeks I would be finished with sixth grade and move on to junior high school, where mothers began to specialize, becoming band boosters, football fanatics, or cheerleader chums.

Mr. Bell was the music teacher. He had a raspy voice and used a small, round tuner he blew into to get us searching for the correct pitch, twice a week when he visited our room while Mrs. Sowers disappeared for forty minutes.

We sang "Dixie" and "The Battle Hymn of the Republic" and "The Marine Corps Hymn" from the stapled book full of uplifting songs we stored in our desks. Mr. Bell told us we were all blessed to be born under a fortunate flag. For our first music exam in October, he'd listened to us sing, one by one, "The Star-Spangled Banner" from memory, placing us exactly under the flag for our performances.

There was more to it than moving our mouths, he'd explained, showing us the proper posture for singing the National Anthem, his back as straight as a soldier's. All of us had kept eye contact with a spot slightly above his head so we looked patriotic and proud, working our way through the a cappella praise for home.

In January, for an earlier PTA meeting, he'd chosen four of us sixth graders to sing "America the Beautiful" and "Over There" for a room full of mothers. By

September my voice would crack and turn into something embarrassing, but on that January night I could carry a tune in close harmony with Paula Phelan and Nancy Housel and Jimmy Dunmire, all of us soprano and alto. Mr. Bell had introduced us, and we were a hit.

Upstairs, after we'd finished to applause and been allowed to leave so we wouldn't have to sit through the "business meeting," the four of us watched the *Tennessee Ernie Ford Show* on the television that was kept in our classroom because Mrs. Sowers was also the principal. Tommy Sands was the guest. He sang "Teenage Crush," and Jimmy Dunmire and I sang along while the girls stared at Tommy Sands. "I wish Tab Hunter was on," Nancy said. "'Young Love' is my favorite song, and he looks so cool." Jimmy Dunmire said he wished Mr. Bell would hand out a rock-and-roll song book instead of one filled with the second, third, and fourth verses nobody ever sang to all of those patriotic tunes.

Three months later, when my mother said Mr. Bell was as good as dead, she added, "Isn't it something that he always has such good posture, and here he has it in his back?"

Instead of leaving while we had music class, Mrs. Sowers stayed in the room all day, except for Friday afternoon art, and taught us something she called "enrichment social studies." We learned all of the presidents in order from Washington to Eisenhower; we learned the names and dates of our country's wars right up to Korean (1950–1953). She taught us Democrats and Republicans, Federalists and Whigs; she had us memorize the states and their capitals, beginning with Albany and Atlanta, Annapolis, Augusta. We needed to know everything about the United States, she said, including the names of the National Parks, their spellings just as important, or we'd become bad citizens, ones that the Communists could brainwash.

Now, more than ever, she explained, we needed to take care of our bodies and minds, and that summer, a year later than my friends, I finished getting my polio shots, my mother smiling as I walked out of the office of the doctor she'd finally made an appointment with because there was no home remedy for polio. "There's one less thing that can jump up and get you," she said, but shortly after school began, the Asian Flu cleared out half the students in every class I had. "We don't have a quorum today," Mr. Wargo said in history, but nobody knew what he was talking about, even when he shook his head as if a quorum was something to be taken seriously, like Communism.

More than a million people around the world died from the Asian Flu, but everybody in my school returned within a few weeks. In October, just after I

stopped singing in seventh-grade music class, moving my lips like the rock stars on the Saturday night Dick Clark show, the Russians put Sputnik into orbit, and nobody at school cared about music anymore, or art, or even English and history. Everybody in the seventh grade took a test, and by February, thirty of us were assigned to advanced math and science, the chosen ones out of the three hundred or so in the seventh grade.

Our math book had letters as well as numbers in it. We said algebra instead of arithmetic and carried slide rules and copies of the periodic table. In ten years, we were told, we needed to be in charge of outer space, because if we weren't, the Communists would be, and they would be certain to make our lives miserable from "up there." "Somebody better learn something quick," my father said, "or we'll all be under the red boot."

It didn't look good. One U.S. rocket had blown up on the launch pad; one had just sat there until it toppled over. "We have Elvis Presley," our science teacher said. "The Russians have Sputnik." In November, the Russians sent a dog up in Sputnik II. "Laika," the newspaper said. "The dog's name means *barker* in Russian." The dog spinning around the world made us study harder, but after a week it died when the oxygen ran out. "Just like the Communists," my mother said, "to let it die like that."

"How do we know it was inside?" my father said. "How do we know that dog didn't die as soon as it blasted off?"

My parents gave me a microscope for Christmas. By the end of January, when the police were hunting for Charles Starkweather and his fourteen-year-old girlfriend Caril Fugate because he'd killed eleven people, I was tired of looking at bits of dust and strands of hair and drops of my saliva. By the time the police caught both of them in Wyoming, the United States launched Explorer into orbit. "Our first satellite," the science teacher said. "We should all be proud." Except in science and math class, all we talked about was murder, how Charles Starkweather looked like a hard-nosed rockabilly singer, somebody with a haircut like the high school boys who didn't take any science classes at all. And Caril Fugate was only a year older than we were—what girl did we know in eighth grade who would ride off with the boy who killed her parents? Vanguard, the next satellite, went into orbit in March. "Now we're cooking with gas," my father said.

In April, my old grade-school building was declared hazardous. Its fire escapes were unsafe, something we'd all known the year before, but now a corner of the roof had torn loose and fallen into the playground ten minutes

after recess ended. Jimmy Dunmire and I still played basketball there, stuffing balls through the eight-foot-high baskets we'd been happy to grab with our hands the year before.

We looked up at the missing corner and talked about where we'd stood for nut fights during fifth grade, when it was a craze to slap drilled buckeyes threaded through a shoestring against each other until one of them split and fell to the ground. It looked as if those bricks would have fallen right about where everybody stood around to watch the short, small duels.

We'd looked down from the second-floor windows from fourth to sixth grade, and not once had either of us said he would jump for a dollar, or even for five dollars. You could tell, just from looking, that we were too high for safety. Jimmy Dunmire wanted to see more bricks fall. "That would be cool," he said, brushing his hands across his new flattop haircut. "I bought 'Kiss and Make Up' yesterday. It's so cool, I played it fifteen times in a row."

Mr. Bell, my mother heard, had returned to teaching. "A miracle," she said, but we didn't see him because he only taught music at the grade school, and by May the talk of miracles had dissolved because Mr. Bell had suddenly "retired." Jimmy Dunmire stopped going to the school playground with me. He joined a singing group called the Coachmen, who dressed in black and red and sang doo-wop songs like "Come Go with Me" and "Speedo."

Starting in July, I played "Summertime Blues" by Eddie Cochran over and over. "Now you can't use the car 'cause you didn't work a lick," I'd sing along in my deepest voice. I bought Chuck Berry and Little Richard records and had a flattop pasted into shape with some pink gunk that came in a tube I twisted up like lipstick. When I heard a doo-wop song like "In the Still of the Nite," I thought of Jimmy Dunmire and the rest of the Coachmen singing it, how they would sound.

I started to slouch like the Coachmen did when they walked in the halls. "You walk like a bum," my father said. "Stand up straight."

"You should be glad you're so tall," my mother said. "It's not good for a man to be short." She looked me up and down as if she was measuring me for a suit. "Your grandfather's short," she said. "And what's worse, he never stands up straight." I knew what was coming next—slouchers were the men who wasted their lives. They stayed in the shadows like the dead we didn't know. They curled like old women who crept to the pews they reused each Sunday. I nodded, agreeing that those women were bent like the hunchback who shined shoes at the bus station, where my friends and I bought magazines sealed in

plastic to carry behind the humps of sumac and locust, where we slouched into the strange tongue of silent lust.

There were no magazines at our houses but the goodnesses of *Readers' Digest.* But there, in the magazine pages that followed the last nude woman, were photographs of "The Man Who Grows!" Nothing in his shoes to trick us, he promised six inches in minutes, if we paid.

In one picture, he stood smaller than the unschooled men who flanked him, and then he rose, through two panels, past those men who wore the white shirts of our fathers' good posture. Knees, hips, chest, throat—there were body parts enough to restretch ourselves after years of recklessness with slouching, with love for the reliable return of desire, what we stooped to, slumping our shoulders, saying *yes* to the curved spine that pulled us toward the joyful four legs of thoughtlessness.

The nuclear submarine *Nautilus* sailed under the North Pole, something that was sure to scare the Communists, and the first nuclear power plant at Shippensport, less than an hour away, was cranking out electricity. "See?" my father said. "See what America can do when it puts its mind to things?"

When eighth grade began, we learned simultaneous equations in algebra and created graphs that took on shapes besides straight lines. In science, we stood beside Bunsen burners and wore goggles and followed directions, no exceptions, in order to see, first-hand, how the world worked. "Science is war," our teacher said. Soon enough we'd see what he meant by that as he marked the map of the world hanging from the back wall with a flag that represented our class. When everyone had mastered how to calculate the lifting force of levers, he advanced our flag toward Moscow. When one of us mislabeled the water cycle, the Communists moved closer to our homes.

During the battle of electricity, AC and DC and the reason our light bulbs let us learn in the dark, the Soviets swept across Europe while he repeated, "Filaments, incandescence, amperes, ohms." When he returned our unit tests, he smiled and moved the Communists back into Poland where they'd begun. The room was an atlas. We all drew accurate diagrams of a battery, ready to invade.

Outside of class, I didn't say one word about algebra or the intricacies of an electric circuit to anyone. I memorized all the verses to "Stagger Lee" and sang them to myself while I practiced my jump shot on a regulation basket Dave Tolley's father had put up on a nearby street.

On the first day of December, there was a huge fire in a school in Chicago, so big that it was on television. For once, I watched the news, and my mother even bought a newspaper on Tuesday, something she never did, to read the story and look at a page full of pictures. There were more the following day, and though that school, Our Lady of the Angels, was three times larger than my old grade school, it looked, from the side, to be identical. It had the same tall windows; the newspaper said the second-floor windowsills, like the ones at my old school, were twenty-five feet from the ground. The outside was brick, but the inside, like ours had been, was all wood that was dry and brittle from years of service. In fact, my old school was even older. Our Lady of the Angels had been built in 1910; Glenshaw School had been constructed in 1899. I remembered that date from the cornerstone close to where the roof had fallen, because anything from the nineteenth century seemed so old it was like it had never happened.

There were almost a hundred dead students and nuns. "God have mercy on their souls," my mother said.

"And the ones burned and still alive," my father said. "They're in for it."

"Why didn't they all jump?" my mother said, but I didn't say a word about the formula for acceleration that I'd learned and what it was like to hit the cement from twenty-five feet up. Though the windows weren't as high off the ground at the junior high school, I had most of my classes on the third floor. That Tuesday I looked down from the windows of each room I entered to see where I would land if I had to jump. Two of the drops led to cement. Some of those nuns had told their students to pray while they waited for the firemen to arrive with ladders—even the eighth graders like me, who surely, I thought, would have ignored that advice and rushed for the windows no matter how far it was to the ground.

And then I started to list all of the times I thought I'd been in mortal danger, beginning with crossing the street in September 1951, when first grade began. Each morning and afternoon during the first two weeks of school, when Jack Mehringer, a policeman with a huge belly, had stopped traffic so we could cross the highway two blocks from our school, he'd told me to check twice for cars or I'd wind up a grease smear. Finally, on the last morning, he'd said, "You've got a first-class cowlick there, little fella," and I'd looked down at my shoes because I had no idea what he was talking about. I felt like yelling, "Fatso" or "Lard Ass," or asking him how it felt hiding behind that telephone pole my aunt had told me about.

In Etna, Pennsylvania, before I started first grade, bank robbers were trapped across the street from the hardware store where a friend of my mother's took

dictation from the owner. Jack Mehringer, at the end of the block, was a hundred pounds past being protected behind the telephone pole, where he turned himself sideways, his gun in his holster, while the bandits fired a few shots toward the state police, who had taken positions closer to where the robbers were holed up. "Something like a baby who covers his eyes and believes the threatening world is gone," my mother's friend said. She watched from the upstairs window; she gave her boss a face covered with sweat each time she told my mother the story, kept his lips trembling through the thirty seconds of gunfire, none of it supplied by Mehringer.

The summer after Jack Mehringer survived behind that phone pole and I'd finished first grade without being hit by a car, years before I ever knew Jimmy Scharf or he decided to sit on the railroad tracks, I learned something else about time and place and the power they have to single you out.

Everybody I was playing with went in to lunch, except Linda Truman. She had the same name as the President—"Good riddance to him before too long," I heard at home—who wasn't going to be President much longer because Eisenhower was going to straighten things out. I didn't care about Eisenhower the week before I was starting second grade; I wanted Linda Truman, who would be in my class, to think I had better things to do than go straight home to cheese sandwiches and milk.

"Let's go to the railroad tracks," I said, and she didn't hesitate. She walked beside me down Angle Alley—so we looked, from behind, like those sentimental paintings of children you see on the walls of pediatricians' offices. It was only two blocks. It was only crossing one street where cars had to slow down for the right-angle turn where the alley merged with the street adjacent to the one we lived on.

But there, just crossing the railroad tracks toward us, were three older boys we didn't know because they were Mickies who went to the Catholic school. Mickies—everybody had a name like that: Wops, Hunkies, Kikes, Niggers, Spics. What made them different was they had BB guns, and they pointed them at us like we were riding in a stagecoach with a loaded strongbox.

They backed us against a door, and Linda Truman grabbed my hand. I thought somebody lived behind that door, that he would open it and say, "What's going on here?"

Nobody said a word until one of the boys lifted his gun to his shoulder and chanted, "First-grade babies, stick them in the gravy." The other two laughed. They fired their pellets at our feet and yelled, "Dance."

I danced, like all the cowards in cowboy movies. Linda Truman cried, like all the women who listen to the gunfire from another duel in the dusty street. The two boys who'd fired at our feet lifted their guns to their shoulders, and the three of them took a stance like a firing squad, shouting, "Five, four, three, two, one," before shooting BB's into the door six inches above our heads.

I didn't tell anyone. They'd fired a volley so close to simultaneously I wouldn't have known which one shot my eye out or peppered Linda Truman's face. I had no idea whether or not any of them had fired because he felt he had to or face ridicule or gun barrels. And I didn't know if one or more of them had to force himself not to point his gun directly at my face.

That house belonged to somebody who might be home. That door had three sets of pockmarks six inches above our heads. Ten years old, and all of them so accurate, as if they'd been trained for combat at the Catholic school, as if Mickies were better prepared for life around the corner than I was.

By the day of the Chicago fire, Mr. Bell had been dead for three months. My mother found out a week after he died, two days after he was buried, because his death notice had run on Saturday and Sunday when we still didn't get a newspaper. Since the beginning of school, I had spent less time with Jimmy Dunmire because he wasn't in the accelerated classes, which were filled mostly with boys who lived near Mt. Royal Boulevard, where, according to my father, the uppity-ups lived. They'd gone to the new grade school, which was slung low like the houses they lived in, ranch-style with big lawns that never had dandelions. On December 1st, the day of the Chicago fire, we started junior-high basketball practice, and I felt like I was playing alongside a stranger.

Just before Christmas vacation, Jimmy Dunmire sang with the Coachmen in the junior high school talent show. They took first place, and girls crowded around them in the hall, the four of them in matching chinos and shirts. In Cuba, Fidel Castro was winning a war my science teacher was worried about. "He's with the Communists, just you wait and see," he said, "and here he'll be right next door to us."

I got a chemistry set for Christmas from my parents. Between Christmas and New Year's, I made up my own experiments and stunk up the house when I started a small fire. "Don't you know what you're doing?" my mother said. "What are they teaching you over there?"

I listened to the radio from noon to six on New Year's Day to hear the Top

100 songs of 1958. I sang "For Your Precious Love" and "Little Star" in my head, where I sounded exactly like Jerry Butler and the lead singer of the Elegants. I played air guitar to Duane Eddy and Link Wray. "Rebel Rouser" sounded like the South would rise again; "Rumble" sounded like the world would end in a gang fight. When school began again the following day, I walked out of the locker room after basketball practice with Jimmy Dunmire, making fun of the whiz kids in my science classes, boys who didn't even try out for basketball, boys who, even now, couldn't touch the rim of the eight-foot baskets at our old school playground.

And the closest I came to dying during those years was riding in a new jeep that Gene Hodge owned. Nobody else I knew owned a new car. Gene Hodge, a year older, lived in the corner of the school district where the houses were set back from narrow roads at the end of curved, tree-lined driveways. Nobody over sixteen from those houses rode the bus to school, and Gene Hodge, two days after he passed his driver's test, hauled the rest of our mile relay team home after practice.

We called him Sergeant Hodge and told him to take us to the front. I sat in the back like all the colonels and generals I'd seen in movies, and either the jeep or Gene Hodge was a little clumsy, because each time we skidded out of a curve, I felt better about having one less hazard between me and my house, set close to the street where I lived.

A few weeks later, just after school ended for the summer, Gene Hodge slid off the road where those rich kids lived, ran up what was left of a road crew's bank of cinders, and flipped over—Gene Hodge and one passenger thrown clear, the other two pinned underneath, one with minor injuries, and Dan Watkins, killed instantly, his head nearly torn from his body.

That May, in the shower after track practice, Dan Watkins had danced the Mashed Potato while a couple of us had sung, "Please, Mr. Postman." He was astonishing, keeping his balance on a floor so slippery with water and grit from the cinder track the rest of us minced our steps while he ground his feet to the rhythm of our approximation of the Marvelettes. Ten minutes later, he showed me the grade he'd received on the story I'd written for him in Latin after he agreed to pay me to cheat for him. "B+," he said. "Way to go, man. I can't even pronounce these words, let alone say what they mean. Five bucks is the all-time cheap price for first-rate work like this."

When Dan Watkins got killed, I was sure the radio in the jeep was tuned to a station that might have been playing a song you could dance the Mashed

Potato to; but the first thing I thought, when I heard the news, was *God exists and I am next.*

The second thing I thought was I knew my Latin, and I'd earned my A.

What was wrong with me was I couldn't manage relief I'd survived and use it to work harder and apply myself. I couldn't even manage guilt and penance. All I managed was believing Gene Hodge deserved to be punished, that anyone so stupid and careless should have to turn himself into the Eye-for-an-Eye Court, the only check and balance that works.

When school began again, the Coachmen were singing folk songs in close harmony, sounding like the Kingston Trio and the Brothers Four. Everybody talked about Dan Watkins for the first few days, and I remembered that one night in April, the year after Linda Truman and I were shot at, my father spoke quietly to my mother about the fat policeman who'd been hit by a train at the crossing two blocks from the Wilson Street School. He'd stepped into the path of a north-bound approaching a couple of seconds after the south-bound had passed. "Something a child would do," my mother said, before I could walk into the living room to start talking about looking both ways.

Old man Krause was one of those neighbors we thought we hated. Because he came outside to curse at us when a foul ball rolled into his yard. Because he'd hidden behind his shrubbery once and leapt out to pounce on a rolling softball, refusing to return it.

One afternoon, while we sat around complaining about adults, Charlie Schneider explained the theory of dog shit, how a burning bagful would draw the people we targeted to their front porches, where the men, especially, would stamp out the fire while we watched happily from a safely distant shadow. It seemed like such a great idea that the next weekend, Dave Tolley and I watched Charlie scoop a week's worth of his golden retriever's dog turds into a paper sack and followed him across the vacant lot where we played to stand beside him in the summer darkness while he lit the bag and rang old man Krause's bell.

The Theory of Dog Shit

We hid on the street side of the same shrubbery Krause had used earlier in the week. But when Krause flung open the door, he didn't stomp on the fire. He just yelled at us. "I know who you are. Young Tolley and Schneider. I know your fathers."

I was glad to be excluded because I didn't live on the same street, but we didn't bother Krause anymore that summer. Instead, we tried the theory of dog shit on a dozen enemy houses—the fathers of effeminate classmates and girls who ignored us, but mostly men who trimmed their lawns so perfectly and so often we thought we hated them as much as we did a softball stealer. We moved out of their neighborhood and mine to give our victims more would-be vandals from whom to choose, and though there were men who cursed into the darkness, launching the great obscenities of anger, not once did the person who answered the door step on the bag of shit.

It was the summer of 1959, we'd just finished eighth grade, and a whole new set of neighbors had moved in during the past two

years because the farm between my house and the housing plan where Dave Tolley, Charlie Schneider, and old man Krause lived had been sold and divided into lots. Three years earlier, when there were huge drainage pipes set in place to accommodate the changes in landscape and the demands of sixty new families, we'd used those pipes to entertain ourselves.

Each one of the pipes eventually led downhill to The Flats, where the township's poorest families lived. Pine Creek, which flowed among those houses, flooded them each spring. There was an abandoned strip mine at one end of that neighborhood, and a busy highway bordered another side. All three of us could see that drainage from the housing plan would empty itself onto the hillside above The Flats, one more reason to be happy to live on high ground, although never once did we burn dog shit on the front porches of those who lived there.

What we did that earlier summer was crab-walk through those enormous storm drains, pretending we were following a lead-lined tunnel to a bomb shelter, like the ones people were beginning to build because the Russians were threatening to nuke us. Overhead, the model home that had been built before any of the lots were sold was unlocked for the wives of steelworkers and mechanics and truck drivers, men who worked with their hands like our fathers did. Once, we'd watched those women brush their fingertips over the slick Braille of appliances before they parted the gold and green patterned drapes to appreciate the view, but quickly, in the darkness of those pipes, we forgot the simple geography of their corridors, and all three of us raised our voices as if volume was a vaccine for the sudden amnesia of being underground.

We couldn't get ourselves properly turned around. For ten minutes we sweated and swore our mild fifth-grade oaths like "damn" and "hell" and "shit," and finally we skidded out of a pipe fifty feet above a backyard full of old tires and two abandoned cars.

One neighbor we didn't harass was Jack Hall, who was building a bomb shelter in his backyard because he was a veteran of nuclear testing and said he knew exactly what was coming for the families whose fathers thought the only possible use for the A-bomb after Hiroshima and Nagasaki was stock footage in movies and television shows.

He'd done a hitch at Camp Desert Rock, where he'd witnessed a bomb test called Shot Smoky by standing in the open with a group of other soldiers four

miles from the tower where the A-bomb ignited. He'd watched two other earlier tests and been discharged shortly after Shot Smoky with sores and loose teeth, dizzy enough, he told us five times that summer, to tumble down his own steps like a baby.

"Like a hurricane full of shit," he told us. "Dirt and wire, sagebrush, rattlesnakes, and what not. We hugged God's good earth and then we stood up and marched to ground zero to make sure that tower and everything around it looked like nothing."

He talked to us because we stopped to see how his shelter was coming along. Our fathers didn't work evenings and weekends on a place to hide when the missiles were launched. They didn't say a word about the duck-and-cover we learned in school, nothing about doing what our junior high school teachers taught, nothing whatsoever about purified water and canned food, generators, a thick cement wall, and the rest of what Jack Hall's family would have by the end of the summer. Better to "go like that," they said, using the finger snap my mother made to demonstrate the way an old woman on our street had died just after school had ended.

That summer, Congress reaffirmed something called the Captive Nations Resolution. The newspaper said it had been passed in 1953, and Eisenhower, for the seventh time, was proclaiming a week of prayer for those under Communism. "Good timing," my father said, "what with Nixon off to the Soviet Union. Maybe he'll lead them all in prayer."

I didn't care about Nixon's trip, but I worried that my father would announce there were evening church services to ensure the community's compliance with prayer. That the government's edict would end up with me enduring another week like the one before Easter—a second Holy Thursday service, the Good Friday three-hour marathon, and worse, sunrise service, getting up at 5:30 to sing the praises of democracy, filing out to the breakfast of pancakes and sausages before we filed back in for Sunday School and regular church.

In Moscow, Nixon and Khrushchev argued among the dishwashers and televisions in the pavilion on technology sponsored by the USA. The United States, Khrushchev blustered, was a bourgeois department store. "Good," my mother said, watching the news. Nixon didn't have to tell us the USSR was an armory. In Florida, that week, to show how likely it was for the Soviets to launch an attack, newlyweds named Minison were spending their honeymoon in a bomb shelter exclusively for *Life* magazine. We could expect the photographs soon.

Later that week, Jack Hall's nearly completed bomb shelter, after the summer's heaviest rain, flooded like the root cellar under our porch. "If there's a war," my father said, "he'll be in the soup, all right, only it will be radioactive broth."

For once I thought my father was right. He knew as much about survival as anyone on the streets I could walk to, including Jack Hall. He was a scoutmaster, and everything he owned for Boy Scouts was survival gear—flashlights, canteens, first aid kits, lanterns.

None of it seemed like it would help anybody last for the next seventy years like I wanted to, but the nearby hardware store sold a crowbar as an "instant fallout shelter" because, their sign said, you could use it to pry open a manhole cover and clamber down to safety. "Fat chance," my father said. My friends and I had never gone back into the confusing storm drains, but now, because Charlie and two other boys in my class knew it would lead to manholes, they entered the mouth of a large storm drain behind the only McDonald's on our side of Pittsburgh with such confidence that I had to follow. A hundred feet into it, I started to worry about the stream of water we had to straddle, the stains on the inside of the pipe that showed water, at least once, had reached more than halfway up the sides, enough to flush us out, maybe drowned along the way.

It was raining outside. If it suddenly fell harder, maybe things would add up to the sort of flash flood that swept away thirteen- or fourteen-year-old fools. We worked our way to a sort of intersection, and I followed those three boys up the ladder to where Charlie popped up the manhole cover that turned out to be near Gimbel's, the department store that anchored the shopping center next to McDonald's.

"Maybe Jack Hall will put a pipe like this under his shelter now," Charlie said. "And then we could pop up inside after the war starts and make ourselves at home. He couldn't open the door to throw us out."

"Fat chance," I said, but what we all agreed on was we needed guns. We watched television shows depicting the dilemma of admitting neighbors and diminishing the chances of survival. Even so, we all knew nobody would actually finish a bomb shelter except fanatics like Jack Hall. "Two days after the blast," the civil defense manual said, "only 1 percent of radioactivity is left, but the radiation may be so intense at the start that 1 percent may be extremely dangerous."

"When does the last 1 percent go away?" I asked my father, and he spread his arms as if he was describing the world's largest fish-that-got-away.

That summer, Pennsylvania was invaded by tent caterpillars. Trees sprouted gauzy nests that promised disaster, and those caterpillars had dozens of nests on the crab-apple tree by Paul Kress's driveway two doors away. I looked into the nests, where through the web-like covering, I could see hundreds of thin caterpillars swarming as if they wanted to break out and get to work on the leaves of that tree or my body, if I was foolish enough to let them cover me. "It's creepy how you can see right inside these things," Paul said.

"They're translucent," I said, remembering the word from my eighth-grade science class and the quiz on *transparent, translucent,* and *opaque.*

"The better to see them burn," Paul said, lugging a gallon can of gasoline out of his father's garage. "Let's nuke them. Let's do Hiroshima on as many as we can."

The caterpillars were hideous. I had no trouble finding a stick and helping Paul lift cocoons from the tree and drop them into a puddle of gasoline he'd poured into a low spot where his driveway widened near a small pipe that took runoff water away from the garage. Most of the nests stuck to our sticks when we nudged the ends of them, and if they didn't, the caterpillars spilling out as we walked them to the puddle, we stepped on as many as we could.

When we had ten of those nests in place, it seemed as if there were thousands of caterpillars, most of them still inside their translucent houses. Fumes from the gasoline Paul had poured rose around us as we leaned over to look. The mouth of the pipe looked hazy. "This stuff is like dope," Paul said. "People sniff this to get like they're drunk."

I nodded. Paul's father, according to mine, "liked his drink," but no one in my house drank, so I had to rely on old stories about The Prince to have any idea of what it was to "get like they're drunk."

I took a step back and then another as Paul splashed more gasoline on the mess. He leaned back down and scraped one of his big wooden matches that lit when dragged across any rough surface. A cloud of flame blew up so close to his face that he arced back like a gymnast, sprawling among the loose caterpillars as the flame roiled for a second or two and then sucked back down to campfire size.

"Shit," he said. "Holy shit," and his hands went to his face, resting on his cheeks and then his forehead like my mother's did when she tested me for fever.

I shook a caterpillar off my shoe. "That was close," he said, laughing, getting up, and leaning over to look at the roasted worms. "Look at them all," he said, "the dumb shits."

Already, the fire was nearly out. The caterpillars looked like the snakes we lit on the 4th of July, only way thinner. Nobody knew what those snakes were

made of, but we loved the picture of a coiled cobra on the box, and every summer we bought packages of them, lighting the dark, thick pills and watching as dark gray snakes emerged, curling up, getting longer until they started to collapse on themselves while the stump from which they'd issued hissed and spit and then went quiet.

"They're totaled," Paul said. "The little shits."

One afternoon, Jack Hall told Dave Tolley and me that Shot Hood was seventy-four kilotons. "You betcha that one was big," he said. "Hiroshima was thirteen. You boys can do the math."

And we did. And we were reading all about bombs, discovering, to our delight, a description of the excrement bomb of ancient China. In his *Military Encyclopedia, 1044,* Tseng Kung-Liang gives his recipe:

> 15 pounds of human excrement—dried, sifted, and powdered
> 8 ounces wolfsbane
> 8 ounces aconite
> 8 ounces croton oil
> 8 ounces soap-bean pods
> 8 ounces arsenious oxide
> 8 ounces arsenic sulfide
> 4 ounces cantharides beetles
> 16 ounces ashes
> 8 ounces tung oil

All of this wonderful mess was mixed with gunpowder and catapulted into the enemy, where it was supposed to irritate the skin and raise blisters. The ingredients were mysterious enough for us to believe that those blisters would cover some enemy's body and cause him unendurable agony. In the book we read, it said the artillerymen who fired those bombs were told to suck black plums and eat licorice to protect themselves.

"Fat chance that would work," Dave Tolley said, but already we had decided to add ashes and lima bean pods and hot pepper when we made our next dog-shit assault. Nothing looked different as the bag burned, but this time, at last, one man stomped on the fire and then ran directly at us. At ten o'clock Friday night, he was wearing a white shirt and a tie, deserving shit on his shoes for sporting a

costume like that so late. And though we wanted to bolt, we knew his accurate direction was an accident, that if we stayed behind the thick, fat junipers across the street from his house, we could watch him slow down when he reached the asphalt, then stop and scream again, adding, "I know you're out here" to every scatological expletive, as if hearing him would make us reconsider the deployment of shit.

Life magazine published "Their Sheltered Honeymoon" during August, the Minisons smiling for the cameras as if a bomb shelter was a swell place to start a marriage, the three of us joking about how they must have had the world's greatest honeymoon because there wasn't anything else to do but have sex. Khrushchev, declaring more Communist technological advances, had told Nixon, "When we catch you up, in passing you by, we will wave to you."

"The world doesn't seem to know itself, Gary," Jack Hall told me one afternoon before I met up with Dave and Charlie. "You march toward ground zero and everything clears up in a hurry. There's nothing at all to worry about except the next step, and then the next and the next after that. Everything else is gone. Vanished. Vamoosed."

I nodded, thinking of the desert and tumbleweeds, the sheriff in a hundred movies showing his deputies where the outlaws have gotten to. "You'll see when the time comes," Jack Hall said finally. "Your old man ought to get his ass in gear. He's got a family worth saving, and he's out mowing his lawn."

When school started, our social studies teacher gave us a problem to solve:

A bomb shelter can hold eight people long enough for them to survive World War III. However, there are sixteen people inside, and they have to choose, in the thirty minutes before the missiles arrive, which eight will get to live and which eight will get pushed out into the holocaust.

We threw out the politician, the lawyer, and the minister. We were ninth graders now, so we shoved the teacher outside. It didn't take long to add the artist and the soldier, taking for granted that we had the guns, not him. Finally, we evicted the two people who were over fifty years old.

Who did we keep? Inside, waiting out the years until that lethal one percent

dissipated, were two teenagers (a boy and a girl), the engineer, and the survivalist. Besides them, we kept two small children, a carpenter, and a mechanic. They were good choices, nearly everyone agreed. Only the engineer wore a tie to work, and he could be persuaded, we thought, to never wear it again.

God

ottlob Lang, my grandfather, is locked out of his house. He tries each of the three doors and the four rear windows at street level, returns to the front porch and the door to the kitchen, where he knows his five children are sitting with his wife, her father, and two of her brothers; but he refuses to pound or threaten to break it down or shatter the glass on any one of the fourteen windows of the house on Prospect Street in Etna, Pennsylvania. He shouts, "You kids will regret this"—that he's certain my grandmother wasn't the one who snapped the bolts shut, because she knows what marriage means.

"This isn't the old country," his oldest daughter Margaret says through the door. "You're not taking us to hell in a hand basket with you." He listens to her shout "souse" and "stew pot." He hears his wife's brothers comforting her in their soft, effeminate bachelors' voices. He looks up to where his father-in-law, in German, hollers down from an upstairs window that he should thank God for Roosevelt, who gives rewards for the weakness and sloth of the likes of Gottlob Lang.

God of Our Fathers

"*Gott im himmel*," my grandfather says, despite himself, and empties the change from his pockets, opens his shirt and tosses it on the porch. All he can do is make metaphors and go back to his brother George, who will keep him a week, no more. Later, he will retrieve two stuffed suitcases, his overcoat, his watch, his Victrola, and the enormous ship-in-a-bottle he'd won in a raffle. Before the year ends, he learns, in a letter from Germany, that his cousins are happy, finally, they didn't follow him to America. "We are men again," they write, block-printing in perfect English to show him anything is possible.

His youngest daughter, my mother, is in high school. After she was born, he'd promised himself "no more children," hauling ashes and shoveling sidewalks, sweeping and mopping the floors of the neighborhood grade school, and later the high school, before paying to drink in the private clubs of Prohibition. And then, accustomed to those clubs, keeping that habit after it was repealed until the night he was expelled.

The Saturday before Christmas, 1952, my father took me and my mother along while he delivered leftovers from the bakery to the St. Barnabas Home. My mother disappeared upstairs, but I followed my father into a lounge with a television and an enormous ham radio. "This is Archie," my father said. I was seven years old, but I thought Archie looked out of whack, even for a man in a wheelchair. "Did you hear me?" my father said. "Say hello to Archie."

"Hi," I tried, but all I could do was stare at how Archie's left arm was inverted at the elbow as if the hinge of it were nailed on backward.

Archie grimaced and swiveled in his chair. "Hi there, fella," he squeaked in a child's voice. His other arm seemed to work fairly well. He used it to push a button on the chair, turning it toward an elaborate ham radio set.

"Archie made this whole getup," my father said while Archie was busy activating some controls. "He's a regular genius with this stuff. Ask him anything about it. You'll never stump him."

I didn't want to ask Archie anything. My father was here to deliver leftover rolls and coffee cakes, something he'd started to do that year on every slow Saturday, choosing a charity home run by men who were all called "Brother Paul" or "Brother Hance" or some other Brother, each of them wearing an identical dark, hooded robe. The bakery wasn't open on Sundays. Doughnuts and sweet rolls and coffee cakes went stale more quickly than anything else my father sold. If I trailed behind my father through three pans or four, he let me choose one roll to eat while we waited for my mother, who never talked to my father on the ride home. She said "Later" to him, but babbled to me about Roy Rogers, the Lone Ranger, Hopalong Cassidy, and the Cisco Kid.

Two-and-a-half years after these trips began, at Woolworth's, in Pittsburgh, there was seventy feet of Davy Crockett—coloring books, T-shirts, and a stack of coonskin caps. All I owned was a lunch box I carried from New Year's to June when even Eisenhower sported a Davy Crockett tie, and I had long ago memorized all the verses to the three-minute ballad by Bill Hayes as well as the serial biography on a set of bubble-gum cards, from born-on-a-mountaintop-in-Tennessee to hero's-death-at-the-Alamo.

He was "the king of the wild frontier," and I sang along with each verse while I sat in the back of our green and beige '54 Chevy Bel Air on the Saturdays we visited St. Barnabas, where by now, I knew my mother visited the mysterious Prince of Etna. There were legends enough about him to fill a string of verses

in a ballad. If only he'd died a hero's death at some Alamo before he'd spiraled down to a room in a charity home, he might have remained tall and strong in the second-hand memories I constructed from hearing my mother and her sister tell stories.

Instead, I listened to my Aunt Margaret mutter, "The old stew. I had to shovel his sidewalks and carry his ashes so he kept a job." She meant the 1920s, hard winters for a school janitor like The Prince who drank weeknights. Hard winters for the oldest of my mother's sisters, who passed on those chores to her younger brother just before the Depression set in.

Because of their help, The Prince kept that job, even "moved up" to the new high school, but by the early 1930s he lost that job anyway, replaced by a man who didn't show up an hour after my mother's brother had finished the sidewalk, stoked the furnace, and walked inside to go to class.

My Aunt Margaret hated The Prince, and that anger made her a wonderful storyteller. "He brought home a handful of chickens he won at cards. He threw them into the kitchen like he was the great provider. 'Kill them or keep them,' he said to Mother, and when I wanted to open the door and shoo them out with a broom, your Uncle Karl built them a coop in the cellar."

"Right there on the spot, he made that coop," she said. "The old souse. You should have seen his face when he saw those chickens penned up down there like we were farmers now. He thought he'd brought home the bacon. There's not enough time in the day for all the stories I could tell about that pantywaist."

Even so, she always came back to the story that happened the week before they locked The Prince out of the house for good. One night he'd stolen the two silver dollars my mother had earned by writing about the pleasures of her hometown and having her essay published in the *Pittsburgh Press*. He loved the taverns in that town, and sober, he tried to tell her the logic of spending her prize on local beer. "Get me to swear I'll never steal from you," he said, "and I never will again. I never drank in this house after I swore not to. Never once. Never." As if he might jump, he leaned over the porch rail that ran twenty feet above the bricks of Prospect Street. He was a drinker because it was "his fun," and a man needed to see things differently at night.

What he did for pay was like homework he left behind. "Your mother, don't you know," he said, "only tithes to me." Which was what led him to stealing. Didn't she see that his need was more than God's?

It's in the genes, my Aunt Margaret always insisted, who, because she was nearly twelve years older than my mother, had been stolen from for years. Even

The Prince's younger brother George was a legend. When the trolleys ran along every main street from Pittsburgh, when they reached all of the nearest mill towns, George collected fares and kept the change belted to his waist. So long ago, he carried dimes, nickels, and pennies. He punched transfers, took the slug-sized tokens, and drove it all to the roundhouse in West Etna, where shifts ended for the motormen who made the Etna–Pittsburgh round-trip run.

According to Aunt Margaret, he sipped whiskey for lunch. He broke for drinks and made his mistake between two trolleys, standing in the blind spot of nose-to-rear, so when the cars lurched together, he was crushed so badly the coins from the changer were imbedded in his stomach.

"It was as if he'd swallowed them," my aunt said, "can you imagine? They gave up on him at the hospital, but when he didn't die right off, they operated. And wouldn't you know, he lived to tell about it."

The Prince descended from janitor to odd jobs to farmhand, and finally, from the top of that silo my aunt never tired of describing, into the fortunate haystack of the stuntman. Nobody helped him to a hospital or his feet. He entered the St. Barnabas Home, where weakness was watched like money.

What was most remarkable was that I'd only learned my connection to all of this since just before my tenth birthday, in the summer of 1955, when I'd started complaining, one Saturday, about waiting so long in a room full of sick old men and Archie and the Brothers who looked like they had just stepped out of a comic book. Archie fiddled with his ham radio and let me listen to voices speaking in foreign languages. "That's Russkie talk," he'd said. "That's the Commies." And then he'd suddenly slumped forward in his wheelchair, tangling himself in the ropes that helped prop him in place. "Unhh," Archie had said. "Unhh."

He'd quivered and twitched, but he couldn't manage a word, and I sat staring at him until an attendant swiveled in his chair by the television and saw Archie's predicament. "Unhh," Archie managed once more as the white-coated man untangled him, sat him up, and said, "Archie's had enough for this evening," wheeling him away.

I spent the next half hour wandering through the dining hall, eating two of my father's coconut rolls, and inspecting the metal plates and cups. When I opened the enormous refrigerator, I didn't find anything but the same packages of pre-shelled eggs my father kept in his bakery refrigerator. There wasn't any orange juice or milk. There weren't any apples or bananas. In the cupboards, though, were packages filled with the oatmeal I hated—those boxes so large I thought it would take me the rest of my life to choke down even one of them

while my father chanted his clean-your-plate observation, "You don't know what's good."

"I'm not coming anymore," I said in the Bel Air. "It always takes an hour to do a five-minute job."

My father, without turning his head, said, "You don't know anything." My mother stayed quiet while I whined.

"Think before you talk," I heard. "Grow up," was repeated. And still I insisted, until my mother said, "Gary, you've heard us talk about The Prince a thousand times over. We come to see your grandfather."

"I know all about The Prince, but who's my grandfather?" I said.

"Don't act like you never heard us talking. Your Aunt Margaret especially. She's been telling stories on The Prince for years. Surely you knew."

Surely. I understood I was the champion of bad listeners, the fool who didn't get the elementary punch line. My aunt had been telling stories, not on some local character, but on her father. "What did you think?" my mother said. "We kept a boarder?" And beginning the next week, she took me with her upstairs after I'd listened again to how obviously my Aunt Margaret placed her Prince stories inside her home, in the same rooms with my grandmother, the house where I stayed over nearly every Friday night while my mother worked with my father in the bakery to prepare for the busiest day of the week.

The Prince, it turned out, was small and shriveled and quiet. He looked like nobody I'd ever heard of and said, "Ruthy's boy" to me when I shook his hand and when we stood to leave.

He said nothing could hurt him now but "the sugar" and time. He asked for doughnuts, the long crème-filled crullers baked every night but Sunday.

"Ruthy," he said, "in a place like this you could live forever," locking the door behind her after we entered, hooking his thumbs in the loops where anyone else's belt would slide.

"He knows she's dead," Aunt Margaret said, five years later, on the first morning my grandmother was laid out at Ogrodnik's Funeral Home. "Those Brothers out there at the Home read the papers. They follow the death notices. If that pantywaist shows up, I'll throw him down the stairs myself."

I believed it. I was fifteen when my grandmother died, but Aunt Margaret was muscular enough to still beat me in arm wrestling. That afternoon, I walked around the Ogrodnik's block in Etna with a girl who came to the viewing with

her mother and hoped she would be so moved by death she might think she owed me some display of sympathy.

We held hands, and I repeated the stories about The Prince in order to seem like a chip off the old block. In the alley behind the funeral home, during our second swing around the block, she leaned over and pecked my cheek with her lips, pulling her hand away as she said, "You poor thing."

"Well?" my older cousins said when I walked back inside. The girl had gotten into the car at the end of the alley where her mother was waiting. Her mother had smiled weakly. Before the car turned the corner, I heard "The Twist" turned up and then suddenly turned down. I flashed what I hoped was a mysterious grin at my cousins and sat in a chair to contemplate another failure of nerve.

By then, everybody knew The Prince had been standing across the street by Isaly's, a deli and ice-cream store, for the whole afternoon. "The old souse," Aunt Margaret kept saying. "Let him bake in the sun." When he wasn't there the morning of the funeral, my mother knew he'd talked Ogrodnik into letting him in after hours for a quick look, but even my Aunt Margaret didn't say a word to Ogrodnik. Nobody wanted to know for sure.

After the funeral service, my grandmother's three surviving brothers, her two sons, and my father were pallbearers. As they carried the coffin down the short slope to the gravesite, one of her brothers slipped on the grass and tumbled onto his back. My father and my uncles grimaced and held steady while he gathered himself and stood up. Aunt Margaret, standing beside me, said, "I thought we were going to have a second funeral there for a second."

She and that brother who slipped were the last to leave that house on Prospect Street, moving out within a month. My aunt, standing on the front porch, said, "Right here, the old stew stood. He didn't know what to make of being locked out. And then he just hightailed out of here. And now Mother's dead, and he's so pickled in his drink that he'll live forever."

On the railing were a dozen stones of a size that fit my hand. I hefted one, and she smiled. "If a cat cut through the yard," she said, "we could use these up on it." I pitched the stone far enough that it landed outside the property line. "If that old stew showed up, we could drive him down the hill to the Circle Bar."

At the St. Barnabas Home, just before the fundraising picnic that summer, the destitute and the crippled were led to be seated in the middle section—so near the front, all the summer visitors could watch them through the scripture

readings and the shortened, outdoor sermon. There were men hunched over to cough and spit, men strapped into wheelchairs, their free hands shaking with tics and palsies and alcohol's delirious daydreams. There were men who sat upright in frayed shirts and trousers once worn by the heavier and the taller, all watched over by the dark-robed and hooded Brothers as if they were bunched for an enormous high school assembly. In mid-June, a few of them would pass out in the afternoon sun, and one would have a seizure. They were our family, I heard each year; they were thankful we accepted all of them as brothers. But when I searched the crowd for a glance at The Prince, there was no sign of him.

At the end of the benediction, taped trumpets started "God of Our Fathers" as the residents rose and retreated. We faced forward. We finished every verse while those men were locked down for the evening.

None of them carried cups of punch and plates of hors d'oeuvres to shaded benches and chairs, but up two flights of stairs was my grandfather waiting in his room, where outside, the branches of an oak clawed the window as if it were angry he'd refused that afternoon church service.

"Can't make me," he said, spreading my mother's gift of Limburger on a thick slice of onion, handing me a buffalo carved from soap, offering my sister a bear. "Wish me a whiskey," he said, as if the want that had driven him there could be made into a small, secular prayer. He stroked his clip-on tie until it dropped to the floor. "Snake," he whispered, sliding it toward my sister with his shoe. "Snake," he hissed, filling the window with his tight white shirt, all of us staring at the just-waxed floor as if a miracle was being born.

Years later, returning on my own, I tried to see the man who punched six holes in the wall of his living room. By then I'd grown to believe there was something admirable in sustained physical stupidity. One or two holes, like the ones I'd put into the walls of the first house I owned, was passion or drunkenness or both, but six was determination, especially since I remembered the walls in my grandmother's house. They were more solid than the one I'd punctured. Her house was built at the turn of the century by her father and men like him, who thought everything they built displayed who they were. If you hit a wood beam, you'd surely break your hand, and my grandfather, handy with carpenter's tools himself, certainly knew that. No matter how drunk, he must have calculated after the first lucky swing, fixing the odds against how closely his father-in-law had run those beams from floor to ceiling, the consequences of hitting the wrong spot. And no matter, his fist must have hurt so much by the fifth and sixth punch, he would have long understood regret. I was a month

removed from putting two holes in my basement wall, both with the butt end of a cue stick. I lived there for three years and never replaced the wallboard, but my grandfather, I'd been told, had repaired his damage the following day. Not a handyman whatsoever, my way of repair was to promise myself that's the end of one more form of asinine behavior, and after that, I managed to avoid that particular stupidity.

I couldn't ask him anything about "the old days." And he couldn't volunteer. We had to deduce each other from expressions and gestures, clothes, and the language we chose to keep things going.

He sat on the same bed covered by the same spread I'd taken note of for nearly twenty years. "Ruthy's boy," he said again, looking at my wife as if he was imagining what it was like to live with his descendant.

A Bible lay open on his nightstand. I handed him my gift of Limburger. "Long time for that," he said. "I thank you."

The package design, I was convinced, was identical to the one in which my mother's gifts were wrapped. At the store, certainly, there had only been one brand to choose from.

"The bakery's gone," I said. "Five years ago."

"Ruthy said so, I recollect. Not that I'm fixing to stop by for zwieback and crullers." He grinned. "Peg, your Aunt Margaret, she's the one didn't truck with me. She wouldn't sell as much as a sugar cookie to me for my good money. I'd look in the window first, see which one of my girls was standing counter."

I nodded, looking at the Limburger as he turned it in his hands. I imagined it warming, its smell spreading through the room. A chemistry teacher had told me that it had the same smell as the stuff that builds up under toenails.

"I recollect you sitting there in short britches with a mitt full of raisin-filled. Kept you quiet a spell so Ruthy could red up the store in peace."

I nodded, but I didn't have any memory of him in the bakery—not surprising, since whoever he seemed to be during those visits was not the grandfather I had met when I was ten.

"So why wasn't I told?" I'd asked my mother a few weeks earlier than that initial meeting, when I'd announced I'd decided to sort out his story for myself. It had been nearly twenty years by then he'd lived in that home.

"Of course you were told," she said. "Who did you think I was talking to up there?"

I could have asked additional questions: And who were we visiting when I

was a small child and my grandfather lived on the farm before he fell? And who did I think was the man who brought her a dozen eggs or a head of lettuce or a handful of red beets wrapped in old newspaper when he visited four or five times a year, driven in from the farm by the man who'd agreed to give him a roof over his head "as long as he earned his keep"?

He still had a shelf of soap carvings; he chose one for my wife, a whale, and handed it to her like a corsage. "Get tired of having him around, you can wash him down to minnow size."

When I stood up to leave, I took two steps forward as he pushed off with both hands, and then I looked away while he struggled, a year away from turning ninety years old. The Bible was open to the first page of Matthew, all of the "begats" taking the reader toward Jesus. The Prince could have been doing a sort of homework, or he could have turned to the beginning of the New Testament and said, "Here's a place to start."

Thirty years later, when I visit the family plot, I see that my grandfather, dead for nearly all of those years, isn't buried beside my grandmother. The space has been left unused. "No way," my sister, who still tends it a few times each year, said about his chances of him being there. "You still have one uncle left alive. If he lived forever, he'd rather waste the space than allow The Prince in there."

My father, when he makes excuses for The Prince, repeats some version of "lack of privacy" that always ends with him asking me to imagine my grandparents in their upstairs bedroom, their boys on one side, their girls on the other, her brothers on another. Each time, I put them in that room my grandmother slept in by herself when I was a child. The room's only wall that didn't have somebody listening ran up against the back alley. My father reminds me that my grandmother's father lived there into an age old enough to hold me after I was born. "Who wouldn't go out at night?" my father, the teetotaler, adds.

The Prince would have shared the one bathroom with five other men and his wife when he moved in. There would be more privacy if he used the bathrooms in the taverns he frequented.

By the time The Prince moved into St. Barnabas, the smallest upstairs bedroom in his former house was a makeshift guest room. It was nearly identical in size to the one he lived in for the last twenty-one years of his life.

I remember the size of that small room because it held a bed that ran nearly

the entire length of the wall, and there was just enough room to walk alongside between it and the dresser, which stood against the opposite wall. It was the sort of room old men rent above bars and restaurants, hobbling down to get the mail, or shuffling to the end of hallways to use a shared bathroom.

I sat in the audience, once, while a professor explained the Shroud of Turin to a hundred senior citizens. He had slides and sources. He waved a wand of light to trace the face of Jesus in case someone didn't see it. "Look," he said, "the eyes, the curve of lips exactly the same as in the pictures you know of Christ."

He ran overtime with the possibilities of belief. Except for the professor and me, there wasn't a person in the room under sixty, and I was betting myself that very few of them would stay for the second half of the program, a poetry reading I was giving to publicize my latest book, *Inventing Angels*.

That week a patient had discovered the face of Christ in the grain of a hospital door, and the citizens of a nearby town had witnessed Jesus on the side of their municipal water tower. People gathered, some of them joyful, some of them apprehensive about the inevitable skeptics.

The Faces of Christ

Those aren't the only sightings. Certainly, they're not the oddest. For instance, Mrs. Edward Rubio, in 1979, in New Mexico, discovered the face of Christ seared into a burrito she was cooking for her husband. She enshrined it in a room in her house—flowers, votive candles—and worshippers and the simply curious came from all over to look long and hard at that burrito.

If my parents had lived in New Mexico then, they would have come to see that miracle on any day but a Sunday, something that explains why the first movie I ever saw on a Sunday was *El Cid*. I was nearly sixteen years old. My friends were going, and some of them had convinced me this was a movie not to be missed. My mother, when the car pulled into the driveway, told me she was disappointed; my father refused to speak to me.

I was uncertain then, and still am, about the logic of such belief. All the way until her death, I had always understood my grandmother's disapproval. She refrained from card playing and restaurants as well as movies on Sundays, but my parents played Canasta without a care and ate out every other Sunday after church. They had no difficulty watching television, which showed films of

its own to their approval, so I'm left with the image of Charlton Heston as the dying Cid propped on his horse to lead his inspired men to victory, and the sense that I took one step closer to damnation because I sat in a Pittsburgh theater on a Sunday afternoon.

Our family, in the years preceding my defiance, went regularly to the movies on Saturday night. There's hardly a film from the 1950s I don't vaguely or vividly recall. We saw whatever films happened to be showing in Butler or East Liberty, depending on whether we went north or south. If there was a choice, my parents opted for biblical epics, costume dramas, Westerns, musicals, or comedies. What I missed, I've discovered, were B-movie thrillers and film-noir dramas. If I saw them at all, I saw them on Friday nights with my Great Uncle Bill, who didn't even know what was playing at the Etna Theater, except it was Friday and seven P.M., so off we went, walking in mid-feature or near its end—no matter, because we just waited it out to watch until the story returned to the point where we'd come in. For years, I thought this was how everyone went to the movies, knowing the endings before the beginnings. For *El Cid*, my friends and I were seated during a set of previews. I didn't know about the Cid's heroics until the final fifteen minutes.

Certainly, I didn't know there were film critics, production budgets, or films in foreign languages, but I knew movies on Sundays were sinful, and I knew a film that showed the face of Christ was blasphemous. After the first one we saw of these, my father had had enough. He started reading about movies to ensure it wouldn't happen again.

The movie that changed our viewing habits was called *Day of Triumph.* For the first time, the actor playing Jesus turned to face us, instead of looking at crowds of disciples and followers who gazed at him in awe while we stared at his back and flowing hair. The actor's name was Robert Wilson. It was 1954, but it was the first crucifixion-and-resurrection film since Cecil B. DeMille had made a silent in 1927, so my parents had sought this one out, not knowing that Jesus, played by an actor who looked old enough to be playing Joseph, was going to face us.

From then on, my father refused to sit through another film that showed the face of Christ. Christ was a flowing robe and outstretched hands; he was a beatific voice and sandals. No actor could possibly take on the role of Christ if he allowed himself to be filmed from the front.

It was worse than nudity. It would be doubly worse on a Sunday. In 1959, five years after *Day of Triumph*, we went back to a film that featured Christ called

The Big Fisherman because Jesus was depicted as the sleeve of a white robe and one blessed hand.

Howard Keel, a singer who starred in some of the benign musicals my father loved, played Simon Peter; I don't know, even now, whose arm, clothed in baggy white, rose and fell, but watching that film years later, I noticed a vaccination mark on one of the women, something of a miracle.

My father started choosing the films for his family more selectively. We passed on *King of Kings* the same year I saw *El Cid* because Jeffrey Hunter, unlike previous film Christs, acted as if he were just another character, facing the audience, turning in profile, but worst of all, acting as if he were an ordinary human being.

A year later, when, as a family, we had nearly stopped going to the movies altogether, we sat through a film called *Whistle Down the Wind.* It featured Hayley Mills—so wholesome, in my father's view, that anything she starred in was a safe choice.

Instead, it centered on a character, played by Alan Bates, whose identity was ambiguously linked to Christ. Hayley Mills and enough other children to suggest the twelve disciples begin a sort of cult after they find him in a barn. So strongly does it appear that the vagrant Bates plays is Christ-like that there are scenes that prod us to remember the three denials of Peter. My father grumbled. He leaned over and whispered to my mother, but we didn't walk out. There was uncertainty after all, although my father, after that, refused any movies unless he knew the entire story for fear he'd be subjected to blasphemy by metaphor.

Since then, there has been a family in Texas who saw the face of Christ in swirls of plaster on their ceiling, and there was someone in Ohio who saw that countenance on the side of a soybean oil tank. In 1983, a woman named Josephine Taylor saw the face of Christ on her bathroom floor in Ontario. Three thousand people came to witness the miracle, although someone from the church eventually concluded that the face had been formed from the scars of old linoleum adhesive. Regardless, Arlene Gardner, in 1987, in Tennessee, saw the face of Christ on the General Electric freezer sitting on the front deck of her trailer. Her neighbor's porch light, apparently, caused a bearded face to appear, so it took a bit of inadvertent teamwork to generate that miracle.

Now, when I visit my father, we watch whatever's on one of the two channels that come in clearly on his television. No cable, no antenna—he lives on a hill near Pittsburgh, or there would be no picture whatsoever. I've sat through soap operas and made-for-television movies where the characters could have used the

behavioral adjustments a sighting of the face of Christ might bring. My father never criticizes the sins of these characters; he doesn't say a word about violence and sexual innuendo. The brightness and contrast on his television are nearly gone. The color is the kind I remember from the 1950s—fields of primaries washing into each other. Everyone is garish in a sort of colorized comic-book effect. In these shades, all of the women look tawdry, all the men threatening—if the face of Christ appeared on his television, it would be sponsored by NBC or CBS, and it would appear as unnatural and unconvincing as Jesus on a burrito or wood paneling.

Last night, on one of the tabloid shows that intersperse with the melodramas, I saw a photograph of a tumor excised from a woman who had somehow denied its presence and growth for years. She had dressed and lived her life until it sickened her irrevocably, and the excision had made no difference. "Look at it closely," we were told, "and what do you see?"

"Death," I said at once, and immediately described to my father the literal apparition of a troll-like figure, his arms and legs spread in a sort of frenzied jig of triumph, like Hitler in France, his face set in the bearded leer of the satyr.

"The face of death," the announcer said, but I didn't need anybody to corroborate what I was witnessing. That woman's tumor, malignant or benign, was clearly anthropomorphic. Immediately, I thought of all the faces of Christ, the hysteria and worship. I reminded myself of foolishness, turned away, repositioned myself, and looked back on the same troll still dancing with the glee of success.

My father didn't say a word about trolls and cancer, but he can see the recent history of weather in a field where I'm busy with insects and thorns and poisonous leaves. He understands the effects of variations in rain and heat; he names the plants that thrive or decline accordingly. If the face of Christ appeared in that field, created by design or accident, he'd say blasphemy or miracle, depending on which technique proved to be at its source.

He told me, later that evening, the story of Saint Wilgefortis, the patron saint of women who wish to be rid of beastly husbands. She prayed for deliverance from her forced marriage to the brutal King of Sicily and sprouted, on her wedding day, a full black beard and mustache. She was crucified by her father, the king of Portugal, who had arranged the marriage for all of the standard reasons of wealth and power. "What do you think of that?" my father asked, and I told him it sounded like another face-of-Christ story—most likely a man dressed as a woman, the explanatory story fabricated by the church to accompany it.

"You'll see some day," he said, and though I kept my silence, I think my father was right about the face of Christ on film. By the time I watched a Jesus movie on my own, Christ, once veiled and awe-inspiring, then mellow and human, had become flawed, and worst of all, silly.

Just out of college, I sought out *Johnny Got His Gun*, in which Donald Sutherland portrays Christ as a sort of hippie, laid back and unable to intervene in any meaningful way in the miserable lives we lead. Two years later, I watched *Jesus Christ, Superstar*, the film version of the rock opera, and a man named Ted Neeley opened and closed his film career by singing badly and suggesting, by the fixed expression he carried throughout, that Jesus was stoned for most of his waking hours.

There were other full-frontal Christ films released within a year. One of them was seriously pious, but unintentionally stupid. Johnny Cash, the country singer, made a film called *The Gospel Road*, which featured a nonspeaking Jesus, played by a nonactor named Robert Elfstrom whose deep meditations are interrupted by Country/Christian tunes written and sung by Cash himself. My father would have demanded his money back.

Shortly thereafter, a film called *Him* was released, with the promotional line: "Are you curious about his sexual life?" My father would have picketed the movie theater that showed this one, a film featuring a homosexual Christ—crosses gleaming, in the advertisement, from his aroused eyes.

Watching the holy hand of Christ in *The Big Fisherman* had been ludicrous in its own way, something like watching, during that era, the papier-mâché hand of Allison Hayes, the enraged housewife in *Attack of the Fifty-Foot Woman*, or the one movable claw that represented, in close-up, the terrible threat of the giant vegetable space invader in *It Conquered the World*. Just like those monsters, however, Christ had more power when I couldn't get a glimpse of him. The fifty-foot woman is stupendously comical when we see all of her; the terror from outer space turns out to be physically challenged, obviously pushed forward on wheels when it decides to attack. Seeing too much is risky.

I've never told my father about any of these blasphemies, the religious and the artistic. I tell him, though, about the face of Christ that was seen in the construction site for a bridge a few miles from where I live. Some of the landscape slashes have merged into cheekbones; some have turned into hair and a beard, running toward the Susquehanna River.

Planes appeared overhead, people paying fifty dollars to judge that symbol

for themselves. Below them, they claimed, was a face in the Rushmore soil, and many of those who witnessed it said the bridge was better left unfinished because it would surely collapse.

For a brief time I lived near where progress paused while priests debated whether we had been handed a shrine that would surely erase itself regardless. The bridge, of course, was completed, but what I believe now is, we need a sighting of the face of Christ turned away from us. There, the witnesses will say, is the back of his head, trusting in instinct reinforced by faith. We look away and turn back, and still we see. We change angles and distance, and continue to believe. And when the back of Christ's head crumbles, or caves in, or is erased by wind and water, we know that underneath us, the ridges and troughs go on aligning themselves in persistent, suggestive ways.

Church came first. God, then family—and my father was often furious with my failure to keep things holy. Silence was warm-up for worship. Sitting straight. And staying that way for an hour.

He told and retold the story of his father's hand on his thigh, the tourniquet that clotted movement during church in order to make sure I understood that each Sunday began in discipline. Always, my sister and I sat on the left side, third pew from the back. My grandmother's pew. Where she always sat on the end. Where my Aunt Margaret positioned herself between my sister and me. Our parents sat in the choir loft above and behind the pastor. They looked for us after the processional hymn. If we were late, just once, would strange children be sitting there? If we were ever absent, would another family slide over, inching into the inexplicable void? And if we misbehaved in any small way, they could be watching from up there without us knowing until they spoke their unhappiness as soon as they took off their choir robes and found us standing exactly where we were told to stand, beside the door that opened from the basement where they stored those robes.

Say It

Some Sundays the flowers on the altar reminded the congregation of the church's shut-ins. They signified a sorrow that equaled death—the crippled, the crazed, the ones so aged they had taken permanently to bed. And their names, almost always, were as shut in as the past: Esther and Pearl, Florence and Ida; Amos and Zachariah, Otto, Laird.

Even their physical problems often sounded as if they'd originated in an earlier century. Besides cancer and heart disease, there were vague rumors of lumbago; whispered stories of neuritis, neuralgia, and the strange neurasthenia of hysterical spinsters. Regardless, all of the victims suffered and were buried, entering the threats and promises of the Apostles' Creed, leaving behind their mysterious fear of the out-of-doors, their sudden shakes, their palsies, and their eyes' refusal of daylight. They were joining the dearly departed who were listed in the bulletin for monthly bouquets,

including the three ancient sisters who lived near the church and opened their back door to groceries and Pastor Sowers, who told boys in the congregation to mow their grass and shovel their sidewalks—so astonishingly free of footprints, we half believed those sisters capable of flight.

When it caused a sensation for a few months, my mother refused to buy *The Most Wonderful Story Doll*, Jesus lying in a gilded Bible watched over by cardboard replicas of Mary and Joseph. "Sacrilegious," she hissed, and so did a million mothers who didn't want the family dog to chew off the arms and legs of Christ, refusing and refusing until Ideal Toys bought Jesus back from America's dealers, all those faces of the Christ Child rendered into the dimpled smiles of mortal dolls, ones that wet themselves when they guzzled down a bottle, ones that wailed when my sister turned them over her knee for punishment.

Mothers wanted their daughters to play with ordinary infants, dolls they could love without fear. They didn't want their daughters to be awed by handling Jesus, to be afraid to drop Christ down the stairs, or even to find him floating face down in the bathtub, learning the terrible stillness of doubt.

One Sunday I recited the names of the Bible's sixty-six books. Both testaments. All the pronunciations from Habakkuk to Ephesians as a way of signifying everything I was willing to learn. I worked through a psalm a week, memorizing, and nobody in my family complained about having to listen to me stop and start up again when I raced through the words as if I'd forget if I spoke more slowly.

My grade-school friends didn't envy me. They weren't wasting their time trying to match verses with the minister's chosen one, even when I total-recalled Genesis, chapters 1 and 2, and carried the creation to the pulpit for my star turn on Children's Day.

I was descending from heaven; I was apprentice to salvation, and I memorized until the sky became a scroll that unrolled before my eyes like another miracle I doubted when I began, in fifth grade, to learn there were alternate myths for this world, and to ask questions that were met with "Faith is the answer."

The alphabet of absolutes drifted downwind like a morning's cirrus skyscape. The church stuffed itself with mill hunks and their bloated wives, and I was the son of nobody but a pair of people who sold bread and cakes to this congregation descended from the fisted thunderheads of lust.

Hymns, sermons, litanies—the church windows thrummed with passing trucks; the town's brutal clamor climbed the chancel while the words left me like my parents fleeing Eden. Suddenly, I lip-synched the blue signature of doubt, listening to the audible mural of the streets, for the raffle equation of worship, while another careless coal barge foundered in the river downstream from that church, the language of its failure waiting for an elegy of explication.

My parents, on Saturdays, played cards until midnight. They said goodbye to their friends and slept until Sunday School, church, and the long, dress-and-white-shirted wait until Sunday dinner. The Blue Laws shut the stores and taverns; the Pittsburgh Pirates were stopped at six o'clock, the second games of doubleheaders suspended for months—no matter, because good people didn't stay at Sunday baseball past that time.

Television, though, was free and showed films, sports, and Ed Sullivan, who came on after the Pirates quit for the night as if the Blue Laws stopped at the door.

And when the Soviets launched, when they shot their second Sputnik on a Sunday, spinning a dog through space, my father raged about how the godless never rested. "They'll see, those Reds," he said. On television that night, some congressman said we'd have to work seven days a week to catch the Soviets, and my father cited the black smoke of Pittsburgh, the last of the coal-fired trains spreading soot through the open windows of Sunday worship. Already, there were men who risked their souls for steel because companies couldn't afford to bank a blast furnace to honor God's day. "God help us," he said. "We haven't a choice."

There were punishments for the weaknesses of the mouth. Relatives had killed themselves with salt and fatty meat; a neighbor had slaughtered himself with sugar; my grandfather had made a public fool of himself for liquor. "Each of them knew," my mother said, and she meant I was growing toward the bone-stunting temptations of tobacco and coffee, the festering pimples that erupt from excessive candy and greasy food, gobbled when I went out with friends.

"God's way," she said, and she warned me about the pack of gum I'd found and chewed, explaining that there were dope dealers who seeded the desire of sixth graders with the drop of good fortune, waiting for their next day of expensive need.

I didn't bring up anything about the warm dance of tongue and lips, the moistures driven by lust; but the first beer I swallowed poured warm from three

bottles I found in the half-razed house where used rubbers told me there were willing girls nearby.

I had such weakness, I finished a fourth, long-opened bottle—and stepped, minutes later, through the lost heat register's empty hole, sticking at the shoulders instead of tumbling to the cellar's glass and nails. I went down to check where I would have landed. It would be seven years until my first cold beer, reversing the Pharaoh's dream, famine first, refusal urging my mouth to open.

For adults in our Sunday School, there were two age-group grades. The men and women decided for themselves when they were promoted from one to the other. The women woke up one week and waved their mumbling husbands to the Men's Booster Class before they turned the other way with the church's old women to the Sunshine Bible Class.

As they approached the afterlife, the sexes separated. Those men sold lilies, wreaths, and seasonal graveside greens. The Sunshine Bible Class sold maps of the Holy Land; the Sea of Galilee, the Dead Sea, the River Jordan, and all the other water ran light blue, while the land lay pastel like the summer dresses of women.

Those charts were wall-sized. They explained how Christ connected the dots, one to thirty, on his missions, so I could follow the journeys of Jesus until they seemed as simple as the mulched trails in the city park.

And what did anyone do with those maps, large as home-movie screens? Where were they stored, and who threw them out with the deflated basketballs and headless dolls that grew in garages? After the Sunshine Bible Class was death, all of those women turning to names on the golden plaques they bought for the basement walls. And each year, on Pentecost Sunday, the members stood to call roll from those perfections for absence, edited quietly as if they were translating ancient stories colored into twilights, the hush we imagine in that time of day, soft, then softer.

After the choir passed, after the tenors and the bass men sang themselves to the nave, the recessional's last verses were sung only by the women, who stood among the pews. The stanzas wavered. The hymns turned shrill and reedy with alto and soprano faith. The men who didn't sing in the choir moved their lips as if

learning to read, but my friends and I forgot to move our mouths at all while we watched the breasts of girls rise and fall through the last couplets that let us stare.

I listened to the huge promises of those verses; goodness and gold, wings and light and every earthly pleasure I wanted dropped like ballast from the hot air balloon of resurrection. If singing aloud helped you to heaven, I wasn't going—not even for hosts of women who piously warbled, leaving husbands behind; not for all of the girls who might die young.

On the front page of each hymnal were the names of the dead—Swope, Kleeb, Haman, and the rest who'd departed, according to the inscriptions, to their great reward. By seventh grade, whatever faith I had was mute, but I knew which song of praise would open my mouth, how men sang for women's bodies, how recessionals were formed in the throats thrown back in temporary joy.

The summer before seventh grade, I still believed a hillside of trees behind the houses across the street meant we lived close to where wealth and leisure lived, that there was a chance the bakery made more money than I imagined, that my father earned like a lawyer. I was about to enter junior high school, where the road to college began—like it had for a neighbor boy, who said the two of us should walk naked in the darkness of trees behind his house. Wasn't it exciting, he asked, to be so free? Didn't I feel different nude?

By then he was hard, but even when he touched me, I was soft and small, suddenly knowing how skinny I was, how weak, that he could strangle me if that's what gave him pleasure.

"You shouldn't be afraid to feel good," he said, but I kept my hands at my sides while he examined me like a doctor. When his hand slipped away from me, he stroked himself, crooning, "Look now, look now."

And I did, using the faint back-porch light of his house to see him explode between my black tennis shoes, all I was wearing for five minutes, not moving but turning my head as if I'd just murmured goodbye, as if he was standing in the open door of a train.

Going to church meant my mother, like a surgeon, slipped on white gloves at the door. They said she was ready, and it was time for me to get in the station wagon, sit in back, and remember to keep the window rolled up. She held a tissue to the

handles and knobs between our house and our pew. She wore them once and washed them; she owned a second, identical pair, three ridges along the back that matched the two pairs in boxes she would save for Easter or Christmas or weddings that requested extended hands.

"White gloves," she said, "are like glasses," what she needed to see past herself. She wore them like lipstick, her hands bleached by etiquette. She prayed with her fingers gloved; she held the hymnal as if it were ice. The pairs that waited in boxes were like the souls of the unborn.

My confirmation class always listened to Pastor Sowers, learning the Bible's major numbers, one through the nine-sixty-nine of Methuselah, who lived eight times longer than all of us put together. We memorized the three parts of the Trinity, the four Gospels. We recited the Ten Commandments and the names of the twelve disciples, subtracting Judas the Betrayer before we matched them to the eleven of ourselves, the future fishers of men.

Pastor Sowers told us sacrifice stories, the number of ways to be crucified, including upside down; but all five of us boys wanted to know the number of minutes Jesus lasted on the cross, the number of stones it took to slaughter Stephen.

Pastor Sowers made us recite the Nicene Creed and the Apostles' Creed, listening for lapses because we were the future of a faith that could spout, in unison, the three temptations of Christ in the wilderness and the seven words of the Cross.

That year I wanted to ask the number of men who'd taken Mary Magdalene to bed, and how much she charged. And not asking, I counted, on my own, the years I had to three score and ten, learned the date for Easter in 2016, when I needed to rise from the dead and be repaid for the 10 percent I'd been taxed by God.

Because I didn't see myself among the nine groups blessed by the Beatitudes, not the boys who were poor in sirit, not the meek we taunted, not the six girls who were pure in heart, their bodies numbered by breasts and thighs when the boys picked partners, choosing until one was unchosen, becoming the Virgin Mary, shifting in her chair as if she were already counting the two heart attacks of Pastor Sowers, the forty-two years he lived, including the 134 months he lasted after he laid his hands to our heads and declared us saved.

About to be confirmed, we learned the perfect position to receive the body of Christ, kneeling to lay one hand open upon the other, supplicants. We learned

the proper way to reach for wine, letting the blood of Christ be passed down to our half-raised hands from the minister's tray of tiny cups.

Each Sunday, Communion sounded like pity on the part of God, some charity approaching us with its patronizing sack of coins. The next winter, the new minister changed his technique and laid the wafers directly on our tongues. My hands, unoccupied, gripped each other and waited for wine to be sipped from the common cup, wiped dry after each upturned mouth had touched it.

All of us were infants at the rail, our hands used only for balance as we rose, steadying ourselves, returning to the hardwood pews where we sat in silence, Christian families with histories, ready to hear the benediction and sing the recessional hymn, verses releasing us into weather that waited outside, regardless of communion and prayer—our fathers retrieving their cars like valets, their wives and children relaxing in the doorways like the wealthy.

Week after week, "He's Got the Whole World in His Hands" was number one on the Top 40 Countdown on KQV. For once, my father sang along with a popular song, because Laurie London, the singer, meant we were all being watched over by a benevolent God.

I hoped not, because if that was true, God would know that before sleep each night, my hands loved the brief pleasure they made as I remembered the beautiful parts of girls from my invisible place in their lives. I stiffened and swelled as I imagined girls who would shudder and cry out and not care one bit about whether or not God was watching.

For a month, two other boys from my street and I played a board game that let us become owners of the whole world, in part, and then in bigger parts if we outsmarted each other, clever enough to consolidate our power like an army.

In history class, during our six days with myths, Atlas held the whole world in place, using his legs and back, looking unhappy in his work, so much a man underappreciated by his boss.

The newspaper declared the whole world smaller, the globe shriveling from the cold of technology until it fit in the soft palms of the wealthy.

What small hands, a girl told me, for someone your size—and I clutched her body, denying what I took for weakness by a show of desire, running my hands over the whole world of her clothed body.

Where I wasn't kept expanding. Stars multiplied. They lived in neighborhoods impossible to reach, so far away I wasn't even a story in their sky.

At last the world chilled and contracted to something so small I thought I could carry it like a pen, one hand free for the future's essential labor, the difficult, the lamentable, and the loved.

That summer, I bought a copy of "Willie and the Hand Jive," by Johnny Otis. He used the rhythm that Bo Diddley had made famous and insisted that everybody could do that crazy hand jive. Roseanne Meenan, who lived next door, could do the hand jive, and so could her friends. They were all a year older than I was and went to a private school where they wore white blouses and plaid skirts every day until summer, when they sunbathed in two-piece swimsuits that made cutting the grass a joy to drag out as long as possible.

I took my shirt off and looped slowly around the yard. When I was finished, I put "Willie and the Hand Jive" on my suitcase-sized record player and bounced a tennis ball off the back of our garage, pretending I was too busy to make the motions, but watching their hands moving to the music while they lay on their backs in the sun.

By August I learned about the doctor who cured patients by long-distance, sending sickness to limbo through the power of belief. Thousands, he said he saved, from far away, and those who couldn't call sent writing samples, clues enough for healing—though I needed the miracle for those who stayed mute the afternoon I failed the buddy system of the church camp pool, following the wall to fourteen feet where the water deepened for diving, pretending I could push off to the backstroke of buoyant faith.

Reach and pull, I thought, reach and pull—strokes so simple the animals used them. Suddenly, jostled free of my handhold, I reached back and sank in the stoical splendor of silence. I touched bottom and rose. I said nothing and reached, sinking again and floundering up to the white inner tube of the lifeguard as if I'd been swimming for hours and cramped. As if I were expert but tired, brought ashore like the exhausted channel crossers who refuse aid with the beauty of courage—teaching me, that day and the remainder of that week, the rewards for faith: health, hope, significance, and salvation.

I listened, but the ministers didn't say anything about the second coming of the Balm of Gilead and how that cure was marketed, before the phone's invention, as something that would save thousands from sickness, from drunkenness,

debauchery, and the horrors of the unhealthy mind. God's gold, the salesman said, was suspended in solution, and its miraculous properties fixed the problems brought on by inattention to health and studies. The rest of that popular potion, however, was the distraction of brandy, something like *Life-Savior Jesus*, "scripture message included," the candy I bought for a nickel ten minutes after I was saved by the O-ring of the lifeguard.

There's no escaping the Huns of Time, my great-aunt said, or seemed to, her teeth as badly fitted as her accent. The Huns of Time, she said, are never satisfied, no reasoning with them—intending, I thought, to make me see the way the Huns had invaded her.

They'd sacked Rome, I knew, come from some place like Germany where my great-grandfathers had been raised, speaking a dark language of coughs and growls, and some afternoons, when I was doing nothing but slouch in front of a small television, I thought I could hear the Huns of Time muttering among themselves outside.

Some evenings, when the Huns slipped inside, I could tell they'd quit school, that they moved a lot because they couldn't hold jobs. Always, though, the Huns were having fun—more of it, at least, than the parents like mine who were punctual as dawn.

They laughed a lot and stuffed turkey legs in their mouths; they swallowed wine and beer in gulps. Wasn't there always plenty of time? And didn't it return the next day? No wonder the Huns looked so happy. Their families were sure to join them, coming from over the horizon where they pillaged like darkness or light.

Though everyone in my family knew we had to go upstairs for hot water, "Wash hands after using" was taped above the rust-stained sink beside the terrible basement toilet in my father's bakery. Fourteen years old and working on Friday nights now, I knew bacteria closed businesses like my father's. They hid inside the near future like the stark, rogue cells of failure.

Just before closing, my mother scrubbed pans while steam spread around her like heaven's immaculate floor. When it vanished, my shift began its long high arc toward midnight while I handled tomorrow's food and waited on men who believed, leaving bars, they needed doughnuts or cookies, entire cakes and pies, each of those drunks sending me back to the sink where I scrubbed because

my father made it clear that the hands that touched coins were tainted, that the hands that touched others were stained.

Some nights, there were women who laughed, leaning across the glass counter, their loose blouses falling open as if they were luring my hands to their breasts. Seeing them drove me downstairs for a few minutes of fantasy that demanded another scalding to keep from spreading whatever was carried by desire, finishing the things I owed my father just before my mother returned to drive my soft hands home, dirty for sleep, giving the secret sins that wanted to kill me ten hours to plot while I slept until near noon, waking to lunch without washing, holding a thick pressed-meat sandwich, stuffing it down my selfish throat with my filthy, soiled fingers because now I wasn't working for anybody but myself.

The Sundays I was an acolyte, I bowed to the Cross, lit the candles on each side of it, and then extended the wick from the gold-plated lighter and reached toward the first of fourteen candles I needed to fire up before the processional hymn.

There were two sets of seven, running higher than my shoulders and ending among artificial ferns and palm leaves, and one Sunday, the fourth candle to my right, no matter how I positioned the wick, refused to ignite. I moved on, but a moment later, when the sixth candle balked as well, I began to sweat.

Whoever had been acolyte the week before had mashed the wicks into the melted wax, and now, the wax hardened, I needed either the time to melt each pool or the nerve to reach up and scrape the wicks clean with my fingers.

I couldn't manage either. By the time I discovered I had six balky candles, the organist had begun to crank out "Faith of Our Fathers," bringing the congregation to its feet and the choir down the center aisle. I extinguished my flame and shuffled down the side steps to the front pew, where three of my friends were ready with junior high school humor about limp wicks and flaccid candles.

OK, I said to myself, it's not my fault—and that would have been that, except that Pastor Sowers, while the choir sang its weekly anthem, lifted a book of matches from under his surplice and lit one as he stood and reached into the plastic foliage to put the flame to one of the unlit candles. My nearest friend poked his elbow between my ribs, but I was horrified.

The candle blossomed fire, but Pastor Sowers shook the match out and lit another, pushing a palm leaf to the side and extending himself on one leg for the most distant wick. Nothing. The anthem was winding down.

Just then, Clifford Weisel, the president of the church council, stormed down

the aisle, lurching slightly from the remnants of childhood polio, and hobbled up the steps to hand Pastor Sowers a cigarette lighter. "Weisel's old man smokes," my friend said, poking me again and laughing, but the anthem was over, Pastor Sowers refused the lighter, and I had another thirty-five minutes to think about the importance of symmetrical light before I walked up those stairs, bowed my head, and snuffed eleven quivering flames while counting down to the zero of pledging, "Never again."

"You stick to it," my father said when I vowed to quit.

Three weeks later, when it was my turn, I checked the candle wicks before Sunday School. I made sure every one of them was standing up straight. I lit all of them successfully. The following week, I announced my resignation as an acolyte. After all, I explained, there were younger boys ready to take my place. The next thing I wanted to quit was sitting through church.

"Say there's no God. Go ahead, say it."

Mr. Haberline's hands were wired to my wrists like a polygraph. He was the homeroom teacher who read the Bible so badly during opening exercises, I laughed. He'd recited, morning after morning, his trinity of Korea, the flag, and God, and this time he'd followed it up with "adult-airy" right after he'd led the Pledge with one fist over the valentine location of his heart.

Mr. Haberline breathed cigarettes and coffee into my suspect face. A bell rang, but thirty tenth graders stayed seated to hear what I had to say about the meaning of our lives, whether or not I thought we had a purpose besides allegiance to rules. He leaned in so close I couldn't see anything but the gap between his front teeth. Behind me I matched every scrape and rustle to someone I knew: the stockings of Carol Baker, the silk blouse of Sally Sloan, the tapping of a geometry book by Jack Williams, who sat a step back to my left while forty-four shoes shuffled in the hall.

"Say there's no God and go to hell. Say it," he repeated, and I said "cavalry," "tabranacle," and "spelacher" to myself, lip-sealed and breathing through my nose, what I could keep doing, alone, until the late bell rang, autonomic as a steady pulse through the mispronunciations of belief.

Any Sunday morning, eight forty-five, from 1958 to 1963—my father sits in his Chevrolet station wagon with the engine running, my mother beside him, my sister in the back seat. I'm half dressed in my room, slowly buttoning my white shirt and hoping this will be the week he backs out of the driveway and leaves without me.

Instead, my mother, every time, comes inside and says, "Hurry now, before trouble starts," and I finish knotting my blue or dark red tie, pick up my hand-me-down beige sport coat or, finally getting rid of that, my bought-new gray blazer, and give her time to close the car door before I follow, dropping into the seat behind her. I can watch my father for the ten minutes we spend on the nearly empty roads to Emmanuel Lutheran Church. He stares straight ahead as if he's handling the Bel Air wagon for the first time. Nobody says a word, but trouble doesn't materialize.

The Technology of Paradise

From the Sunday after I was confirmed until the Sunday before I went off to college, I was last in the car and had perfect attendance, arriving early for both Sunday School and church. For nine years preceding those, I'd gone without complaint. Fourteen years altogether. *Seven hundred and twenty-eight Sundays*—I've counted them to be sure of the repetitions, because to this day I can sing the lyrics of a hundred hymns, recite the litanies as well as the Apostles' and Nicene creeds. And I can call out the answers to Bible questions before any *Jeopardy* contestant can push a button. Who is Zacharias? I say to "Father of John the Baptist." Who is Joseph of Arimathea? I blurt to "Provider of tomb for Jesus." Who are Shadrach, Meshach, and Abednego? I recite to "Survivors of Nebuchadnezzar's fire." For a bonus, I can sing a Gospel song that uses the rhythmic names of those would-be martyrs for its chorus.

What I've learned since that time is that in another part of the world, during one initiation rite, a dozen small cones are arranged in a mystical pattern on the shaved scalp of the novice. While he

prays, they're lit and slowly burn down like candles until they sear a profound scar into the flesh of the would-be priest.

Another group of monks demonstrates devotion by amputating their fingers, at designated intervals, in a prescribed sequence. They give up the index finger, the ring finger; they eventually relinquish the thumb and show seniority by the severity of their stumps.

I sometimes shake my head and smile, but what I know best is that some disciples will flog themselves and carry a cross along the highways of America like this former priest who sleeps in a lost school-bus shelter, who wears burlap and bears a cross of X-logs that look so heavy I would say lunacy, except we played tennis through college and he touch-volleyed with the soft hands of the expert, used slice and drop shot and lob as if he could win with the ascetic's repertoire.

I say "George" now, standing two steps from him a mile from my father's house, although he's abandoned his name like a pope, and since he's no longer talking, I begin to babble like somebody who's heard a beep, somebody who's leaving his name and message on the tape unspooling behind his eyes, waiting for him to return so he can get back to me.

Years ago, his family had built a clay court in the lot beside their house. When I visited, I'd help George lay down lines or, if I was early, roll and sweep the court to a sweet perfection that made our first footprints seem intrusion.

That house, a year after I graduated from college, burned to the ground—one of those total-loss blazes that transforms a house into rubble. Bad wiring, I heard, but by then it was the hearsay of my mother's letters to Oxford, Ohio, where I was busy reading a list of books for my master's degree oral examination.

He's Zydesh now. The spelling is mine. He refuses to write as well as speak since he explained to his brother, who had a hundred-mile-an-hour serve with a wooden racket in high school, how he was atoning for his sins by taking on a name from the bottom of the alphabet. My father has suggested I take advantage of knowing Zydesh when he was George. "Who knows," he's said, "it may do you some good."

George looks like the red-herring suspect in a B movie—long hair and beard, and the prophets' look of possession in his eyes. I keep myself from staring by examining the bus shelter, a place where in three weeks, children will gather at 7:30, pushing back, in case of rain, to where he is sitting.

The cinder-block walls are splotched with gray and blue and green paint. Periodically, someone slathers over the obscenities that appear on such walls. In

a couple of weeks, I imagine, somebody will roust George out of here, sweep and disinfect and repaint in bright school-bus yellow, maybe repair the hole ripped out at the top of the back wall, where a vent was built in to keep air circulating.

"I'm Gary," I say. "From college. Tennis." I'm not equipped for either banter or interview. I think, if he speaks, it will be to curse or bless me. I feel like a tourist in an AIDS ward or a cancer hospice.

I want to say something now that might cause George to smile or at least raise his eyes to mine. I run through old tennis matches and the new ones I've coached at a small college, mentioning that my son played for me, that he hit two-handed from both sides, that I write stories and poems, occasionally referencing tennis, going on and on like a devotee of a new immortality scheme I've been reading about, one in which you recite everything you've ever thought about to a computer. The scientist who champions this version of heaven means us to record emotions, tastes, personality, and attitudes. He intends for us to recreate what's stored in our brains so we can be called up by our descendants. He means aspirations, sexual urges, religious doubts and whatever else is necessary for us to be ourselves as eternal software, a confessed, box-set of disks called up in paradise for conversations with the living.

Fat chance, I think. We might as well begin genetic engineering for the masses. We'll end up with the expurgated and the overtly confessional. The insufferably perfect and the tediously grotesque.

An hour before I walked the Middle Road to where I'd learned George lived, I watched a retrospective feature about a racer who woke up with amnesia after crashing his car. As if the retaining wall were birth, I thought, considering his software angel, the disks with no past. And now I'm observing the split-life of flagellant George, who, if he spoke to a computer, would disregard, probably, everything except the trials of Zydesh.

In England, in 1752, the government decided, belatedly, to shift to the Gregorian calendar after years of lagging behind the developed world's abandonment of the Julian calendar it subscribed to. So many years had passed with the slightly slower calibration that England was now eleven days behind the rest of Europe. What else to do but decree the disappearance of those days, declaring September 3 changed to September 14?

Simple perhaps, though enough people believed those eleven lost days had shortened their lives that a riot began. The Calendar Riots claimed whole lives of its own, but the change, nevertheless, remained. And here is George shortening his life by abandoning his identity. And here I am confessing to thousands of

games of *Aardy the Aardvark* and *Tetris*, weeks spent mastering the patterns for excelling in a reality more artificial than any George could be imagining.

In the first game, the aardvark's tongue searches for ants; it extends and absorbs them through more and more complex anthills while the feeding time is diminished until there is no possible way Aardy can succeed unless you have memorized the likely alternatives with which the computer will test you. Likewise, with *Tetris*, the varying geometric shapes drop so rapidly, you need nerve, anticipation, and hundreds of games played in order to recognize the perfect fits instantaneously.

Not to mention the hundreds of hours spent on the mastery of tennis. Not to total the months of playing time, the initiation of lessons and defeats, fatigue and injury. It's no surprise that players argue line calls made eighty feet from where they stand. Play long enough, repeating the strokes, and you recognize, to within an inch, whether or not a ball traveling the seventy-eight feet of a court will strike its target.

Earlier, before the feature on the racer's amnesia, I'd driven the four miles from my father's house to where George had lived. I'd parked and crossed the road to examine the house someone had built on the site of the destroyed one. The name on the mailbox was different. For all I knew, there had been two subsequent houses, five different owners; but the lot next door was eerie with familiarity.

The fence was gone. The net and the lines were gone. Yet there was no mistaking that a tennis court lay under the short, thick grass. I thought I could sense, as soon as I stepped onto the surface, where the baseline ran, where George would stand to receive my serve.

The ground, of course, was remarkably level, but what astonished me was the easy recognition of the constructed rectangle, how there were no weeds. The red clay might account for the pattern, but what herbicide would allow grass but prevent weeds for decades? It made me reconsider the technology of lawn care; it made me aware of the possible consequences of rolling on the perfect lawns of my neighbors.

Whether or not George had been a successful priest, I didn't know, but I thought about herbicides and the human body, tennis and religion. And then I walked off that odd grass and scraped the soles of my shoes with each stride back across the highway to my car.

There have always been people who see the body as a hindrance: sinful, inefficient, obsolete. If only the soul were free; if only the mind were free.

Religion and science are often siblings. On a simple scale, it's like one of those horror movies from the 1950s where the fanatics save Hitler's brain in a jar for the resurrection of Germany, or the scientist saves his wife's brain while he searches for a beautiful body in which to transplant it.

The technology of paradise, we might say, knowing enough now to put the body aside and replace it with machinery. As long as the mind can be reduced to a set of mechanical ideas. As long as we are willing to say goodbye to our senses. As long as we don't give a damn about the way we take things in, how each of us synthesizes those sensory details in a particular, distinctive way.

One study explains that the brightest among us have the earliest memories. From age three perhaps, or even from age two. Better, if something can be called up from the days before walking, a sort of MENSA by retrieval. Snow, I think, the winter of 1947. Christmas, how our blue-bulbed tree tumbled onto the carpet the night before I received a tricycle from Santa.

My mother's fur collar, the eyes and noses of the sewn fox pelts that formed it. My ringworm head-shave, the black salve that was slathered on my skull. My steel-braced shoes to correct pronation syndrome. The neighbor who drowned in pneumonia being carried off under flashing lights.

On the radio, "Near You" and "Open the Door, Richard." After church, driving across Pittsburgh on Sundays, my father singing, "I've got a lovely bunch of coconuts."

The high IQ of nostalgia. The reaching back for the complete file. If you want to talk with me in a hundred years, you'll need a book of trivia, year by year, beginning in 1947, to verify whether or not I'm another liar or one of those rarities who record the past with accuracy.

Software package indeed. Once, I paired with his brother against George and his father. We were big hitters, but our best shots were blunted on clay. We had trouble getting to the net behind our second serves. My idea of tennis was to let the ball bounce as little as possible, but George welcomed half volleys, spun serves wide and into the body, moving like someone who understood the nuances of nylon strings, how they received each shot. His father, despite his bad knees, had perfected the lob and the low, slice service return. George's brother and I lost two quick sets, firing two dozen outright winners and enough unforced errors to keep the score from being close.

When I was paired with George, every gentlemanly gesture on our team belonged to him. Every flare-up on the court was mine. All of the sensible

strategies were executed by George. All of the overstruck, low-percentage shots were mine. George was a saint. He lifted my level of play by refusing to allow me to embarrass myself with racket throwing and curses.

Once, after a week of foul weather, George was busy, when I arrived, with small pegs and string. He was relining from scratch, remeasuring the distances, squaring the corners. Before he laid down one line, the court was outlined in twine. It looked like the floor plan for an agility drill, and when I started spinning out lime along the singles sideline, I grew nervous, as if I'd somehow forget to stop or turn, drawing lines where none belonged.

Just over the hill from the school-bus shelter is a freshly seeded swath of grass. As little as a year ago, I know, there were two asphalt tennis courts there. When he was twelve years old, my son had happily hit forehands and backhands for hours on those courts. By the time he was fourteen, he refused to play there, making me drive another five miles when we visited my father, because someone, when the courts were built, had miscalculated the area, had laid down one court and then discovered there was room only for an additional singles court. Not so bad, but the sidelines of that court ran less than two feet from the fence. You had to play up to receive serve; you had to take balls on the rise and rush the net because otherwise you'd be beaten or injured. It wasn't strategy that made him refuse to play. He was embarrassed to be seen on such a court.

"George," I say again, "take care," but he's Quasimodo among the bells. When I retreat from where I've been standing just outside the doorway, Zydesh doesn't follow. His cross is propped against the back of the shelter. Before I can reason with myself, I stoop, put my shoulder in the crook of the X, and heft it carefully, like a novice.

I think of all the lies and silences I would record on my permanent record. I think of the fictions I would enter through the keyboard. In all of these lamentations for the brain, there is a moment, finally, when it locks the fire exits for intelligence, when memory is jammed, smoke-frenzied, against each inward-opening door. After the Coconut Grove for thinking, after the Happy Land for inference, each of us vows smoke alarm, sprinkler, fire escape, multiple doors—as if our chant could free us from the flaming high-rise of impermanence and we could ascend the precarious air.

Work

"This is where I fell and tore my arm open," I say. "The time it got all infected."

My wife smiles. She knows this story, how I scraped my arm playing with Keith Osborne, and because he was three years older, believed him when he said, "You'll be OK," after he ran water over it and covered the worst abrasions with Band-Aids so we could run back outside to chase a rubber ball we slammed against a wall to simulate a baseball game. I wore a long-sleeved shirt for the next two days, not telling anyone about my arm until I noticed, that second day, gobs of yellow pus oozing from underneath the Band-Aids. My mother scrubbed those wounds with nearly scalding water. She performed an amateur debridement while I screamed and writhed in the arms of Aunt Margaret.

I was six years old, just finished with first grade. In the summer of 1952, this block in Etna was busy with pedestrians who walked from their nearby houses or parked on either side

Clemente Stuff

of the street to purchase jewelry, shoes, or appliances; candy, ice cream, or baked goods. My father had bought the bakery business two years before and was building a house we'd move into before Christmas. If there were traffic jams during rush hour each day, that was just what you'd expect from the Etna bottleneck on the way to and from Pittsburgh. If those snarls became worse each year, that was what people put up with if they moved into Shaler Township, the first, fast-growing suburb north of Pittsburgh where our new house was rising.

Six years later the Etna bypass would open and doom this block, parking banned during four key hours per day. But it was still a bottleneck. Traffic, enormous by then, backed up, beginning at Butler Street, further than it ever had. Ten years after I recovered from my arm injury without antibiotics, hardly anyone parked to shop, even during the legal hours, but horns honked and drivers cursed, and my father's bakery, as well as most of the other businesses, gradually shut down.

A familiar story, nothing remarkable, but I've come back to

walk the block because my father, more than thirty-five years after he left the bakery behind, has told me the road, finally, will be widened—that eighteen months from now, the opposite side of Butler Street will be leveled.

"Carlos Funeral Home," I say, pointing to the first building across from where we stand in front of what used to be Miller's Tavern. Immediately, I know that's not chronologically accurate. In 1952, the building housed McIntyre's Funeral Home. To my parents, the change in names, after the bypass was built, seemed another sign of times gone bad. You didn't go to a stranger named Carlos. Now that McIntyre was gone, you went to Neeley's or Ogrodnik's. My mother would check the names to see who had allowed their relatives to be laid out by Carlos. She would shake her head when she recognized someone she knew.

Now the building has been converted to apartments, nothing that makes me consider the ethnic connotations of an owner's name, but I remember my father's family was laid out at home, so it didn't matter. My uncle who died young before I started school, my grandmother while I was in fourth grade, my other grandfather, the one so stern and straight-laced I was unable to speak to him as a child, in 1965, the year the bakery closed—all of them on display in the living room of the house on Greismere Street, which runs along the cliffside overlooking Butler Street.

The year the bypass opened, I became a teenager. My mother sent me across the street to Ben's, a mom-and-pop store, on the Fridays I waited for her to close at six o'clock. The *Press*, not the *Sun-Telegraph*; the late edition, not the home edition. There were times when I was sent back to trade one "edition" in for the other, and I learned to check in the upper right-hand corner for the proper label; but on one particular day, I forgot a more important warning and darted from between two trucks bottlenecked going north and dashed directly into the path of a car going south that was somehow not backed up at the light.

The car squealed and stopped, just bumping me. I took a step back and caught my balance. It was almost a stuntman's perfection, me frozen, the driver relieved, and then one of the truck drivers yelled, "You big, dumb, shitty bastard" at me, and immediately afterward, the driver of the car that had nudged me shouted, "Yeah, what's wrong with you, you big, dumb, shitty bastard?"

It was an odd version of call-and-response, the near tragedy turning into a profane lecture on caution. The rush-hour traffic, even against the flow, jammed up behind the braked Ford, and then I ran, without looking, through the last lane, where no cars, by good fortune, had swerved around the stalled line to speed along the curb lane.

Horns rippled back both lines while I opened the bakery door. Did my mother see or hear any of this? Was she so thankful, she accepted one moment of good luck wrapped in epithets? She said nothing and never did.

My wife, skipping a half dozen empty or apartment-converted buildings, reads a set of hand-made signs: *Beer Cans. Barbie Dolls. Clemente Stuff.* I tell her I have old Clemente stuff. He signed my scorecard after three different games; I was still collecting baseball cards when he first broke in with the Pirates. She says that before too long, Barbie will be fifty years old; that despite being young enough, she'd never owned one; that she remembers how our older son, when he was nine years old, insisted we go in the beer-can store. He was collecting cans. We'd walked the sides of roads and covered the trash receptacles of parks until he had several hundred cans, all of them problematic in value. My son wanted to see what they were worth, but none of the cans he owned were on display in the store I kept seeing as Ben's—candy and soda, ice-cream cones, and newspapers to run back across the street.

Next door, where Zip used to load cases of beer into the trunks of cars, somebody is selling *Used Bikes*, someone is promoting *Artistic Carousel Horses*, and Michelle is advertising *Furniture*—not one car parked from those doors to the bypass, not one pedestrian on the sidewalk from the old funeral home to the gas station, which, my father says, might be spared.

One generation removed from Etna, I live among people who define themselves through where they've traveled, where they've lived before, and where they've been educated. Here, the people remain recognized through their presence: the work they do, where they live, and the family they come from. None of them, even now, work for large companies; few of them travel, except by car to hunting camps and a summer week on the shore of a nearby lake. Like my father, many of them no longer subscribe to the Pittsburgh paper, getting the news they need not from a computer, but from the weekly that covers an area whose perimeter they could walk around before the next issue is released.

For the most part, they're not aware of Emerson's advice to make their place an "axis of the earth," but their concerns are similarly centered in an age when many people see that focus to be as quaint as old beer cans and carousel-horse collections.

What there still is on this street is optimism. The block of independent, small businesses. The absence of brand names, franchises, and conglomerates. And every storefront but one filled with goods, every door but one open despite bleak prospects.

And if these men and women know that the location, at least, is doomed, that two years from now they'll be relocated, they seem little different from the men and women who flipped over the cardboard signs in the windows, turning *Open, Welcome* outward and *Closed, Come Again* inward—Nucera, Klueh, Tripani, Keller, Toner, Ackerman, Fincke.

In 1952, Hoburg's was the anchor store of this block, the tallest building in Etna, five stories. Hardware, I remember; farmers' supplies, my father said earlier, enough of a change to explain itself and who lived in Shaler Township before we did.

It still stands, renamed the Peer Building, ironically empty and soaring above the renamed but busy Huntz' Tavern. There was nothing so remarkable that year, on the doomed side of the street, but it featured an appliance store, a barber shop, a shoe repair shop, a soda fountain, a beer distributorship, and a real estate office—small, privately owned businesses. The families lived upstairs or in the back of the rooms where they worked. Ben Hughes and his wife stepped out from their living room to scoop ice cream. George Seale could leave his lunch on the kitchen table and talk about available property. Zip could lock up his beer and go upstairs to watch television or read the paper. He could look out his living room window at the same view he had all day from his office.

None of these men put on a coat and tie and entered the bottleneck to Pittsburgh. The women worked the storefronts, tending the cash registers, chatting with their neighbors or patrons walking a mile or more from West Etna. Two of those women, Anne Hemmerich the beautician and Florence Ackerman the shoe saleswoman, doubled as owners. Their customers lingered to share stories with them or other customers. My mother seldom sat down, because she talked the spaces between customers full with anecdotes.

What these people had in common was working alone. Nearly all of them welcomed the responsibility of having to "be there" or go belly up. My father, from 1950 to 1965, baked five nights a week, year-round. Or else the bakery couldn't open. The butcher, the barber, the shoemaker, the hairdresser—you were there; or if you were fortunate, you had a wife to open up.

An exception? The Burnells lived in a house above but separate from Keller's Appliance Store, which moved in after Edgar's Grocery closed, and I

don't remember anyone in the family working there. Whatever Charley Burnell did for a living, I didn't know, which made him seem a stranger on that street, a customer instead of a neighbor. On a picnic, once, the Burnells brought two cans of baked beans—nothing unusual, except they ate them cold and direct from the can, scrambling for the piece of pork fat in each that floated among the beans. Mr. Burnell claimed one; Charlotte, who was my sister's age, two years older and turning thirteen that year, won the other.

Even the bars were neighborhood-centered—Miller, Peluso, Petroska. My father reminded me that they drew men from their homes and distracted them. They encouraged heavy drinking, and the evidence stumbled past the bakery at the law-required two A.M. closing time. If a man could get up and punch in for his seven A.M. shift, he could handle it; if he was late or absent, he had a problem. Next door to the bakery was the jewelry store where the wife took care of things on the days her husband was "out of commission." A man like The Prince, my father would say. A man who couldn't take care of himself.

Men trudged to Miller's or Stanley's or Peluso's through all of the weather the post office claims to deliver in. "It warms the bones," they said to my father on those Friday nights I greased pans and rolled sandwich buns, most of them reeling in the sudden heat of ovens. By that time I was in high school, the bypass completed, and I arrived shortly after ten o'clock and stayed until five-thirty the following morning. By that time, I knew those men, the jeweler included, warmed by the first flush of alcohol heat, would be more vulnerable to the cold before they finished their shuffle home.

The space where the bakery was is a parking lot now. It funnels the wind between the old feed store and the jewelry shop, enough that I shiver in July. Nancy Willard writes, "Our stories stitch the living and the dead into a single fabric, a coat to keep us from the winds that blow through the spaces the dead once filled." I've spent the morning listening to my father's stories weave their warmth. He paused to apologize each time he came to something he thought might offend. "It was called Hunky Alley," he says about the street that will be truncated by the widened highway. "George Seale was called Gum Toby because he always chewed on an unlit cigar."

I told him names are voices and then let it drop. He doesn't need a lesson. He went on, talking about Stanley's Saloon, which stretched alongside the shoe repair shop and the barber shop. "Petroska's," he said. "One daughter was

something. She played the accordion in the bar, but the other girl was the nurse for your sister's delivery."

Finally, my father took his stories back to his childhood, Ben Hughes's store becoming Mag McCooney's, where couples went for soda after going to the movies in the 1930s. Keller's Appliance Store turned into Edgar's Grocery. "They delivered," my father said. "They carried baskets of food to your door, but the new A&P didn't have to deliver if it saved you 10 percent on everything and carried ten times the stock."

He paused before adding, "Keller married Edgar's daughter," and then his bakery became the butcher shop where E. P. Seitz, the man from whom he rented, got started—half of the building holding Sarah Miller's Notion Shop. "Needles and thread," he said, leaving the rest of the notions to me because he'd gone next door in his memory, changing Best Feeds to the Welfare Store, "where people with bum luck went." He didn't mention The Prince, and I thought of his pride in never taking anything from anybody, no matter what. How The Prince's unforgivable sin had been taking, literally and figuratively, from his family.

Grace Paley instructs, "If you say what's on your mind in the language that comes to you from your parents and your street and your friends, you'll probably say something beautiful." I think of standing on the railroad tracks with Keith Osborne behind the bakery. He lived above Toner's Candy Store, and when he told me to close my eyes, turn my back, and listen with my feet for the train, I followed his directions, just like I'd done with my wounded arm. Keith Osborne said, "First one to jump is a crybaby," and I stood my ground while the engineer sounded his whistle.

Each time I was the crybaby. There was always a moment for Keith Osborne to wait after I landed before he jumped off the tracks. Unless I caught my foot, like characters did in books and movies, I was in less danger than I was crossing the street. One afternoon, no train vibrating the rails, I tried to catch my shoe in the tracks and couldn't do it. Those stories were lies, I thought, but when I felt the first tremors, I pulled my foot away from danger.

E. P. Seitz lived across the street from the bakery. He'd risen from butcher to car dealer to landlord without moving from the only house with a small yard instead of a business in the front. As an old man, he sat on the porch nearly every day, watching cars and passersby who I never saw stop to chat. If he leaned forward, he could see both the site of his old butcher shop and his former car

dealership. He sat on that porch when I was running through traffic, but he didn't yell anything after my foolish dash from between the trucks. Now, an old woman sits there as if she's accepted the legacy of sentinel for Butler Street. I learn she's married to the old barber, that they moved "up in the world" before the barber shop closed, becoming owners themselves, acquiring a front porch and its swing, getting a chance to sit thirty feet back from the sidewalk instead of on a front stoop.

Tripani, the retired barber, will have to relocate. The house, the most attractive building on that side of the street, will be leveled like the others. Tripani was the barber my mother refused to send me to after I'd caught ringworm the summer before I tried to sell colored paper by the sheet. "You can't start school like that," she said. My head was shaved and livid. My father and uncles called me "baldy wiener." My mother and aunts tried different home remedies, including salves concocted by the gypsy above the Circle Bar.

"That Tripani," my mother repeated, sounding just like she did, years later, when she said, "That Carlos." I want to tell Tripani that story—that my mother, almost certainly, was wrong. Those ointments were useless; it was more likely I'd picked up ringworm from resting my head against the filthy seats at the Etna Theater, where, as my mother put it, "Who knows who was just sitting there."

Just after two A.M. on one of the first Friday nights I worked through until morning for my father, a voice called from what seemed like underneath the bakery. It was possible—half the bakery, including the room in which we were standing, had no foundation, and there were places where a man, if he wanted to, could lie on his back and squirm under.

Outside, though, there was three hours of heavy snow, six inches or more drifted thigh-deep in spots. "Baker, baker!" we heard—me, my father, and Johnny Kosher, who worked for him even though he'd developed "a bad case of the jitters." My father waited for another call while Johnny Kosher, a former full-time baker himself, began to pound the rising dough for rye and whole-wheat bread into shape for weighing and fitting into pans.

"Baker, baker!" the call came again. Whoever was moaning was prone in all that snow, sick or injured or so drunk he couldn't rouse himself. Johnny Kosher flopped a mound of rye dough on the bench and started chopping off one-pound segments. "It's old man Moyer," my father said.

I shrugged, and Johnny Kosher clipped so quickly at the dough I wanted to

grab his wrists. "Baker, baker!" the voice from the snow repeated, and my father forced the side door open through a snow drift and stepped out into the narrow walkway between the bakery and the jewelry store.

That door stood open for two minutes, long enough for my feet to start stamping and Johnny Kosher to begin lifting pans of sandwich buns from the oven. Finally, my father backed into the oven room, hoisting old man Moyer onto the chair I pushed his way. "Drunk as a skunk," my father observed, and then he added, "Johnny, your hands," shifting my stare to where his assistant had just pulled his sixth rack of sandwich buns bare-handed from the oven.

Johnny Kosher jumped back then and lifted his hands to inspect them. "Nothing," he said. His gloves were in his pocket. He'd forgotten them and yet his hands weren't burned.

It was a movie script by now—the near-death, the rescue, the miraculous unmarked hands. The next time old man Moyer spoke, he said my father's name and nodded, and then he slept without tumbling from that armless folding chair, a miracle of its own.

"OK now," my father said at five A.M. "OK now," jostling old man Moyer. He wanted him out of the bakery before customers might slog through the snow to buy sweet rolls and bread. Old man Moyer needed to find his own bed now, and without speaking, he felt his way erect, pulled his jacket tight, and restarted the ten steps to his own side door and the stairs that led to the rooms above his shop.

The street was a limited version of the frontier, and Franklin Roosevelt, even posthumously, was, according to the small businessmen who filled the storefronts with goods, the worst thing that had ever happened to the United States. It was straight Republican. George Seale, the real-estate man, was on the "up and ups" with the Republican hierarchy. He made deals while he sucked on his moist cigar, and for years, I thought voting was a one-stroke process.

In a setting more exotic, with steep mountainsides and river gorges, travelers will stop to talk with residents whose lives are tied to one street for generations. Continuity, a sense of permanence—if Nucera made shoes by hand, if Zip brewed his beer, if Ben Hughes churned homemade ice cream, tourists would park the bottleneck closed to wander and buy. Without sufficient credentials, quaintness turns depressing and expendable. Nothing on the side of the street opposite from the leveled bakery demands to be saved.

We drive up to Greismere Street, where my father spent most of his boyhood in a house overlooking Etna. None of the houses are new or significantly changed from when I was a child and we visited once a month. The available land pitches so steeply toward Etna, no developer could construct another dwelling. At the end of the street, though, is where the cliff will have to be cut back for the additional lane.

On Sunday night, November 12, 1950, Etna's fire bells sounded, reaching the house on Greismere Street while we were visiting. There was a bell code that told the town's listeners which call box had been sounded. My parents knew the neighborhood of every fire without getting out of their chairs.

That night the bells said Butler Street, and my father, who had turned on the ovens three hours earlier, joked, "It's probably the bake shop." Everybody rushed to the upstairs window that looked out over Etna. Smoke was roiling up from the rear of the bakery; fire was visible.

My father skidded his delivery sedan down Kittanning Street, past Hunky Alley. The rest of us watched the firemen as if we could make the scene a fantasy by staring from behind glass. The bakery, for the most part, was saved, though the refrigerator had shorted out and created the need for a repaired rear wall, new paint, and a re-tarpapered roof the following spring after weeks of having #10 cans catch the worst of the leaks. My father reopened the bakery on November 21st. My mother, as she always did, recorded the sales figures in a notebook—$48.93. The following day, she recorded $126.54, and though the building hadn't yet recovered, the business had. For months, the old blue refrigerator sat out back, giving off its exotic odor of electrical fire even after a winter of snow and freezing rain.

Now, if I knocked on the door of the Greismere Street house and asked to go upstairs, I could see the parking lot where the bakery once sat, but *Fincke* isn't on the mailbox. Neither is *Cubbage* or *Bannister* lettered on the mailboxes on either side, so none of these people would likely welcome me. No matter; what I want to see is the cliffside that's supposed to be coming down in eighteen months.

Below where we stand, the businesses stop. Taking twenty feet will pull the edge right back to the property lines of these houses, and without the maple, locust, and sumac trees, the owners will look out their second-story windows as if they were living in hotel rooms in city high-rises.

Protected by ADT Security Systems, it says in the yards of the two houses nearest the edge, and I imagine a clause in the contract to cover the landscaping of

convenience. While the bypass was being built, the adjoining cliffside cut back, boulders tumbled onto the future site of the roadway, and one Sunday morning a mudslide covered the two houses closest to the construction.

These houses sit above such hazards, but all along the edge, just beyond the guardrails, enough decomposing trash has been piled to create a precarious extension of the cliffside. Covered with a film of grass clippings, it sits more like ancient, deep, wet snow than careless landfill. Just beyond it, jutting out at a suspect angle, one old maple still carries the remnants of a tree house, which might have been abandoned before I made my first trip to Greismere Street for family gatherings more than fifty years ago.

You wouldn't be careless in that tree house. You wouldn't come back ten years later to grow nostalgic with a friend and a case of beer unless you were the kind of teenager who climbed water towers and trestles and dove out of motel rooms into swimming pools three stories beneath you.

But if you cleaned up the broken glass and kept out the cars where the street fades into a set of tracks in the undergrowth, you'd have the start of a public park. Twenty steps down the path, the scenery turns idyllic: maples and oaks and ash, rhododendron and junipers towering a generation after being planted and left behind by the families who once cultivated the land well beyond the property lines that we see marked by crumbling walls fifty feet to our right.

My wife, doubling back, shows me how all the old guardrails are still in place, that they're in pairs along the edge, the cabled and uncabled, as if they do double duty to reinforce where drivers are most likely to need something to keep them from tumbling with their cars into Etna.

In the alley above these houses, my cousin and I played basketball, using a hoop nailed onto a telephone pole. If we missed to the left, somebody had to retrieve the ball before it rolled downhill to the guardrail. If I played by myself, I never shot from the right side for fear of having the ball tumble all the way to where Butler Street merged into Route 8.

Losing the ball will be a certainty in less than two years. A rolling ball will pitch out and straight down among the cars, which, once the highway's complete, won't have to slow and stop. A basketball landing on a car from this height would do some damage, or it could distract a driver, start a chain-reaction crash.

Like any freshly opened bottleneck, the new road will attract thousands more cars, working its way back to stop and go. That basketball, for a moment,

will look like a comet fragment slamming into Jupiter, and its destruction will ripple back the lanes like sound or meaning until the drivers of undamaged but stopped cars will curse the designs of the new expressway, believing its construction flawed.

Building a tennis court was a dream I shared with my father. Constructing it ourselves was his dream alone. But it seemed so easy, standing beside him in the middle of June near the edge of the twenty acres of land he'd just bought as an investment in his distant retirement that I estimated the end of July, August tops, and the two of us would be spinning out lime along the boundaries, getting things ready for play. He had me captive, because tennis was all I had wanted to do since May, when I'd reached the quarterfinals of the biggest junior tournament in Pittsburgh, my rocket-flat serve and forehand good enough to be successful in the 15-and-unders, even against the kids nearly two years older, the ones lucky enough to have birthdays a month or two after the cutoff date of October 1.

The nearest house was a hundred yards away up a dirt road, and my father said there weren't any zoning ordinances that discouraged using your land any way you pleased. "Look at all that clay," he said, and I agreed it looked like we could hold the just-finished French Open right there on our new property if they had postponed it until September. "And this place is nearly level to begin with. We just push this bank over to there, fill in this low spot here, roll it, get some fence, and we're in business."

The Handmade Court

"All right!" I blurted. I was willing to give up a month of weekends to shovels and wheelbarrows and the heavy, water-filled roller that the residents who rented that nearest house allowed us to store in their garage. This was going to be country-club stuff: a clay court, privacy, hours of play without some jerks wearing street shoes telling me and my friends to "get the fuck off the court," meaning any of the only three public courts in Shaler Township in 1959.

Three weeks earlier, my first time in a tournament, I was dressed in plaid swimming trunks and the same white T-shirt I wore under dress shirts on Sunday morning. Up until that Saturday,

I'd never worn shorts to play tennis, because I didn't own any. I played in old black chinos, faded to near-white at the knees—mostly with my father, who wore his green work pants to the pay-by-the-hour county courts ten miles from where we lived.

I wore a pair of black high-top tennis shoes, and the first morning at the tournament, I learned that "tennis shoes" was a figurative expression. I wasn't allowed on the clay courts where the youngest entries were being shuttled, so I had to wait (and so did my angry opponent) for a default on one of the hard courts for us to play. Tennis shoes, I was told by the tournament director, had flat soles. They were low-cut and lighter, and they weren't black like my Keds.

I had two tennis rackets at least, the ones my father and mother used. They were right off the discount store counter, pre-strung with string so cheap it shredded into what looked like unraveling cardboard. No one else in the Pittsburgh Metropolitan Tennis Tournament wore shorts that weren't white.

Where I played tennis with my friends, there were nets with holes so large they resembled the webs torn by the struggles of victims captured by giant spiders in the movies I watched on late-night television. Men in blue jeans who used the same skinhead balls all summer would lean on those nets to swill beer after thirty minutes of loping around bare-chested. By the end of May, even if the park service repaired the worst holes in April before they put the nets back up after a winter in some storage garage, the net strings would tear away from the tape that ran across the top, so you might, every once in a while, skid a shot through a hole without fluttering a bit of cord. If your opponent wasn't paying attention, the point continued.

For placing legitimate shots, however, cross-court was best. Although there were times we found the net pulled straight across by men who thought it needed to be the same level from side to side, it always sagged, when we lowered it, into a sad, shallow U because there was no center strap to adjust for tension.

The second day of that tournament, I added a cardigan sweater that was a cheap knock-off of what Perry Como wore on television every Saturday. It had red and blue cuffs and a similar stripe where it buttoned up the front. I'd noticed that the better players had V-neck sweaters; they had racket covers, and strings that were gold or clear. And their rackets said Wilson and Bancroft, rather than

Best Craft like mine—the least of my worries, because when I laid my mother's racket on the ground by the net post, it wobbled slightly from being warped. Worse, one of the strings was broken and tied off—how my father saved a few dollars, waiting until at least three strings broke before he took the rackets to the Honus Wagner store in Pittsburgh, where they were replaced with those same woven-nylon shredders.

The second time my opponent served, he looped a short, underhanded shot into the service box that I caught on the second hop. I thought he'd lost track of the score and was slapping the ball my way, until he moved to the other side of the court to serve. During the next game, standing six feet behind the baseline, I caught a ball still in the air like I always did so I wouldn't have to chase it. "My point," my opponent said, and he walked so casually to receive my next serve that I was sure he was right.

"Don't be discouraged, son. He's seeded #4," the man who collected the used balls said from outside the fence. I didn't say anything. I didn't know what "seeded" meant. Ten minutes later, when that boy sprained his ankle, I took my default win and moved on. My mother, when I got home, presented me with a pair of white tennis shorts and a shirt with a collar to wear the following day.

I won that match, too, defeating a boy who was as unseeded as I was. He threw his racket over the fence four times during the match. His mother retrieved it each time. When we finished, he dragged his V-neck sweater by one sleeve, sweeping a path from the net post to the gate.

Fourth of July weekend, a couple of days before my fourteenth birthday, I found myself starting the first work I'd ever done that amounted to anything other than earning an extra dessert or the dollar-an-hour I received for greasing pans. As soon as I filled one wheelbarrow and hauled the clay to be dumped, I was sweating. In half an hour, I had blisters, and there was no sign of an ice-cream break.

My father's new property was farther from our house than the county courts. Once we'd taken the forty-five minutes to drive there, my father was committed to a full day of work. After another half hour of digging and dumping, the only antidote to pain was planning lines I could use on girls when the muscles that would surely come from the hardest work I'd ever done bulged and rippled beside every swimming pool I could get myself invited to. I had reason for my hope. I'd just been invited by Janet Cook, who lived near Mt. Royal Boulevard, to a semiformal dance at the club her parents belonged to.

Another half hour passed before I nearly speared myself as my shovel struck rock. "Dammit," I said, and my father spun around with his shovel loaded. I ducked, thinking I was eating a face-full for swearing. "Sorry, Dad," I said, when the dirt stayed put.

"What's the problem?" my father asked, so tolerant that I turned nervous.

"It's like there's a road under here, a big rock or something."

"Work around it. Find the edge and pry it out. Nobody said there wouldn't be any rocks. You can't expect everything to be simple."

I poked around with the shovel blade, and when I'd measured the perimeter of the rock, I understood that we were not going to finish this court in time to help my chances in the 15's. "Dad," I said, "it's four feet across; it's twice that around."

My father stood staring at me, performing a quick mental assessment of the personification of his genes. He didn't look like he was enjoying the evaluation. "You work over here, if that's what you want," he finally said. "No boulders over here. No mountains."

"Really," I said, "there's no moving this thing."

"There's always moving. It doesn't go down forever like a hole to China."

"You'll see."

"Over here, then. Over here, so you can at least be shoveling while I get the Himalayas out of your way."

I didn't back off very far. This was an opportunity to rest for a minute. My father was about to recognize that this project was a disaster. He'd cancel the remainder of the work order before he'd remember to complain about me standing around.

"Looks as if you're going to learn what real work is," my father observed after he'd probed long enough to make it look like he'd done the measuring. "Get the pick from the garage."

I was in the quarterfinals. This boy was seeded #2, but by now the strings on my father's racket were frayed so badly it looked, from a distance, as if there was a hole in the middle. During the last game of the first set, three strings broke during one point, my last forehand slingshotting over my opponent's head as if I'd imagined him Goliath. I picked up my mother's racket, my ready-made excuse for losing in the one-sided fashion you might expect if you used a lightweight racket that was warped and missing a string.

The truth is, I would have lost even with a Wilson Jack Kramer Autograph

Model in my hand. I had a fast, flat first serve and a forehand I hit harder than any boy my age. But I ran around every shot to avoid my backhand, and then dashed back to a makeshift middle I created five feet to the left of center. It was easier to sprint to wide forehands than to run around backhands, and my opponent had made certain I was doing both on every point.

The other boy's father, sympathetic perhaps, took me aside to explain that I was using what was called a playground grip, the same grip my father used. I could only slice a backhand. If I tried to hit a backhand hard, the ball traveled directly into the bottom of the net. "You get yourself some lessons," the man said. "Learn how to play the game."

It was the same summer one of my father's brothers took me aside after church and said it was time I stopped tying my tie in a "nigger knot" like my father did if I was going to a semiformal dance at the private tennis and swimming-pool club where Janet Cook's parents and their friends had two well-kept courts for themselves. He stood me in front of a mirror in the men's room and had me master the Full Windsor. "There," he said, and he left the rest to my memory without saying a word about the origin of the name of the knot I vowed never to tie again, the same technique he'd used a few years earlier when he'd taught me to play chess. "You think you're ready?" he'd said, and when I nodded and moved my first pawn, he proceeded to checkmate me in four moves. "That's called the fool's gambit, Gary," he'd said. "You remember that the next time you think you know something."

I walked into that dance with confidence in my tie, but I didn't need my uncle to explain to me that I was badly dressed when none of the boys was wearing a sport coat like the one I'd gotten that week. "Just like new," my father had said, but my cousin had worn it for the past two years, and before that his older brother had worn it for three more.

It didn't matter that it was a good fit. The difference between being new in 1954 and 1959, from lapel width to pattern design, was clear.

Walking away from my struggling father, I maintained a steady cadence up the lane toward the garage by telling myself it was worth it having to split stone like I was on a chain gang just so I didn't have to hear again how stupid I was for claiming the rock unmovable. Nevertheless, I took as long as possible finding the

pick. I wasn't in a hurry to swing anything that had the feel of the John Henry legend about it.

I lugged the pick back down the lane. The head of it looked to me like it had been forged in the nineteenth century and dragged across Pennsylvania while its owner had to scour the countryside for Indians. Though it was the only pick I'd ever handled, I was suddenly sure my father owned something from the Iron Age. I carted it across the clay to the monstrous rock, and before my father could start instructing, took what I thought was the correct stance, swinging the ancient tool up over my head the way I'd seen it being done in all those *Boy's Life* features on diligence and fortitude.

The heavy head slid down the shaft and split open two of my fingers. "Dammit, shit!" I yelled.

"Being ignorant doesn't mean you have to be stupid," my father said. "You ought to count yourself lucky you had one hand up so high, or you'd need more than swearing to cure you. You break your hand and there's no point in us finishing this thing here."

"I'm hopeless," I said. "I'm too dumb to live."

"Sarcasm doesn't help anybody."

"I need leg irons. I need a striped suit and one of those beanies."

"You go for a walk," he said. "You get your head clear while I take care of this." And I did, walking to where the people who lived in that nearest house were watching television on their porch. As soon as I paused to look over their shoulders, they invited me to sit down. The Pirates were on. I watched five innings while my father swung that pick against rock.

My next tournament, in early July, was entirely on clay courts, but by then I had real tennis shoes. Like the big tournament in May, it was held in an area of Pittsburgh where the streets were shaded and the yards were professionally landscaped. The mothers who sat along the fences were dressed in stylish skirts and blouses, and all of them wore sunglasses. The fathers who watched all wore dress shirts and ties, their suit coats left on hangers that were hooked to the inside of their cars.

By now I had a knit shirt with a collar to wear and a Bancroft tennis racket (with lousy spiral-nylon strings because my mother had bought it pre-strung). My father, foregoing sleep before his night shift in the bakery, stood throughout the two matches I played before I lost in the round of sixteen to an unseeded

player, double-faulting fifteen times because I was trying to serve with the proper grip. Both days my father wore a white T-shirt and his dark green work pants. Those courts were so perfect that when I saw a set of small green leaves pushing up through the clay at the base of the fence, I bent down and uprooted them.

The next weekend my father and I worked on the court, we discovered another stone stretched out like the continental shelf. I decided to give logic a try: "I say we give this up," I repeated three times, hoping that the tumblers in my father's brain would fall. I saw that the summer was going to disappear while we slaved in this rock garden. The weekend's late afternoons, when I should be perfecting the shots that would bring me trophies, were going to repeat themselves as times for physical exhaustion.

"We did one giant, we can do two," my father added, using an inaccurate personal pronoun.

I didn't see the proof for his syllogism. "The first one's still in the way," I pointed out.

"It's almost done," he said. "It's a day's work now."

I estimated how many times we'd have to split the newest discovery in order to size the pieces for carrying. "You keep at it with the shovel," my father ordered. "I'll work the pick. An extra weekend or two is all. You'll see."

My mother was the one who drove me to the next tournament because its starting times were in the morning and early afternoons on weekdays. Even at ten A.M., though, there were fathers in ties at the courts. What did they do, I wondered, that let them sit charting shots at every tournament?

My mother had sunglasses, at least. She brought a folding lawn chair because, she explained, she knew how long these matches could take. But after one round I drew the #1 seed, and even with half as many double faults as I'd had in the previous tournament, I won three games altogether. "He's a year older," my mother consoled me. "He'll have to play with the older boys next year."

I shook my head. There was only one more tournament before school started, and it was played at a country club my mother had described as "snooty." It didn't matter. I lost in the first round to the best player in the 13-and-unders, a skinny boy who was playing the 15's, his mother told mine, "for the experience."

By the third week of August, the tennis-court project was a shambles of strewn rock from seventeen boulders we'd found. On the next-to-last summer weekend, I stood among them, not one trophy in hand for my first year in the 15's, and I was thinking about how useless my work had been, how flat and unstable my ground strokes still were, how every court but the ones I practiced on had nets that rose, as they should, six inches higher on each side.

The stunted beginning of a stone wall ran along one side of the court. "It will get high enough we won't even need fence on that side," my father explained. "People can sit on it while they're waiting to play. Your friends, if they have a mind to come out this far for a day of tennis."

"Nobody wants to sit on a bunch of stones, Dad," I said.

"They do it all the time. In parks. On hikes."

"In old clothes they don't care about."

"You play tennis in a suit?"

"White shorts, Dad. Think about it."

"I'll sit on it, then. Your friends from the swim club can stand. They can make sure they don't sweat, too."

My mother, after I told her I wouldn't go anywhere ever again in my lousy hand-me-down sport coat, said, "Only if it doesn't fit."

Because our church wasn't air-conditioned and there hadn't been another dance, I hadn't worn the coat in over a month. I put it on and concentrated on the sleeves, extending my arms to give them every chance of being too long.

"They're OK," she said, but she tugged the fat lapels together and frowned. "It's tight in the chest," she said. "You'll look silly in this before you know it."

I inhaled before she could let go of the material. "OK," she said, "but don't tell your father. It'll be our little secret until the weather turns cooler. All that digging in the dirt must be doing you some good."

Over Labor Day weekend, I watched my father loop a chain around one of the thirty leftover fragments from the biggest stones we'd found, a midsize one that was going to be a test. I followed his face while he worked, noticing how his jaw jerked, how his lips and teeth told secrets about self-absorption. Each time my father yanked at the chain, the stone heaved and slid a few inches. It could have

been the cornerstone for a pyramid. "See," he said. "Just a little bending of the back is all it takes. Just some elbow grease."

It took my father five minutes to stop and start his way thirty feet to where the stones stretched along the lane. I watched him walk backwards and tug, walk forwards and pull, horselike, and I grew certain that I wouldn't be able to shift one of those stones more than the length of my body, that my father was going to be forced to remove every one of them unless he expected me to kneel and push each boulder from behind while he was dragging it with the chain.

During the first week in ninth-grade geography, we studied farming practices, how different cultures worked to prevent erosion, and as I looked at the pictures of ruined croplands, I could see how the tennis court was going to wash away with each rain because water poured over the bank we'd cut and the knobbed end of another huge stone we'd exposed, a delta of small channels branching into where a service court would be.

I knew I needed a backhand, too, and a second serve that had enough spin so I could accomplish something besides pushing it into play next year and having kids who understood plane geometry smash it back past me for winners.

"See?" my father said the next weekend, pointing to how only a half dozen stones were left on the court surface. "You see how things get done?"

"Sure," I agreed.

"And see how high that wall's gotten? A fence would be a waste there."

"I don't know, Dad."

"How many balls you miss-hit high off to the side like that? Two, three a match?"

"Something like that. Maybe more. It depends."

"You're fourteen already. Maybe next year you won't miss-hit more than one or two balls a match. Maybe none."

There were networks of furrows from the dragged stones. My father saw me looking at them. "You get to them with the roller and it's good as new."

"Yeah."

"We're playing here in two weeks. We don't have to wait until everything's perfect for that. It's not a country club we're building here."

I calculated how much of an advantage it would be to serve toward the end where the water was eating at where the service court would be. My father jerked

at the chain he'd wrapped around one of the last boulders. Somewhere in one of the trees across the lane, there were squirrels I couldn't see scrabbling along branches, but my father was straining so close to where I stood that I started to count his steps. He stopped and started twenty-three times before he worried the rock to the wall, never taking more than three choppy steps on any lunge.

W hen I was in seventh grade, I stole things from stores. Second-hand.

A lot of seventh graders shoplifted. Sometimes I stood an aisle's length away and watched them slip stuff inside their jackets, but I never touched one item. Other kids were eager to steal. A few of them, incredibly, were willing to steal for me.

What I coveted most in seventh grade were records—45's. With my own money, I had to discriminate, make a choice between Buddy Holly's "Maybe Baby" and Jack Scott's "Goodbye Baby." But when somebody at school wanted to show off, I accepted records by the Diamonds and Brenda Lee because they were free. Stevie Hoak even stole an album for me—Buddy Knox/*Party Doll*. I'd missed buying the single in sixth grade, but now I could have "Rock Your Baby to Sleep" and "Hula Love" and nine other songs as well.

In the Bakery

"See?" Stevie Hoak said, handing me the album as we walked down the sidewalk in front of the shopping center. "It's easy." On the cover of the album, Buddy Knox was wearing a red sweater with a shiny black shirt that spilled out of the V-neck; Stevie Hoak was wearing a topcoat like the one I wore to church over a suit. It was Saturday afternoon, and there weren't any other twelve-year-olds wearing topcoats at the shopping center.

I handed the album back to him. "You keep it," I said, suddenly believing that real stealing started as soon as the price was more than a dollar. A week later, I bought that album with my own money.

As far as I could tell, Stevie Hoak was the dumbest boy in seventh grade. He was fourteen and couldn't read, but it looked as if stealing really was as easy as Stevie Hoak insisted. The day after I bought the Buddy Knox album, he gave me a book about the greatest baseball players of the twentieth century. I wasn't even with him when he stole it. "I know you like baseball," he said, handing it over. If I had wanted to read that book, I would have checked it out of the school library. But a boy in my class named Chuck York, that same week, stole a gun for me.

There was a time that spring when half the boys in our suburban junior high school wanted to make a zip gun, boring out the chambers in toy pistols to create something that might be lethal. Or at least threatening. It was cool to talk about making a zip gun. As if I had even the remotest idea how to manage it.

Chuck York came back from the Woolworth's a block from our school with two toy guns while I was waiting for the late bus to take me home from band practice. They were small. I could palm one and then flash it like I was a real hoodlum in Pittsburgh. I was wearing a hat tugged down over my forehead. It was black and had a little feather through the band. I punched Chuck York on the shoulder and said "Cool," and I carried that gun around in my jacket for a week or so before I sold it to a sixth grader for a dollar, staying within my self-imposed limit.

I thought it was stupid to shoplift. I could receive cheap stolen property and get the same things as the thieves without the risk. For a few months, I saw myself as thrifty, even when my father suggested that I go to work for him from seven to ten o'clock on Friday nights for one dollar an hour. "It's time you earned what you spend," he said. "It's time you know what real work is."

I thought he meant to keep me busy on Friday nights. Away from trouble, as if he'd inspected my room and found too many things unaccounted for by my meager allowance. No one would believe my greatest sin was receiving stolen property that I never asked for and never, by itself, cost more than $2.98, the price of the Buddy Knox album.

Three years later, when I earned a driver's license, I was still being paid a dollar an hour when he asked me to change my hours and lengthen my shift. For ten dollars a night, I was to start at 10:00 P.M. and work until 5:30 in the morning. It was a raise of sorts, working out to about $1.25 per hour if I counted my driving time to and from work. The government's minimum wage was eighty-five cents an hour. I hadn't received one stolen item since I'd started to work for him.

Once I began working all-nighters, I learned that I could sing along to myself with almost any song on the red plastic radio when my father lowered the first doughnuts into the hot grease. Those hit records, even if they were by Bobby Vee or Connie Francis or some other pop singer I'd never listen to at home, were a celebration, because doughnuts were the last sweet things I laid my hands on before my seven-and a-half-hour Friday-night shift was over.

My father, always working with two or more items at once, would busy himself with icing cupcakes or filling pastries with jellied fruit while those doughnuts deep-fried. I'd wish for the Isley Brothers or Ernie K-Doe or Jerry Butler, singers I listened to on WAMO, Pittsburgh's black station that went off

the air at sundown and didn't return until sunrise, so even in midsummer I never heard that station broadcasting from that grease-crusted radio.

In my father's bakery, I measured time by how high the bread dough had risen, how browned the crusts of the first sandwich buns had turned, and the number of pans of coffee cakes and pies I carried to countertops in the sales area, none of them strutting off those trays to sing and dance and smile like the ones in television ads for my father's national-brand competition. After doughnuts, while my father was preparing to fill some of them with jelly or custard, I stepped into whatever weather was waiting a few minutes after 5:30 A.M., inhaling with the joy I thought I'd earned before dawn, driving the station wagon three miles to where my mother was drinking coffee and eating zwieback or bear claws she'd brought home stale the night before. If I was running late, I'd hear the all-night deejay say "Sayonara" before he played Sam Cooke's "Chain Gang," like he always did, because it was time for steelworkers and other blue-collar laborers who had to work weekends to test themselves by getting out of bed for shifts that began at seven A.M.

In winter, if it was snowing, I'd leave that car on our plowed street so I could say the hell with shoveling our driveway with snow still falling—nothing I could say to my father when he handed me the shovel at 5:15 so I could get the sidewalk cleared out front before I left. Just before 6:00 A.M., I would exhale with my mother before she closed the door of the Chevy, still warm, and steered it back to the bakery in the changing light to sell to men finishing one shift or beginning another at the steel mill two blocks away, each carrying a bag of sweet things into the ordinary hours of morning.

But at ten P.M., when my shift was beginning, I worked in a different room than my father, one with no radio. I had nothing but seven hours until doughnuts while I began my routine by greasing pans. I dipped a brush into the lard that stayed liquid in a #10 can in the steam cabinet until I needed it. It was like varnishing wood, swirling that brush back and forth and not missing a spot that would allow the bread to stick, because then what would we have? I worked slowly, already daydreaming. The grease would coagulate. It would turn thick and white and remind me I was lazy. It would scream that message if my father saw me slide the can into the oven for a quick remelting.

Before long, I was sectioning dough into soft logs of sixteen or eighteen ounces before dropping them into those rectangular pans. Each time I cut off a piece within a quarter ounce, close enough to nip and drop, I'd say, "Yes!" aloud.

Maybe one out of five. My father, if he was in a good mood, would take the black-handled scraper I used for cutting from me and do five of his own, getting four of them within a quarter ounce. If I acted as if he'd been lucky, he'd do five more, sometimes nailing all five.

Twice a night we took breaks, during which we shot a wadded-up, wax-coated bread bag at a #10 can my father hung from a nail eight feet up on the one wall that rose high enough to let us shoot with at least a little arc. The court was a rough square with twelve-foot sides, one boundary the steam cabinet, two sides bounded by the bakery's ovens. It made for sweat, but we played HORSE or 21, games with a minimum of movement. My father tried behind the back shots and over his head facing away from the basket shots, tricks he'd make once or twice a night until he had H-O-R-S, and then he'd move in and call "left hand, bank," "left hand, swish." He knew my weakness from watching me roll sandwich buns one-handed, unable to coordinate my left hand for even the simplest of circular motions. If I didn't make the low-arc jump shot I'd rely upon when the pressure was on, he'd run the game out with his left hand.

Except for that room and the one where things were sold, the ceilings were so low I could bump my head if I stood on my toes. Winter or summer, the heat around my head was at suffocation level. In winter, because there was no foundation under the main work area, my feet froze because all the heat that roasted my head was generated by the ovens, none of it by any heating system except a space heater by the display cases. Which was where an occasional drunk would fall asleep if he wandered in and sat down in the folding chair beside it—the heat, in winter, taking him into unconsciousness.

My father had me wait on the men and women who stumbled in around two A.M., the time when the bars were required to close. Like everything he asked me to do, it had a reason besides the doing of it. He wanted me to see what drunk meant. He wanted me to see how people who drank in bars until two A.M. looked to be out of control.

At two-thirty he locked the front door, and the deep hours began. Until five o'clock and the start of doughnuts, it seemed as if we were the only people awake in Etna. "You can't sit down at four A.M.," he said, "or sleep will get you."

The last Friday night I worked for my father in his bakery, I was late. The only time in seven years, from age thirteen to nineteen, and before I lifted the trays of bread pans and carried them to the grease brush I was supposed to use on them

an hour and a half earlier, I started the excuse of sickness I'd rehearsed while I parked the station wagon outside.

In fact, I did feel a little sick, but I'd managed to spend the previous three hours at a party to celebrate the beginning of summer vacation after my sophomore year in college. I'd been drinking and working hard at impressing girls, and I thought my father should be pleased I had enough self-discipline to drive to his bakery instead of calling in sick from some girl's apartment phone, turning down the music for a minute as if a quiet background near midnight meant I was shivering with fever in our kitchen.

So my story, as far as I was concerned, was convincing and contained a bit of truth. I said I could make up the time, that I wouldn't hold him back, meaning every one of those promises, but my father told me to go home if I thought I was sick, that he'd gotten along without me so far and could manage the rest of the night as well.

Whether it was a ploy on his part or not, I had to stay. It was nearly midnight. I had ninety minutes to make up and jobs he'd finished for me to notice each time I passed the sandwich buns rising under old flour bags and saw the pecans scattered in the coffee cake pans.

My father was pleased, I think, when I found myself feverish at three A.M. I ran my tongue around the inside of my mouth and discovered something abnormal. When I opened my mouth for him to inspect, forgetting about the likely smell of stale beer, he confirmed there was a swelling on one side of my mouth, something that looked to be the result of a serious infection.

So I'd been sick "for real" several hours earlier, though I was enough of my father's son to think, for a moment, that I'd been visited with divine punishment for lying. He told me to sit on the only chair in the bakery, the one my mother used between customers during the day. I expected him to return immediately to his work, but he stood behind a display case that would be filled, in a few hours, with sweet rolls and coffee cakes, looking across the room at me as if I was a customer considering an order. "It doesn't matter," he said then. "In eight days I'm closing the bakery for good."

I waited for him to go on, but he gestured toward the door. "You go home," he said. "If you want, next Friday you can work the last night."

By then I'd been to the dentist, who told me two of my wisdom teeth, looking for space in my narrow jaw, had angled into the soft inside of my cheek and initiated a wound that was indeed infected. He performed surgery on the spot. He pulled the other two as a preventive step, and I was on antibiotics and

a soft diet, nothing that would have kept me from working except that I'd been promised my first union job at the Heinz factory in Pittsburgh, and my father wanted to be sure I was healthy for "the real world." He finished his last night without help from anyone, adding three hours to his twelve-hour shift. I could do the math. I could figure that my work, even allowing for his accelerated pace, was less than 50 percent efficient as his. By August he was a janitor in the high school I had attended.

What had I learned from working in the bakery from eighth grade on, the length of my shifts increasing nearly every year? I thought about how long my father had kept the end of his life's investment to himself, whether he had iced his sweet rolls and cakes more thickly or thinly during that time. Whether he had considered not icing them at all as a way of explaining himself to his customers.

And then I turned to wishing he'd closed two weeks sooner, that he'd finished with that bakery before I'd had the chance to demonstrate my selfishness. Such a small thing, my being ninety minutes late. And after all, I'd had a real excuse, it turned out.

Punctuality. Reliability. Since he'd bought it from the man he'd worked for, my father had opened that store five days a week for sixteen years by being there and finishing the work. Regardless, the business went under, its closing the result of the steel industry leaving town, parking being banned on the street during his previously busiest hours. Most of all, though he never said it, the bakery failed because cheap, mass-produced cakes and pies flooded grocery stores. Even worse, terrible emulsified bread—"Look, no holes!"—became popular, my father cringing each time the television showed children happily eating jelly bread without spilling a drop.

In all the important ways, though, that bakery succeeded. My father, I'm sure, believed he was proving something to himself by baking bread the natural way, by making pies with a minimum of corn starch, by using real custard in his cream puffs.

And responsibility? After a while, I'm sure, he'd managed to "be there" so often and so long that he no longer needed to think of his work as proving anything. He simply did it because it represented him to the world.

The first day I worked at the Heinz factory, near the end of the mandatory physical, I suddenly went cold and clammy. I started to stand, and a few seconds later, I found out I'd fainted when I snapped back to consciousness with the nurse screaming in my ear because I was sprawled on top of her after dragging her to the floor as I collapsed. It was less than half an hour since I'd punched in at 7:45 A.M.

Another voice calmed her screams. "Whoa there," it said from somewhere overhead, and I felt a hand on my shoulder. The company doctor owned that voice of reason, and he rolled me over. He didn't look at all anxious about my health. "Let's give her some room," he said, as if the nurse was the one who'd passed out. A minute later I was sitting in a cubicle sipping orange juice and listening to the doctor ask me if I'd fainted recently (No), had dizzy spells (No), or had eaten breakfast (No). "There's something," he said, pausing after my third "No."

Union Grades

"I got in late," I said. "I wasn't up for eating at 6:30."

"Drinking?"

"Some."

"Some will do," he said, smiling as if he knew exactly how lucky I'd been to manage my parents' station wagon into the driveway at three A.M. after a night of helping my girlfriend celebrate her high school graduation.

It wasn't long before he started telling me stories about his college days, concentrating on the sophomore year I'd just completed without distinction. He was younger than my father, but everything he mentioned that was interesting—Christine Jorgenson undergoing the first sex change operation, girls swooning while listening to Johnny Ray sing "Cry"—happened in 1952, when I was in first grade. Or if it was still going on, surviving into 1965 like panty raids, the fad was so old-fashioned it was only done by losers who actually wore their freshman beanies.

I told him I was premed, not a total lie. I stopped short of adding I'd decided to give up that fantasy and opt for English, the only

subject's homework that didn't encourage me to look for a dorm room where the stereo was playing and cards were being shuffled.

"I've never seen anyone faint during a tine test," he said. "You make sure you eat lunch now."

I'd lasted long enough to have finished that tuberculosis test before I collapsed, so I didn't have to face the nurse again before I followed directions to my first work site. Waiting for me was a man dressed in the same blue pin-stripe pants and white T-shirt that I was wearing, and he instructed me, in two minutes, on everything I needed to know about herding institution-size cans of soup onto racks that would be wheeled into the sterilizing department. To someone as hungover and recently recovered from blacking out as I was, those cans lumbered along the conveyor belt with a frightening regularity. I could see more than a hundred feet of the line as it approached above the corridor from an adjoining building, and there wasn't a break in that parade of cans.

By the time the man hopped down from the work stand, the metal bench in front of me was nearly filled with unlabeled cans. I started gathering and pushing. I pulled a lever and lowered the rack, threw a rubber mat onto the next shelf, and began again. For the next hour, I managed to stay ahead of the cans and the urge to vomit orange juice over the side of the work station.

Just after eleven A.M., a half hour before lunch, I saw someone dressed in a Heinz work outfit who looked familiar. Astonishingly, he recognized me. Jim Brittner walked up and extended his hand over the railing. I shook it and then hurried back to the cans that kept threatening to outrun my sluggish arranging. "What the fuck you doing here?" he said. "I thought you was a smart boy?"

I hadn't seen Jim Brittner since he'd quit school on the first report-card day of ninth grade, celebrating his sixteenth birthday by telling the principal to shove his high school up his ass, and following that declaration by strolling past my group of fourteen-year-olds and out the door to drive away in a car that rumbled and smoked and held a girl sitting inside who looked like she was auditioning for a part in the next Mamie Van Doren girls-gone-wild movie.

Jim Brittner had been driving that car without a license since school had started two months before. He'd said maybe three sentences to me in the two years we'd been in the same grade, all of them variations on "Get the fuck out of my way." But now he was acting like an old friend.

"Summer job," I said, sliding cans, pulling the lever, slapping down another mat and beginning to fill it. Brittner reached up and pushed the emergency stop button. "Fuck that for a minute," he said. The cans lurched a bit as they stopped,

and I half expected a domino effect of disaster to come rippling up the line. "What are you, then, a college boy now?"

"Yeah, but maybe not for long."

He perked up. "Yeah? I never even want to see old Shithole High again."

I laughed. "Who knows?" I said like a comrade-in-arms. "Maybe I'll just stay here in September." The cans were stable, but so eerily still, I glanced up the line, anticipating an arm-waving foreman. "What grade you working?" Brittner said.

"I don't know," I said, meaning every word. I didn't even know my job was rated by the Amalgamated Meat Cutters and Butcher Workmen of America Union, the organization I'd been a member of since seven forty-five that morning.

"I'm working Grade 7—been doing this sort of crap a year and a half now. Deliver samples. You know. Carry shit from here to there and take care of stuff—$2.30 an hour."

I thought about the work I was doing and figured it for so unskilled it had to be a lower union grade than Brittner's work. After all, he had eighteen months on the job, and nothing seemed to take less training than what I'd mastered in five minutes.

"I'll ask somebody." Miraculously, I still didn't see anyone who looked like a boss approaching, so I cleaned off the counter before I pushed the button and the line jerked into motion.

"You'll do good here," he said, "as long as you stop looking over your shoulder like some pussy."

At lunch, as I cautiously nibbled a hamburger slathered with Heinz relish and picked at a plate of Heinz baked beans, using nearly all of the forty-five unpaid minutes we had to eat to settle my stomach, I asked a gray-haired guy who I'd seen working another stand.

"Grade 9," he said. "$2.55 an hour. Myself, I'm trying to get to Grade 10, or switch to the second shift because night work pays more."

I hoped I wouldn't see Brittner after lunch. If I did, I'd just shrug if he asked again. Let him find out on his own that a first-day-on-the-job idiot was making more than he was.

I didn't have to worry. I didn't talk to Brittner again until mid-July because after two days I was transferred to the 6:15—3:00 shift, the starting time so early that I rose in the dark even during those longest days of the year. What's more, all of my bad habits disappeared, fleeing like sleep. The only chance I had of seeing

my friends was if on their way home from a party they crashed into me on my way to work.

During those five weeks, I learned that all my jobs were either Grade 8 or Grade 9 because you had to have a proven skill for Grade 10 and above. I also discovered that Brittner was as low paid as a male worker could be at Heinz, because the highest-compensated female worker in the factory was at Grade 6, lower paid than Brittner by ten cents an hour.

The one time I saw Brittner, I was in the basement of a part of the factory called the Power Building, where I was unloading frozen beef into a huge, shoulder-high kettle. At least that beef was frozen at 6:30 when we paired up to tear open the hundred-pound crates and lift them in tandem to dump. By midmorning, puddles of water and blood were forming around my shoes. When Brittner, just before lunch, sidestepped the widening puddle of diluted blood, he gave me a thumbs-up of solidarity. He was carrying another of those sample boxes. He pointed at the puddle and mouthed, "Bullshit."

Before that summer, I'd seen Brittner just once since he'd left high school. More than a year after his swaggering exit from the school lobby, two friends and I, tenth graders now, went bowling on a Saturday morning at the only alley that still had pin boys in 1961. We bowled three games, drank Cokes, and noticed when a guy in the group next to us, during our third game, swore at leaving a six pin and threw his spare ball while two downed pins still lay on the alley. Fiasco fast approaching, I thought, when I saw a hand reach down for those pins just as he released. It was close, whether or not the pin boy got hit, because that guy hit the six pin thin and kicked it up and sideways where that hand pulled back, maybe or maybe not just in time.

Ten minutes later, when we walked outside, there was Jim Brittner sitting on the steps of the bowling alley, smoking. He was dressed exactly the same as he had been the day he quit school—a white T-shirt and blue jeans. "Jim," one of my friends said. "How's it going?"

"Who the fuck are you?" Brittner said.

"Ken Logan. I was in your homeroom last year."

"Ken Logan," Brittner said. "I remember you now. You sucked my cock."

I was glad I hadn't been the one to open my mouth, but Ken Logan had the persistence of a missionary. "You work here?" he said.

Brittner stood up then and dropped his cigarette butt, crushing it under his

shoe in a way that made me think it was his hand I'd seen reaching for those loose pins. I could tell my other friend shared that thought, and we finished walking down the stairs while Ken Logan waited like a dog-pound puppy for whatever answer Brittner was going to give, with his mouth or his fists.

It was light, for once, when I got out of bed the Monday after I was transferred from the basement of the Power Building. Besides getting out of the blood puddles, I got to sleep in. Or at least that's how starting a shift at 7:45 again sounded to me by then. "Banker's hours," the foreman told me after I punched in. "You got lucky." He introduced me to Josh Blakey, a fortyish black guy who drove forklift at railroad receiving.

Blakey took me for new meat fresh from high school. He wanted to know what I'd done for the past four years besides playing with myself, because I was the first white boy to get assigned to him in six years. I told him I was in college, as if that explained my high school career. He seemed to lose interest then, but he nodded. My job, he said, was unloading boxcars full of hundred-pound bags of beans and flour. "You got it made," Blakey ended, "so long them sacks in the cars don't be loose off the boards they married to."

He dropped his skids and lifted the outermost pallet. Eighteen sacks in layers of three, I counted, and then I walked along beside him feeling as useless as I did every time my father changed a tire in the dark while I held the flashlight. "Just be moving all the time," Blakey advised. "You'll get your chance to shake a leg."

Every boxcar, he told me, had its share of shifted loads, and we weren't halfway through the first car before I saw there were piles that were broken down in the next row. By now, the air swirled with dust and flour. Blakey leaned over the wheel and told me how to restack. "Rotate the pattern," he said. "Don't just stack one atop the other, or we'll have ourselves a ton of beans tumbling down soon as I stick a fork in them."

The stack ran shoulder high; the pattern looked like the symbol for Pi. Blakey was careful to park the forklift near the open door, where it was less than 100 degrees. He didn't climb down from his seat as I hunched over the sprawled sacks of dried beans, adjusting the first two layers before I set in to hoist the rest into place without strangling on the cloudy air. "You looking pale, son," he said after I'd heaved the last bag onto the top of the stack. "You looking like one of them albinos."

I coughed and stutter-stepped down the ramp. For the first time, I noticed

we were outside—that if you had the time, you could look up at the sky through the breaks between the boxcars.

"Some job," Blakey said at lunch. "Thirteen years I waited for forklift. Grade 12. It don't pay to look back and wonder."

"I'm starting to look ahead. Six weeks and school starts up again."

"Don't be in such a hurry. Uncle Sam'll have your ass before you know it. You'll be in country."

"I don't think so. I have two more years until I graduate."

"You'll be wishing you had them sacks of beans to hide behind."

"The war can't last until 1967."

"I thought you said you was in college." Blakey grabbed his ass. "I thought you knew how the music goes round and round and comes out here."

Right after lunch, the boxcar we were clearing nearly empty, I counted seven pallets left, but none of them stacked more than three high. "You got a job looking at you, college boy," Blakey said. "You get in them corners. I'll be waiting."

I listened for rats before I put my hands to the pile nearest the wall. I hadn't seen any yet, but if they were there, they had to be crouching behind those final bags, and I didn't want anything feeling cornered where my hands were leading the way for my eyes. Blakey turned and drove down the ramp as if he expected them to charge.

When I had three pallets restacked, enough of a lead to bring Blakey back inside, I went to the door for air and to give him a shout. He was parked beside the forklift that came to take the beans to the kettle room. He and the other driver were laughing, keeping their eyes forward where they had a sightline to the hallway in which the foreman, if he were coming, would materialize.

I figured, What the hell and finished six pallets, getting myself in position for a nonunion break over in sight-down-the-tunnel land, but then, when I hoisted a bag onto the seventh pallet, it split open in my hands and beans mounded beside my shoes just as Blakey roared up the ramp. "You can get yourself a shovel and a short tub from cleanup," he said. "Them other two's busted up bad, so get yourself a couple of tubs."

A half hour later, I sat on the edge of the receiving dock drinking a Coke. "Hey, college boy," Blakey said, "good news. Next car looks to be a virgin. You're as blessed as the pure in heart. Nothing but unbroken cherries all the way to the walls."

The next week, when my job assignment was shifted again, this time to a sealer line where there was little to do but change the packing codes on the hour and watch for jams, Brittner materialized again. "This got to look like heaven after that shit job you had down to the basement two weeks back," he said.

"Yeah," I said. "Grade 8. The same as meat tossing and a thousand times better."

Brittner nodded as if his job had been upgraded since early June. "You quit that college shit yet?" he said.

"I don't think about it much when I'm surrounded by angels," I said, and Brittner looked at the women who boxed the cans and laughed. They were all middle-aged and shapeless.

"You got to get out more," he said.

"I punch out and I'm gone," I said.

"No harm in throwing some down first. The first time we punch out together, you come along, and you'll see you don't need college to learn how to party," he said.

"I'm nineteen," I said.

"Nineteen's good in the factory bars. You see them across the street every day when you park. You have a union card, you can drink. The LCB knows better than to stick its nose in."

So we promised, but by August we still hadn't punched out together and tested the Liquor Control Board's resolve.

At last, incredibly, I was assigned two weeks in the research department, where everything was as wonderful as time and a half. Instead of telling me to look busy when we were between jobs, the technicians who worked there told me to get lost some place in the factory complex. An hour, they would say, spend it wisely, and I headed straight to the locker room, where I made a pillow of all the clean and dirty T-shirts from my locker and read old magazines or the discarded *Pittsburgh Post-Gazettes* I found on the floor.

When I was busy, I set pressures and temperatures on stove-sized cookers, moving from dial to dial according to a chart a child could follow. I logged times and changed numbers on the gauges to coincide with the researchers' needs as they experimented with tomatoes and spices, cooking temperatures, sugars and water volumes, and whatever else had anything to do with what seemed, according to all this care, to be the most important item Heinz produced. It was

the easiest work of the summer, and my good fortune was compounded when one of the men told me it paid more than any other job I'd had.

Even better, the other men talked about books they'd read and movies that didn't feature the police, cowboys, or the army. It was the only time that summer it came in handy to have finished the books by Faulkner and Hemingway and Mailer and Ellison in my modern-novel course. I'd seen *Dr. Strangelove* and *Repulsion* because I'd started going to Pittsburgh's art-house theaters on Sunday evenings, abandoning my beer-swilling girlfriend, who didn't have to get up until noon because her parents could write a tuition check without demanding a percentage from her.

And politics? The war Blakey had insisted was coming my way? I listened closely for a second opinion. "Lyndon Johnson isn't a fool," one of those technicians said when my age and the year I'd graduate came up. "He can't get reelected if this war is going on in 1968." He didn't say anything about 1967, but he made his prediction with such a sense of authority it seemed to account for that year as well.

One of the other men nodded. "You don't have to worry. Even if it's still going on, it won't be fought by college graduates."

At the beginning of the second week, Brittner walked in empty-handed. He was moving so slowly, his hands in his pockets, that I imagined him shuffling into a stylized Hully-Gully, doing "the Frank Sinatra" like I'd mastered during a series of fraternity parties. I gave him a wave that he didn't acknowledge. But after he reappeared from the office on the other side of the room, he carried his new set of samples right toward me.

"What's with this fag job?" he said, not slowing down as he passed. "You suck somebody's cock for Grade 10?"

The last week in August I was sent back to sealing. Good, I thought, knowing I wasn't going to spend my last days in the basement of the Power Building or cleaning out boxcars. And on the very last afternoon, a Friday, two hours before my shift ended, there was a jam on the line next to mine.

The steel arm that swung across the tops of the cases of tomato soup cans to press the glue-covered cardboard flaps together nicked a wrinkled edge, hesitated, and then swung late and caught the next case flush in the side. A splurt of tomato soup shot out from the damaged box, but the guy working the line was at the water fountain, and by the time he ran back to push the stop button, a half dozen cases had jammed together, that heavy hook disengaged just enough to swing

around one more time and open a wound in the second jammed carton, this time splattering globs of tomato soup over the line and onto the smooth concrete floor.

It was a movie. The foreman sprinting. The women who packed the cases cursing. The sealer attendant ripping damaged cases from the line, tossing them onto the floor, where they spilled more than a hundred small cans of condensed soup that rolled a few inches or twenty feet, making trails of red.

The foreman and the attendant didn't pay any attention to the mess. "Get it moving," the foreman kept yelling, and the attendant did, the line cleared in a minute, the sealer arm swinging free again, back in sync when the belt lurched and moved forward. It swung down, pressed the first unharmed box exactly across the seal, and the foreman marched off.

The attendant kicked a few cans out from underfoot, but other than that, he didn't act like wreckage was strewn around his line. Two minutes later I understood why, because Jim Brittner, mop and bucket in hand, showed up. "Get that fucking mess cleaned up," the foreman yelled, walking just out of mop-handle distance behind Brittner. The foreman slapped down a second bucket that I knew had to be for the loose cans that weren't split, and then he disappeared. I knew the salvageable cans would become the dented stock that I could buy for half price in the company store. When Brittner knelt to begin gathering the cans together, he noticed me for what I was sure was the first time, because he gave me the same look he'd given Ken Logan in front of that bowling alley three-and-a-half years earlier.

I looked away. I found things to do that kept me as far from that other line as they could. I wheeled a new pallet of cardboard boxes to the station where the woman who ran my sealer stood. I watched as she expertly fitted the cardboard to the machine she operated, pressed a lever, and twenty-four more cans of soup shot into place before she released that filled box onto the line. I knew she was getting paid Grade 4, fifty cents an hour less than I was getting.

From the very beginning of the line, I watched Brittner swing his mop, streaking swaths of red that gradually faded and then disappeared. Minutes later, when I had to walk closer to him in order to change the code for the last hour of my shift, I thought of him giving me that thumbs-up when I stood in the puddle of watery blood. Surely, I thought, Brittner must know that if I was going back to college, this was my last day, because when this shift ended, Labor Day weekend would begin. I kept every possible gesture to myself.

I wheeled one more pallet of boxes to the loading station, changed the code again at 3:00, and watched the woman load cans until 3:10, when I could ease my

way toward the time clock because my night-shift replacement was on duty. I stood sixth in the line, watching the minute hand hang at 3:14. When it clicked forward, the first card, already in the slot, was pushed down and punched, and then the second, the third, and I felt a forearm in my back that stayed there like a threat until I slid my card in the slot and shoved.

I sat in the locker room in my company outfit for a couple of minutes, watching men hurry so efficiently that by 3:25 I was alone and knew I had six minutes to myself before the small set of men who punched out at 3:30 would hustle in. I pulled off my T-shirt and the dirt-stiffened pin-stripe pants, pulled on my old madras shorts and a dark T-shirt. I left three soiled company paper hats on the shelf, but I tugged out my other pair of work pants and four other T-shirts, balled them up, and laid them on the counter for the uniform attendant to check. "I'm out of here," I said as he started to check the sizes for a fresh batch. "Back to school next week."

"OK, then," the man said, not looking up.

So it was just past three-thirty when I walked out of that factory, and for a moment I considered walking across the street to one of the union bars, buying a beer for Blakey or someone else I recognized, as if he wanted to celebrate with me. As I paused on the sidewalk, I remembered that Brittner would have punched out fifteen minutes after I had, his mop-up shift timed to end just after the shifts of the men and women who were working the production lines. I caught myself looking around for him, thinking that if he was leaving right then, he'd shoulder me as he hurried toward his first beer, that he'd stare at me and say, "What the fuck are you looking at, pussy?" That if I called him by name or asked him what was wrong, he'd start in with a roundhouse right before he'd leap on me, drag me to the ground, and beat me until he was exhausted or someone rolled him off.

Frank Funovitz was throwing a rubber ball out the second-story window to the high school girl who lived beside the elementary school we were cleaning. "Look at that ass," Funovitz said, so I nodded like I thought he expected me to. Her name was Doris, he'd told me, and she lobbed the ball up at us, but this time it bounced off the bricks six feet below the sill. "You wanna get in those pants?" he said.

I watched her retrieve the ball, admiring the way her shorts rode up tight when she bent over, but I didn't want in her pants. From twenty feet away, I could see she had acne, and everything she'd said during the two minutes Funovitz had been playing catch told me she was going to stay in Millvale having babies for one or more jerks who would be laid off every time the economy dipped. She tossed the ball up again, and Funovitz lunged for it, giving him a momentary chance to lose his balance and fall out onto the playground. I estimated he'd land around the edge of the dodge-ball circle, paralyzed maybe, or at least a couple of fractures. My job, while Funovitz slobbered over a girl too young to be his daughter, was to keep an eye open for Alex, the supervisor, who stopped by nearly every day to see if we were getting this grade school ready on schedule for the opening of school in September 1967.

The Theory of Stinks

"We'll make it with no sweat," Funovitz had said in June when I showed up for my first day on the job a week after graduation from college. "I got twenty-eight summers says I know how to work schools." This afternoon was August 10th, and I had to hand it to Funovitz—we were about finished. "See?" he'd said that morning. "We're doing better than those eggheads wasting my taxes on space probes." *Surveyor 4* had disappeared that summer, going silent just as it was touching down on the moon. "Soft landing, my ass," Funovitz had said. "Wait till some of these space cowboys bust themselves up out there. They ought to put my taxes into kicking ass on our city streets." He'd looked at me as if he expected me to complain. "You read about that fellow Rap Brown? What kind of name is 'Rap'?"

I'd shrugged. I had the rest of the week with Funovitz, and then he went on a three-week vacation, what he'd earned for lasting almost thirty years, and I'd be left to cut grass, keep after dust, and polish the floors—routine stuff that would keep me busy four or five hours a day until this summer job ended and my graduate-school deferment kicked in. The rest of the time I could sleep or clown around like Funovitz, who when he caught the next pitch, held the ball and yelled, "You gotta pay for your toy this time."

He glanced over to see if I'd gotten it, but Doris was the one staring up at the window as if she'd lost the reception on our channel. Funovitz made an elaborate gesture of shoving the ball in his pants. "You can pay me anytime," he shouted, though I was sure, because of the angle, she couldn't see much below Funovitz's chest. I guessed that Doris was trying to sort this one out as if it were anything a teacher might say to her next month in plane geometry or world cultures just before she opted for general math and practical history.

Behind us the classroom was all arranged in its rows, everything spotless except for the half-scrubbed wall near the door. "It's for Alex," Funovitz had said at lunch. He didn't have to tell me. We always had something for Alex when he showed up, but Funovitz never stopped explaining. "We got that wall and a couple of bathrooms, and we're done except for you buffing where the traffic goes," he'd said three times since lunch, reducing the list he'd recited in the morning. Now I was holding a dry rag; Funovitz had his in his back pocket. The buckets were right where they were needed to show Alex we were working at making Miss Gempel's room ready for another round of eight-year-olds. "It's almost two-thirty," Funovitz said while Doris tried to reconnect the wires in her head. "Alex's gotta show up pretty damn soon."

"C'mon Frank," Doris finally said. "It's my brother's ball."

"He already has two," Funovitz said.

"C'mon Frank." Doris was letting Funovitz's best lines go right by, but I saw Alex's blue truck down at the stoplight and thumbed a signal so Funovitz could pull the ball out of his crotch and drop it to Doris. "Take good care of this for me," he said. "I gotta go to work now."

She missed it, and the ball bounced just inside the dodge-ball circle. She jumped for the high hopper and gave us one last look at the swing of those breasts the future-welfare-receivers-of-America would be fondling before too long. "Let's get the wall wet," Funovitz said. "One more day to kill and I'm up to the cabin."

We were both working the wall into shape, but as soon as Alex got upstairs,

he called Funovitz over for a conference in the hall. I wiped off the same eight by eight square a couple of times so I had something to do that could end when they were finished.

Alex called my name. I stepped through the door and he started right in: "Frank's gone after tomorrow. You got all this under control?"

"No problem," I said.

"You sure?"

"Yeah." I wondered what Alex had on his mind. Funovitz had made me a list of stuff to be finished, and there weren't any items that took much doing. Now he was standing beside Alex looking pissed off, his arms folded like a boss.

"Frank says you're behind schedule."

"He never told me that."

"Not way behind. But some."

"I know what's left," I said. "I can handle it."

"Maybe you'll have to work a little harder these next three weeks with nobody around to push you. That OK with you?"

"It'll get done," I said.

"Maybe I should check in with you more often. You know, make sure?"

"It's up to you," I said.

"That's right. It's up to me."

There was nothing for me to say then. Funovitz had twenty-eight years. I was summer help, and my plan was to last until the day before I left Pittsburgh for graduate school, because my parents had said "enough's enough" to tuition, and my other choice was allowing my 1-A status to ring an alarm at my Pittsburgh draft board. All I did was stand there wishing for Doris to bounce up the stairs and wing that rubber ball off a blackboard, while nothing happened except I started hating Funovitz for the rest of my life.

"He'll make it," Funovitz said. "It's not like four years ago when we tried that wetback. We're just a little slow this time."

"OK," Alex said. There were only a few more seconds for Doris to show up or for me to say something that would remind Alex how sharp I was. "You know," Alex said, already drifting toward the stairs, "I have half my vacation coming up, so I won't be able to check on you. I've gotta trust you on this one, and all I have is Frank saying he thinks you can learn to work hard. He says something like that, and I've got to believe him enough to trust you when you say this building will shine by Labor Day."

I worked the rag over in my hands until the truck pulled into the street. "Hey, kid," Funovitz said, "you heard him. I stuck up for you. You get this place finished on time and your shit don't stink, get it?"

"You said we were on schedule."

"Alex's schedule is different."

"We could be done with the whole thing by now."

"Yeah, but then we'd have to lay you off, get it? And maybe you wouldna got hired in the first place and got yourself in front of the line for next summer."

I stood there squeezing that damp rag and thinking, like my father had repeated, that work was something that was supposed to exhaust you, nothing like what I'd been doing all summer. My father always said work was a race to see who could do the most and the best, and the guy who won received some sort of pride out of it all. Like eating, he'd said. Like once when I downed a dozen ears of corn, and my father hadn't told anybody at the church picnic because I'd wasted kernels on each ear. Like when I ate twenty-three "junior" pancakes, and my father told the story of the children's church-breakfast food champ for months. "You shoulda seen him," he'd start in. "He looked like Little Black Sambo with those hotcakes piled up in front of him, and when he was done there wasn't a crumb."

Like all summer when I'd been timing myself as I cut the grass in back of the school. I had it down to an hour and thirty-seven minutes, twenty-nine minutes less than what it'd taken me in June the first time I'd mowed while Funovitz slept in the boiler room.

Because it was his last day, maybe, or because he wanted to impress me somehow, Funovitz had us take our next morning's break in the principal's office. It was ten o'clock; we had fifteen minutes to ourselves, but Alex, if he walked in at ten-thirty, wouldn't know when we'd started the break. He'd want to know why we were hanging around in the office, nothing that would happen if I watched out the window for the blue truck.

Some mornings Funovitz read the paper, picking out the stories about the rash of race riots. "What the hell's wrong with the spearchuckers?" he'd say. "Nobody else would burn down their own neighborhood. Erie. New Castle. If they burn down the North Side, they better make sure it's just the coonville section they torch."

Some mornings he'd stick to sports and movies. "*The Dirty Dozen*," he'd say.

"Now that's a movie. Not like this *To Sir, with Love*. You hear that song on the radio? That's a white girl singing to a colored boy. Think about that."

Some mornings he'd just tell me stories. The one he'd saved until the last day was about his neighbor's septic tank getting clogged the summer before. Funovitz spent five minutes telling me how he'd shoveled dirt while I wondered what the point was. "So there we were," he finally said, "looking into this shit hole, and can you believe it, there were thousands of used rubbers stuffing everything up. The guy's only been living next door for five years. How many loads you think somebody can get off in five years?"

I said, "Two thousand" right away, just because it popped into my head; but it made Funovitz stop and calculate what he had to do to reach that kind of record.

"You know, you can screw anything," he said after he'd counted for a while. "Just give yourself three or four days, and you get hot enough to go after even one of these cold-tit teachers." I finished my Pepsi as an excuse for not saying anything. I knew Funovitz would keep going. "But you oughta see Miss Stern," he said. "Second grade. You'd let her sit on your face forever. Or Mrs. Stevens, you could suck on her big knockers all day."

I got up and looked for a wastebasket. Funovitz noticed. "Christ, not in here," he said. "Save it."

"Yeah. OK," I said. There was nothing to do but hold on to the can and walk around as if I was examining the office while Funovitz stuck his feet on the desk and started working his way into a nap. "Keep an eye out for Alex," he said. "You don't want to have him pissed off after yesterday."

I watched Funovitz falling asleep in the principal's chair and measured how far I'd have to roll him so his feet would slip off and he'd pop up and forward with the chair, maybe smashing his face into the desk. With nothing likely to come from that line of thinking, I tried file drawers, all of them locked but one that was stuffed with medical records.

Maybe the secretary had meant it to lock it, too. Maybe she'd meant to check all the drawers before her vacation started, but her husband had been honking the horn outside and flustered her into forgetting one. There were a lot of possibilities, but after I'd read a few folders, none of them mattered much. I wasn't going to report to anybody that Bobby Rhoads had a bee-sting allergy or Betty Kerpewski might tumble into a diabetic coma if she got careless. None of those records listed alcoholism or manic-depression. These kids were doing OK, so far, weaving through the labyrinth of possibilities created by heredity and chance.

What I wanted to read were the records that told how these kids measured

up, whether they had enough IQ points to have a shot at getting out of Millvale, whether they had the A's and B's it took to get smiles from everybody who could change your life.

And you needed teachers to write good things in the spaces marked "Comments." "That's how you'll get scholarships," my father had said when I'd turned ten. "That's how they'll see you're something besides smart." My father had given me a list of chores that he thought I was ready for now that I was old enough to pitch in and help the family, and he commented on every one. "It needs more than just getting done," he'd say when he found something wrong. We'd walk the rows of raspberry bushes along the property line while he tallied how many ripe ones I missed. "Look under here," he said, lifting a clump of leaves as if there weren't any thorns where his hands were. There'd be three deep red berries in a couple of places like that, and he'd drop them in a quart box, covering the bottom, maybe, by the end of inspection. "Anybody can see the ones on top," he'd say.

My father had paid me fifty cents a quart for those berries. I'd slipped the bills between the pages of *The History of the Revolutionary War*, a book I'd won at the American Legion for citizenship, and some nights I pulled that book down and counted them, waiting until I had enough ones to exchange for a twenty-dollar bill, a trade that never failed to draw a smile from my father.

When I'd been accepted to college, I'd been awarded a 20 percent academic grant, but my father, when the time came, wouldn't fill out the financial aid forms for need-based aid. "Nobody but your mother and Uncle Sam gets to know what I earn," he'd said, writing the checks for the other 80 percent of my tuition.

Working at Heinz for two summers and playing janitor had swollen my first real bank account, not just a home stash in a book the American Legion would regret giving me if they found out I was considering running off to Canada if my deferments didn't hold up. All I had to do was not talk back. I knew what I was doing, and once Funovitz was gone, it was as easy as I'd imagined it would be to get finished. I cut grass four times the first two weeks just to see if I could break my record. Getting after it when it was short gave me a better chance. I practically ran those rectangles, chopping six minutes, then three, then two, then two more.

Nobody bothered me. Doris never showed up with her rubber ball. Maybe she sensed how I felt about Millvale. Maybe she'd gone on vacation too, because I didn't even see her in the yard.

The third week, I knew Alex would show up for sure. I got the buffer out and set it up in the hallway I'd saved so I could be busy when he walked in. I

opened the last three cartons of books and stacked a short pile beside each so I could look ready to stamp each new reader with the school name.

A little of this, a little of that. Funovitz called it "the theory of stinks." "You surround yourself with a few bad smells," he said, "and it keeps the major shit from dumping on you."

I imagined he thought he was being original, but I'd heard about the theory of stinks from my father when I was thirteen years old. "It was for the plague," my father said. "People thought that having bad smells around them would keep the black death away."

He told me that the day he found the set of porn magazines I'd bought. "A waste of money," he'd said first, but then he'd launched into the story of stupid hope. "They kept dead goats in their doorways. They let the dogs piss in the house. They ate garlic and took baths in urine when all the time they should have been keeping themselves and everything around them as clean as possible."

Maybe Funovitz had heard that story from his father when he got caught playing with himself while he stared at pictures of women with big knockers sitting on the faces of naked men. I wasn't giving him any credit, though, for something I could figure out for myself, but I hoped he got the morning paper every day at his cabin so he read about George Lincoln Rockwell, the leader of the Nazi Party, being gunned down without the help of anybody who was black.

Alex didn't stop by until Wednesday. Maybe he'd been busy at one of the other schools since he'd used up his vacation days. Maybe he'd checked up on me after hours and seen things were under control. It didn't make any difference. The work I had sitting out for him could get done in one afternoon, so I could save it all the way to Friday if I had to, cutting the grass for the last time in the morning, taking another minute off my record.

The problem was finding something to do besides extra things like digging out the tiny weeds that poked up through the cracks in the playground asphalt. By Tuesday I was going through teachers' desks, thinking it was likely they had something interesting to read in them.

I didn't find anything personal except appointment books—a lot of entries like "Bob's for party" and "Carol's for dinner." Nobody had anything suggestive written down. Not even Miss Stern or Mrs. Stevens.

Alex, when he walked in on Wednesday afternoon, found me swinging the buffer in small arcs, polishing the last half of the hallway to the front door. I snapped the switch and waited for him to look things over. "How's it going?" he

said. I knew he could see I was done with everything. Nobody would be buffing by the front door if there was work somewhere else.

"No problems," I said. "I'll wrap it up with the grass Friday morning."

"Good," Alex said. "You go ahead and finish up."

I flipped the switch and Alex tiptoed down the side of the hall, going right for the basement like I knew he would. The old-fashioned bathrooms were down there. Funovitz had told me he hadn't worked in them for years, leaving that job for whoever was assigned to him as summer help. "The boys piss on the wall. The girls wipe themselves and drop the wet paper on the floor. They think it's a big joke that the shitters stink," he said—but they were just a day's work as long as you didn't mind getting your hands dirty.

I had just about backed the buffer to the door by the time Alex reappeared. I kept it going until he made a motion. "Looks pretty good," he said when I'd shut down. "I guess we're under control here." I noticed that he'd made it down the hall without leaving a mark. I thought about telling him that, but I let it go because I knew he'd been careful on account of he'd seen I'd finished a job that didn't need to be done over.

"You got some books left to stamp," he said.

"That's about it."

"Those downstairs johns are nasty, I bet."

"Not so bad."

"Really?"

"Not so good either."

Alex laughed. "Hey," he said, "you got Friday afternoon off, you know that?"

"No."

Alex looked back at that hallway for a moment, and then he said, "Picnic. North Park. Starts about three, but the time's yours from twelve on to clean up and get yourself out there."

"OK." I didn't know what else to say. I wasn't sure whether I wanted to go.

"I got a map here for you so you don't get lost." He handed me a mimeographed paper with a lot of arrows. "We got a lot of beer to swallow before it gets dark."

"OK," I said again. I waited for him to slide by me and disappear, but he stopped in the doorway. "You want to do this again, you call me. You can have a second summer if you don't get too smart for us."

I raised my hand in a kind of salute I figured Alex would appreciate, but then I said, "I have to stay smart or I'll be drafted," and Alex frowned.

"You a card burner?" he said.

"It's all legal," I said. "As long as I stay in school."

Alex started to scuff at the floor near the buffer. "You somebody who wants to march on Washington?"

"No," I said, telling the truth.

"You know what Ike says, don't you?" Alex said. "You want to win, you use all the power you have. Now that's a real President talking." He kicked the floor and then, as he started to walk outside, spit on it.

As soon as he drove off, I spun the buffer over the last patch, erasing the tiny wet blotch he'd left, and stored all the equipment where I could have locked it up the week before. I wondered who else Alex had in mind for next summer's job now that I'd been eliminated.

I hauled the books to the rooms where they belonged and started stamping the name of the school on the inside of the covers. I wasn't worrying too much about whether I was stamping exactly horizontal. As far as I could tell from looking inside old textbooks, nobody had been careful with the stamp in ten years, and even if Alex forgot I was a Communist sympathizer, I wasn't coming back there for $2.50 an hour.

Lyndon Johnson had just promised eighteen months, tops, before de-escalation. By then I'd have a master's degree, I thought, lucking out with my delaying tactics. On Thursday, when I found an old electric typewriter in the storeroom, I plugged it in, sat down, and started composing letters. I pecked out Miss Stern's name at the top of a piece of paper and typed, "I want you to sit on my face forever."

"Guess Who?" I signed at the bottom.

I typed Mrs. Stevens' name on another sheet and followed it with "I want to suck on your big knockers all day."

I signed that one "Guess Who?" too.

It was easy to personalize them. I remembered everything Funovitz had said about each one of those teachers except Mrs. Cook. I didn't know if she was some sixty-five-year-old fat woman whose husband had died twenty years ago, but I wanted Funovitz on every teacher's mind, so I typed, "I want to look up your dress"—something stupid in keeping with the others. The grades at that school ended at six, and I thought I could at least wish for those teachers to think of Funovitz rather than some eleven-year-old when they read my notes. He deserved being fired for everything he'd never been caught for. And then I came to my senses, balling up all that paper and stuffing it in my pockets to

throw away after I locked up and left for the day. I knew I had as much chance of nailing Funovitz as my graduate school deferment had of keeping me out of Vietnam if the war lasted two more years.

The next morning, when I arrived, the playground was covered with chalked-on graffiti. Something else to deal with, I thought, but then I began to read: "Frank sucks." "Frank bites." "Frank eats it." There were only those three phrases, all of them repeated five or six times inside the dodge-ball circle as if the vandal was afraid to color outside the lines.

Kids, I thought—maybe sixth graders who didn't have the nerve to scribble hard-core language. By the time I was inside the school, I was wishing Funovitz would show up to see how he was viewed by students. By the time I began to cut the grass, trying to break my record, I was convinced Alex wouldn't stop by today. There was the picnic. He'd already checked up on me. I could lock up and leave all of those words on the pavement. There was a chance the brief drought would last through the weekend. Funovitz would see the graffiti first thing next week. I was willing to let those kids speak for me, having said nothing about anything all summer, having just a few more hours before I would never be a janitor again and I could kiss Funovitz goodbye.

My mother reused my father's bakery bags. I carried my lunch in those bags, folded them, and brought them home for another use. Things were kept, according to my mother, because you could never tell when they might prove useful. All nails and screws. Every rubber band and paper clip. Adapters. Plugs. Buttons. String, wire, pins.

And every appliance that might be fixed when she had time to figure out its workings. Radios and televisions. Mixmasters and blenders. "She gets it from The Prince," my father said more than once, "being so handy," but after a while it seemed like primitive cryonics for the inanimate. Some day in the future, when there was a cure for whatever had killed them, those useful things would be revived like the bodies of the long-frozen who were beginning to accumulate in expensive freezers, none of them at all like the worn-out one that lay long and squat like a coffin in the corner of our basement next to the obsolete upright refrigerator, whose tiny freezer compartment, when it stood in the kitchen, used to turn, periodically, into a solid block of ice.

Useful Things

That first refrigerator had cleared the kitchen windowsills of the perishables that were stored there from September to May. Its purchase meant we didn't have to clean our plates because now leftovers could survive in weather warmer than near-freezing.

My mother thought she could turn complaints into silence with wrenches and screwdrivers, that she possessed a toolbox for despair. When she opened her personal hymnal each Sunday, she believed the verses spoke to her. *Hosannah*, she might have sung to herself on her way to repair. *Holy*, she might have whispered to whatever she fixed.

Sunday was a day we weren't to be entertained by movies or amusement parks, but it wasn't, as the Bible suggested, a day of rest. Needle and thread, my mother used on Sunday, darning small holes and patching the large ones, matching the colors of thread to the material in order to preserve the heels and toes of socks, the elbows of shirts, and the knees of pants.

The Prince, nearly every night, drank at the DOH. The social hall, according to my mother. The Hory-Gory, according to my grandmother—a name I was sure, even as a child, was a euphemism, something like gee-whiz or heck or dang. There was a time when my grade-school friends and I tried to guess what Hory-Gory stood for. What kind of whore? What sort of gore? And then I put it aside because my grandmother died, my grandfather was discreetly in a charity home, and I was capable, a teenager, of saying "Jesus Christ" and "hell" and "damn."

All along, though, I was in love with Aunt Margaret's name for the DOH. The Doors of Hell, she repeated, and each time I walked past the yellow-brick building that housed the DOH, I wanted to sneak in and see how damnation was earned. Nobody my parents knew well belonged to the DOH, and none of my friends, after we moved two miles from Etna, had ever heard of it.

Going Inside

I'm thinking about the DOH this afternoon because I've come to take pictures of my grandmother's house at 21 Prospect Street, to walk the neighborhood and give my wife a sense of where my stories about my grandfather are grounded. Liz carries a camera; she's patient as I follow the sidewalk. The block seems unchanged, except that the house next door has been torn down, and large sheets of plywood have been nailed over what used to be latticework under the front porch of my grandmother's old house.

I tug at a loose piece of cement, and it lifts out of the wall that runs the length of the property. I calculate the steepness of the cement stairs that lead up to the front yard of red bricks; by spreading the fingers of one hand, I measure the width of the wall running down each side where I walked as a child, daring disaster, and I know I wouldn't have the nerve to try it now.

It's one way of gauging my grandfather's coordination when he came home. There are so many steps I think his drinking has been exaggerated. A man doesn't avoid falling on stairs like these if he chances them drunk too many times. There are fourteen cement stairs, then two, then seven wooden ones, no matter if he turned

to the kitchen or the living room porch. If he tried to come down the back way, there were six narrow cement stairs, then four more, and after that, the same trip up the wooden ones to the two outside doors. If a man is staggering drunk, he takes a serious fall or spends the night where something less challenging leads to a door.

I pose for a picture, looking back over my wife's shoulder as she snaps a shot of me at the base of the fourteen stairs. I almost wave as I suddenly spot the landmark. "Look," I tell my wife, "the DOH."

She turns and takes a picture so I can see, later, what the building looks like from my grandmother's sidewalk. She's heard me mention it so many times, she doesn't ask me questions. "We'll go inside when we get done here," she says.

"It's private. It'll be locked."

"How do you know?"

I don't have an answer, but I'm surprised to discover I can see the DOH from where I'm standing. My grandmother could have seen her husband enter and leave from her kitchen window or her front porch. She could have, if she raised her voice, called to him and expected The Prince to hear.

We turn up the alley that follows one side of the property and leads to Vine Street. It has, I'm certain, the same brick, the same cracks and creases and folds as it had when I was a child. When I look back, halfway up the hill, I see the storm drain where all of my rubber balls that bounced over the hedges disappeared. Across from me, Mrs. Bondula's side porch looks the same as well—shabby and rotten, as if she'd put one foot through it, yanked it back, and then never used it again.

A pathetic, caved-in doghouse sits next to it, half of BEWARE gone above a faded OF DOG. I can't remember the name of the dog I was afraid of. The sign wasn't there when I was a child, so it's likely Mrs. Bondula owned more after I grew up and away from here, gone for good after 1963. Or perhaps the next resident moved in forty years ago, bought a vicious dog, put up a sign, and began to allow the property to go to hell. Mrs. Bondula, if she were alive now, would be over one hundred, not likely to answer the door and my questions. As far as I can tell, nobody at all would answer that door if I chanced completely falling through the porch to knock.

My grandmother's house, at least, is in better repair. When we reach Vine Street, which runs exactly even with the bottom of the first-floor rear windows, everything, except for a new door, looks exactly the same in the house where I slept nearly every Friday night until I was twelve.

I look up at the bedroom window where I would have stared down at the men who drank and sang along to concertinas on the Kordesich's porch. A year before he was carted away in an ambulance, dying from pneumonia "with a snootful in him," according to Aunt Margaret, old man Kordesich fell down the cement steps when he tried to use my grandmother's yard as a short cut to whichever bar he patronized.

As I check that porch for details, a man lurches out the front door and plunges heavily down the steps to confront us. "You need help with something?" he says, and I smile like a tourist hearing a foreign language.

"There never was a door here," I say, suddenly annoyed.

He follows my look. "If you go back two years or more," he says, slurring his words as if he's been swilling beer since lunch. "My ex-wife moved there—she uses that door." He lifts a cigarette to his mouth and takes a long drag. "She comes and goes like she don't know me," he adds.

I nod. "What's your story?" he suddenly asks.

"Nostalgia," I say, lying.

"The good old days," he snorts. "Sure."

He seems satisfied, but he doesn't go back inside. As we walk away, I half expect him to throw rocks. When we get back to the steep alley, he shouts, "Don't bother talking to that bitch. She don't know nothing about nothing."

The alley is so steep it demands the hitch step I use, going downhill, to protect my ruined knee. The cement steps would be safer than trying these bricks when they were wet or snow-covered. The topography of the neighborhood seems designed to discourage excessive drinking outside the home.

My wife pulls ahead of my mincing steps. She turns left at the bottom, walks to the second building. "OK," Liz declares, "let's at least try the DOH."

"Why would it be unlocked?" I say again, but she's already tugged the door open, keeping her answer, I'm thankful, to herself.

Inside, there's a sign directing us downstairs for bowling, and a set of smoked-glass doors, which, to my perverse satisfaction, is locked. Squinting, I can make out a hazy bar, some figures moving. "That's that," I say, but a buzzer sounds and Liz pulls the handle.

After fifty years, after all the legends and stories, after passing it thousands of times, I walk inside the DOH Club, buzzed in by the bartender, a woman, who seems surprised she doesn't recognize us. Seeing Liz and me in the foyer, the bartender must have thought we were members who'd forgotten our keyed entry cards. Now she has two strangers walking among empty tables to a bar

crowded, just past two-thirty in the afternoon, with men, nearly all of them over sixty years old. Every one of them has a draft beer in front of him. A few are using the beer to chase shots of whiskey. Nobody has a mixed drink or a glass of wine. The only choices here seem to be different shades of amber, and each of the eleven men at the bar gives us the same look of distrust.

I quickly choose a spot between two men who look a generation older than I am. If I'm going to hear anything, I need storytellers who were drinking before 1950. When the bartender sets herself across from me, a commercial ends on the televisions balanced above both ends of the bar, and the men turn right or left to watch Andy Sipowicz and Bobby Simone grill a suspect on *NYPD Blue*. It's twenty minutes to three o'clock. I saw this episode years ago. The suspect is about to confess to kidnapping and imprisoning a child in order to repeatedly molest her. While Sipowicz looks as if he'll spit on the suspect, I explain to the bartender I'm researching the life my grandfather lived when I was born.

"This place was built in the early 1950s, is that right?" I ask the bartender, who is the only one besides me not watching the screen. She draws an Iron City and slides it to a man younger than I am who has materialized to my left, replacing my wife.

"You'll have to ask one of the old-timers," she says. The old-timer beside me holds his beer and watches Sipowicz grimace with disgust.

"Give him a sheet of that stationery from out back," the younger man says, not looking away from Sipowicz clenching his fist and casting a knowing look past the suspect at Bobby Simone.

The bartender steps through a door and returns in less than five seconds, handing me one sheet of yellowed, lined paper with a heading inscribed in elaborate script. "*Freundschaft, lieve und humanitat!*" it begins. I keep my pronunciation to myself, but I guess at its meaning aloud: "Friendship, Life, and Humanity."

"Something like that," the man agrees, looking down at the stationery, then back to the television.

"*Vereinigte Bruder Loge No. 608, D.O.H.*" is more difficult. I fail on the first word, but the bartender and the man beside me shake their heads.

The last line, "*Von Etna, Pennsylvania,*" seems self-explanatory. The address was printed so long ago it doesn't have a zip code.

"Thanks," I say, beginning to fold it.

"Don't be folding that," the man murmurs. "It'll disintegrate."

I run my fingers over it, but it stays intact. "You think anybody here knows German?" I say.

"This got nothing to do with Germany any more," he says.

"The neighborhood?" I suggest. "Friends?"

"Yes," he says.

Sipowicz storms out of the interrogation room, leaving Bobby Simone to face the child-molester. "Before my time," the bartender says, "this club was all at the candy store."

"Pollack's?" I say, remembering the name from selling candy at Easter for the Boy Scouts.

"Sure—two doors down."

I've been inside that candy store. Husband and wife, the Pollacks made their own crème- and caramel-filled chocolates in the back room where fifty years ago men had drunk beer and eaten, I guessed, the same fried-fish sandwiches and hot sausage and bratwurst listed on the chalkboard menu this afternoon.

Steven Bochco and David Milch flash on the screen, the way their names always do at the end of *NYPD Blue*. I've missed the last two minutes where Sipowicz greets his wife and Simone slips into bed with the beautiful detective Russell.

My wife is talking to a man at the end of the bar. I show him the stationery, point to the second line. "United brothers," he translates. He is old enough to have gone to high school with my father and my mother's brother, who graduated together in 1936. "Gottlob Lang," he says, "a long time for that."

"Yes," I say.

"He lived right here," he says, nodding toward the door.

"Yes," I say again.

He shakes his head. "There was the war to go off to, and then things were different."

I wait for him to say something I want to know, but he returns to "A long time for that," before sipping his beer as if it helps him to concentrate. "The DOH," he says, looking at my wife, "it stands for Deutsch of the Hory-Gory." My grandmother's words are spoken where I can hear them for the first time in over forty years. The name, repeated now, is as unlikely as Rumpelstiltskin. I think some secret code has been revealed, that these men will declare, "Now that you know, you'll join us or die."

"Really?" I blurt.

The bartender reaches for the old man's empty glass. "Hory-Gory's in Germany someplace," she says.

"Is that right?" I say, modifying my disbelief.

She pours the old man a fresh draft and looks at me. "Look it up," she says, setting the glass exactly on the circle stain left by the previous beer.

"Gottlob Lang," the old man finally says, "I almost forgot I knew him," and then he turns away.

A minute later, as Liz and I approach the candy store, an old couple closes the door, passes us, and walks into the DOH. The Pollacks, I am certain. They close at three o'clock, I decide. They walk to the DOH and settle in for a sandwich and a couple of drafts. My mother had loved their candy; my Aunt Margaret wouldn't have it in her house. Of course, I think, suddenly knowing another difference more than a decade in age between them meant. The wind catches the paper I am carrying, and I pinch my thumb and finger to keep it from blowing away, gouging a hole in the stationery as if it were made of delicate chocolate.

If I want to see where my grandfather drank as a member of the DOH, I'll have to walk inside a candy store. By the time the new DOH was built in 1950, he'd spent years as a farm hand for room and board, hitching rides, when it was heading toward Etna, on the produce truck and spending an allowance on an hour's worth of boilermakers until, practicing thrift, he bought a bottle to carry back to the farm where, one afternoon, he tumbled from near the top of that often-mentioned silo and survived unhurt.

"What kind of name is Hory-Gory?" Liz asks.

"It's not any place in Germany," I say at once.

"But you'll check on it," my wife says. "Just to make sure?"

Before we leave Etna, we drive past the fire station because my father had told me The Prince "paid for half a fire truck with all the beer he drank there and the raffle tickets he bought."

"I'll check it out," I had promised.

My father had snorted. "All he ever won after I knew your mother was a couple of live chickens and a ship-in-a-bottle."

"A huge one," I had said at once, brightening. The chickens were old news, but I remembered Aunt Margaret describing how the ship-in-a-bottle sat on the mantle like a trophy. "You couldn't touch it," she said. "He did the dusting on that big, ugly monstrosity. Mother hated that thing because it was bought with the drink."

An hour later, my father listens as we tell him about Prospect Street. "We went into the DOH," I say, and he frowns.

"Then you're the first for that."

"It's just a private club. A bar and some tables, a kitchen and a pool table and a bowling alley downstairs."

"Now you know."

"It used to be in Pollack's Candy Store."

"Yes."

"They belong," I say. "They went in just after we left."

"Some people like their drink."

I think of stopping, before I travel back across Pennsylvania to where I live, at each of Etna's bars. I want to order pitchers of Iron City and Fort Pitt and Duquesne, though only the first of them is still brewed. I want to drop a shot of Imperial whiskey into my draft and watch that depth charge plummet to the bottom before I drink. Somebody else at one of those bars will remember Gottlob Lang. The man who remembers will be as old as my father. He will tell me he drank in these bars before the war and after it. That he came home to rant about the Goddamn Krauts and the rotten Nazis, and just what the fuck kind of name, he said one night to my grandfather, is Gottlob anyway?

My father tells me to turn up Spencer Lane, the first time I've taken this road in thirty years. "Why?" I think of asking, but he's sitting up so straight I know I don't have long to wait.

"Look," he says, after we make two right turns. The street is blocked by sawhorses with blinking lights. "Subsidence," he says, "after all these years." *Road Closed* is repeated on three signs, and I keep driving, allowing him to direct me through a loop of roads to the back side of Stoneridge, the housing plan that covers the hillside near his house. "We can park here and walk," he says.

He lives less than half a mile away. We hiked all over this hillside and the woods just below us until the houses sprang up when I was in high school. Now we pass mailboxes tipping toward sunken yards, houses with heavy equipment parked near the shrubbery, a sure sign of cracked foundations. The lights are out in every house; if anyone else is taking the tour, we don't see them.

Subsidence, Mine Fire, Bypass, Golf

Fifteen minutes later, my father has me park in front of the fire hall, where a meeting has already begun with township officials and a set of engineering and mining experts. The hall is packed, every chair taken, a triple row of people I imagine are Stoneridge residents jammed along three walls. One by one, twenty-seven in all while we watch, the homeowners walk to the microphone in the center aisle and voice their protests. After each speech—limited, apparently, to two minutes—a round of applause, whether the speaker is loud or soft, profane or polite. When the first engineer begins to deliver his assurances, my father nudges me toward the door.

"We don't need to hear the rest," he says.

"I didn't realize the mines were that close," I say.

"You were a kid," he says. "When you're a kid you don't know something like that. The closest shaft is at the end of the street. Back when we had sewers put in, forty-five years ago, I thought the Millers were kidding when they said they didn't need to tap

in because they dumped their sewage down a mine shaft. I thought they were cheap, but I never did see any sign of a septic tank, none of that telltale rich green you get from having one."

It turns out the township has mailed my father and the rest of his neighbors a map of the mines in question. If he had bought on the other side of the street, he says, he thinks he would be in danger.

"The map doesn't tell you for sure?"

"You can look," he says.

"You have the map."

"It's hard to read."

When we get home, he starts to search for the map among stacks of old mail he's piled on the dining room table. I've seen dates on those envelopes running back five years. My father, who misplaced his bifocals months ago, can't read the map he finally fishes from stack #3.

The tunnels, according to the map, run along the backyards of the houses across the street. Not so lucky are the residents of Stoneridge, a large part of that housing plan built over a labyrinth of abandoned seams.

"I used to help deliver coal," my father says, and I let him tell me old stories—how, when the truck came, the driver dumped the coal in the alley behind their house. "The basement window was under the back porch," he says. "We had to shovel the coal into bushel baskets, and one of us boys had to get under that porch, take the basket, and hand it down to my father. There's not much worse than breathing coal dust."

I think of worse at once, tell my father about Centralia, the town near where I live that has suffered an underground fire for over forty years.

He thinks I am making it up, but I show him, on the map of Pennsylvania, the highway that is closed now because the fire passed underneath it, causing it to ripple and crack, unsafe for cars and trucks. "Route 61," I say. "See? It's not just some rural two-lane."

The earth, I tell him, is so hot in some places you can start paper on fire. A friend and I, a couple of years ago, chose what we thought were the hottest places, kicked a wad of newspaper as if it were a soccer ball to see if we could score a goal of flames.

"You sound like a couple of kids," my father says.

"A child, once, nearly fell through a small sinkhole into that fire."

My father shakes his head. "Centralia needs to be seen," I say, and then I wait for him to say something that will let me elaborate. There are thousands of

ruined acres, large stands of dead trees, their roots destroyed by heat. The town itself, except for a few dozen diehards, is gone. Literally—the houses razed, the people moved elsewhere because the fire has decades of coal left to burn along the seams spidering beneath the earth. "If you lived where I do," I say, "everything I'm telling you would be old news."

"Why don't I hear about this?" he says.

"People who get heard," I say, "don't live there," and then I launch into my stories and descriptions, finishing with how one of the fields in what used to be the town is full of rows of rusting vents. "It looks like an abandoned drive-in theater," I say, "only the speaker poles left behind; but nothing was ever broadcast there except the hope, twenty-five years ago, that the fire could be stopped by flushing it or smothering it."

"So many mines," my father says, "so many things under the ground we don't know what we have down there anymore."

I agree, but I don't bring up nuclear refuse, toxic medical waste, all of the plastic and such that will outlast us, most likely, by thousands of years. The residents of Stoneridge and Centralia have had their fortunes told by coal: Here, it formed. Here, it did not.

I remember how, ten years ago, I drove back to Pittsburgh to be with my father after his quadruple bypass surgery, something he had to be convinced to have, not because it was necessary to save his life, but because to submit to such surgery meant he'd become weak.

Six months later, we'd played nine holes of golf before we'd had dinner and driven home, by another route, through Stoneridge. "Seven or eight years, maybe, this retread will give me," he'd said, using a tone that told me he'd researched the statistics, and I didn't say anything about how something else could break down, that there was more than one threat under the surfaces of our lives.

All round my father had played best ball of two. Four, he'd recorded after sinking a thirty-foot putt on the second try. Five, he'd written down after he'd driven his second tee shot down the middle instead of hooking it into the woods. By the ninth hole, my father was a stroke ahead and beaming. While we waited for two members of the foursome in front of us to play drop balls over the water hazard, he showed me his scars, the lines and dots of surgery. "The human body can put up with most anything," he said, and then he topped his first iron and watched it trickle into the pond before he lofted his second five iron onto the near-island of green to put himself into position for another par.

After we putted out, I slung his bag over my left shoulder and carried my

own over my right, and he walked, to save his spikes and to protect his socks as well, barefoot across the parking lot. My father didn't hurry. He didn't act as if that asphalt were cooking the soles of his feet. "In the sun," he said, "there's a difference between asphalt and cement," using a tone so placid I freed one hand, laid it to the summer surface, and listened, like the deaf, for the music of the earth.

Alcoholism is often called the "three-generation disease," passed from parent to child to grandchild like hair color, dimples, or the shape of the nose.

"It runs in the family," Aunt Margaret would always say when she talked about The Prince, citing the alcohol-related problems of my grandfather's brother and the caution of her own brothers, how they avoided alcohol out of fear. Aunt Margaret and my mother and my Uncle Karl are long dead, but my father, at eighty-eight, continues to remind me about the evils of "the drink." "I've never taken a sip," he manages to work into our talks, even after fifty years of repetition, following that declaration with a look that says, "And you should stop"—each of those verbal and visual prompts accompanied by a slow shake of his head that seems to be saying, "You can catch alcoholism like a cold."

So it's not that remarkable that I didn't have one alcoholic drink during high school. I was still my father's son, but the most telling reason why I abstained was because, for the most part, my friends didn't drink. We were good students. We were athletes. I began college without having ever seen someone drunk. It does seem remarkable, though, that with or without the example of my grandfather's problems, I didn't have one drink during my first semester at college.

It took some doing. My roommate was "social." There were parties to go to, and he went. Fraternities had their eyes on us, and in the fall of 1963, Greek life was more attractive than any other kind for freshmen like us. In fact, it looked to me as if everyone I wanted to spend time with drank to excess.

I had three goals: Be a Dean's List student. Make the basketball team. Take more chances with girls. Only the last of these had anything to do with alcohol, but before Thanksgiving, without drinking, I went out on more dates that led to "making out" than I had in the previous two years.

All was well. My grades were excellent. And though I was unlikely to see much meaningful playing time, I was a college varsity basketball player.

Drunk, my roommate threw up in our room a few times during those months. It seemed like proof that my father was right. Brothers from several fraternities visited our room, and though I made up excuses for avoiding their parties, they returned and talked to me as well as my roommate.

When Kennedy was assassinated on a Friday afternoon, it wasn't any kind of personal trauma for me. Like I always did at four o'clock, I went to basketball practice, and we had it. That night I walked into town to shoot three hours worth of pool with a friend.

On Saturday we had practice again, and I went to a movie with a girl who seemed happy to spend four hours with me. On Sunday I studied through the death of Lee Harvey Oswald because Monday afternoon the team had its first scrimmage with another college, and I was happy to be riding for an hour each way on the team bus in order to get a few minutes of court time in the second half of the makeshift contest while Kennedy was being buried. Our first regular season game was eight days away.

By the end of the semester, I'd played in a third of our games, never when we were within fifteen points of the other team, and received grades that not only put me on the Dean's List, but also stood me near the top of my class.

Most beer has an alcohol by volume content of about 5 percent. One definition of binge drinking is consuming five twelve-ounce beers in one sitting.

I swallowed my first beer on a Sunday afternoon at the end of the initial week of the second semester. A keg party. I'd never even seen a beer keg before, but I didn't reveal that secret to anyone. Bids to fraternities would come out in a month, and I decided it was time to try my hand at drinking before I risked being declared a pussy.

I finished six beers, getting used to the taste while I disguised how uninitiated I was by moving from group to group before anyone noticed I hadn't finished a twelve-ounce paper-cupful for twenty minutes. At that pace, I didn't get sick, but I definitely enjoyed the buzz I so easily obtained.

A week later I went to a Friday night party and drank until I threw up. I played a game called "Signs" that encouraged binge drinking. The fraternity brothers were experts at making sure freshmen were caught not seeing hand signals we needed to immediately mimic, like "two guns" or "jack off," being given by someone standing at the fringe of our peripheral vision. So I lost frequently

and happily chugged my beer from a glass I'd stolen from the cafeteria. Each time I managed to finish a glassful without pausing, the guys in the fraternity that I most wanted to join cheered and applauded. We had a basketball game in Cleveland the next night, and I still felt sick, even near the end of the second half, when I managed to fire up a few loose shots because I'd come off the bench when we were down by twenty.

The next weekend I went drinking again, this time at a coed keg party. I took a girl who was delighted to drink for free and dance to music played loudly by a local band called Gary and the Houserockers that had the good sense to play a ten-minute rendition of the Isley Brothers' "Shout!" I danced all ten minutes as if demons possessed me. Not satisfied, I worked my way through the Mashed Potato, the Watusi, and the Hully-Gully. The girl danced in a way that I took to be suggestive, and when I wrapped my arms around her, dripping sweat onto her shoulders, she leaned into me like the beginning of a sexual fantasy.

The second semester was three weeks old, and I added a fourth resolution to my list: Find as many opportunities to drink as possible.

I joined that fraternity. My roommate pledged with me. We went to a party where, for the first time, I drank whiskey. Shortly after midnight I thought I might die, but the next day I had stories to tell. I was a frat boy now.

So it went. Basketball ended. Tennis season began, and I became a two-sport college athlete, enough responsibility to drink only on weekends. I survived pledging while my grades collapsed.

I couldn't wait to go back for my sophomore year. My roommate and I were moving into the fraternity house. I was "social" now, too, and I loved it.

Ernest Gallo has said he and his brothers wanted their wine-making company to become the "Campbell's soup company of the wine industry." One strategy was to sell a cheap, fortified wine called Thunderbird in ghettos across the United States. One story claims that Ernest once pulled his car over in an inner-city neighborhood and called out, "What's the word?" and the nearest bum promptly answered, "Thunderbird."

All that summer after my freshman year, on WAMO, the black radio station from Pittsburgh I listened to, were commercials for Thunderbird and Night Train wines. "What's the word—Thunderbird," one ad repeated. "All aboard the Night Train," another one encouraged. And those cheap wines sounded like something I had to try.

The first day back at school, I carried a quart bottle of Thunderbird around with me and thought it was cool listening to James Brown and getting wasted on what someone told me was fortified wine. I had no idea what that meant, except I understood it had a higher alcohol percentage by volume.

Fifty percent higher, as I came to discover when I looked at the label. It tasted awful, but I got really drunk really fast. Before dinner I was sicker than I'd ever been in my life. It was a sickness throughout my entire body, a weakness in the arms and legs. Like a baby—the old phrase settled upon me with authority. I ended up literally lying on the floor.

"Like a wino," my friends said the next day. "Like a bum." My headache stayed. My body was unwilling to do anything useful for thirty-six hours. "Like chemotherapy without the hair loss," I told a friend in my best hyperbole.

He didn't laugh. "That's fucked up," he said.

Somebody else explained that he'd heard the wine was distilled to get the alcohol level higher, that bums, in fact, did drink it because they got more bang for the buck—"Just ninety-nine cents for the full-quart bottle" was another line from the Thunderbird ad. It was the first alcoholic beverage I vowed never to touch again, a promise easy to keep. What's more, I didn't bother to get on board the Night Train. I knew where that express was headed.

When I returned for the second semester, I went to the liquor store with a friend, the two of us telling the clerk we wanted "the cheapest wine you have in stock." It came in a gallon container with a circle of thick glass for a handle that made it look like a moonshiner's jug. The bottle was so dusty our fingertips turned gray. We laughed when we noticed that our lips had turned purple after a few swigs, and we played records loudly in his room for an hour until we simply allowed my brand new copy of Junior Walker and the All Stars' "Shotgun" to play over and over maybe twenty times before somebody walked in and took that record away, slamming the door behind him in a way that suggested we were not supposed to follow.

We moved on to Wilson Pickett and the reliable James Brown. When we reached the bottom of the bottle, we discovered a quarter inch of sludge swirling around like the grit in the bottom of a prospector's pan of dreams. Neither of us was willing to take the final swig.

Though guilt accompanied me like a persistent cough, I thought any time after lunch on Friday was late enough to begin drinking. So what if I had French class at 2:40 on Fridays? During the first semester, I'd sat beside a fraternity brother who copied off my tests even though I informed him I knew nothing. Second

semester, after he failed the class and no longer attended, I moved to the back and sat beside a student I didn't know who drank before class on Wednesdays as well. On Fridays, we thought everything the professor said in French sounded hilarious.

Forty percent of all traffic fatalities in the United States are alcohol-related. The higher the blood-alcohol level, the more likely the traffic accident will produce a fatality.

The weather turned warm in May, and that meant guys in my fraternity would be making road trips to the lake at "Pymy," Pymatuming State Park, where we claimed an isolated section of waterfront as ours. Near the end of April, I'd been surprised—and my friends had been stunned—when a girl I thought was unattainable had gone out with me, not once, but three times. I lost my head trying to impress her, but even better, one Saturday afternoon a friend who drove a Corvette was so infatuated with being close to her that he offered us a ride to the park.

That driver was already half drunk as we left campus, but I thought I'd never looked cooler in my life. An "impossible" girl on my lap, the top down, passing every car we overtook, including one full of fraternity brothers we came up alongside as we entered the state park. The road was narrow, the sort of park road that was dotted with 25 MPH speed-limit signs.

We were doing 120. I'd verified that a few moments before as I finished the beer I'd been holding and let my arm dangle over the edge of the open window as if that lethal speed was something I was used to. I looked to my right and saw the faces of friends so close I could touch the nearest one in the back seat. I pulled my arm inside as the distance between the cars closed to a few inches, and I let loose a whoop of relief when we cleared that car and had to slow down because the road was about to turn to packed dirt and tight curves.

"You looked really scared there for a minute," that sexy girl said. "Like a fawn."

Her simile made me foresee the end of my lucky streak with her, but I didn't try to deny it. Within a few days she had moved on to somebody willing to risk dying at nineteen in order to touch her.

A week later, in that same park, this time unaccompanied by a girl, I watched a fraternity brother have sex in plain sight about one hundred feet away. Nobody in our group of six fraternity brothers moved closer. We didn't yell obscenities or encouragement at either him or her, but everybody stared

until one of our group mentioned that the guy having sex had told him that when he was through with that girl he'd gotten thoroughly drunk before undressing her, we could have her.

"One," somebody called out.

"Two," someone said.

It took me until another guy said "three" to realize what those numbers meant. The six of us were getting in line. I said five in order to save face, but it didn't seem possible that my turn would ever come. I didn't know that drunk girl, but I knew I didn't want to have sex with her in front of my friends.

When the guy who'd called out #1 walked toward the girl as she sat up and began to dress, she saw that we'd been watching and things fell apart. The girl began to cry, and #1 backed off. Whatever we were, we weren't rapists. Half dressed, she wrapped herself in the blanket she'd been lying on, and the brother who'd brought her took her back to school.

A couple of my friends talked as if we'd missed a great opportunity, but I was relieved. No matter how many beers I'd swallowed, I wasn't ready for a public gang bang. A friend who had been #4 and I peeled off from the group and walked along the lake's edge. Neither of us spoke, but I knew he was as thankful as I was that the direction of the day had shifted before we had been forced to become responsible for ourselves. We sat on the bank that overlooked the lake and shared a six-pack, both of us drinking slowly in order to give ourselves something to do besides talk.

Two weeks later the school year was over, and I was on academic probation. I weighed that against the joy I'd experienced with girls who'd gotten drunk with me and allowed me to touch their bodies. I didn't think of The Prince or my father or the consequences of failure until I arrived home and began to watch the mailbox in order to intercept my grades.

They were even worse than I'd anticipated, but I got to work with a black pen and carefully turned my F into what I hoped would pass for a B if I showed it to my mother in the dark of a moving car while she drove.

Which is exactly what I did. "I had some trouble in French," I said, acknowledging my D–. Just below it was my artificial B in Fine Arts, the class I'd skipped more than twenty-five times.

She nodded. "You need to buckle down," she said, and I agreed at once, stuffing those grades in my pocket and throwing them into the trash before the night was over. She'd relay the news to my father, who, thankfully, had stopped asking me about school because he believed, correctly, that I was wasting his money.

"Do you consider the needs of others to the point of neglecting your own wants and needs?"—from a family alcoholism screening test.

The Prince was cited dozens of times that summer as if his name was enough to conjure the evils of dissipation. Moreover, when my father's father died in June, that grandfather was cited as an example of restraint, a model for behavior. "Dad never understood why you didn't talk to him," my father said after the funeral.

"Because he was so stern," I said at once. "He was scary. He always looked as if he was judging everybody."

"He lived a good life," my father said. "It's no sin to expect the same from others."

Shortly after that, the stories about The Prince were supplemented with stories about the drinking problems of some of our neighbors, most particularly a man two houses down who put a shotgun in his mouth and pulled the trigger because, my father explained, "the drink got the best of him."

One night in July, I drove to a keg party at a picnic grove in North Park. I was invited because I played tennis for the park's traveling team, but no one at that party gave any indication they were interested in conditioning. I wore a fraternity shirt that said CROWS across the chest and hoped it would attract girls. After a few hours of drinking, the one who was most interested swayed close to me while I did a dance called "The Hunch," and there was a cheer from the guys at the keg when I was finished dry-humping the narrow space between me and that girl I'd met an hour earlier. It was as close as I got to sex with her, but I gave her one last performance when I fishtailed out of the parking lot at one A.M., speeding away as if recklessness were an aphrodisiac.

The next evening, I went back to that park to play tennis with my father, and the first thing someone who'd been at that party shouted was, "Hey, Crow, how you holding up after all that firewater?"

Anyone within a hundred feet, including my father, could hear. He said nothing, but he didn't talk at all during the two sets we played, changing sides as if we were rivals in the late rounds of a tournament. The silent ride home was an accusation. I didn't get to use my defense, which pointed out that I'd gotten up at six A.M. and managed my shift at Heinz, a sign that I could handle my liquor, that it wasn't getting the best of me.

My father, all that summer, said nothing about my drinking, but then other people besides our neighbor died. People I honest-to-God knew. People my age. A guy from my high school class drove drunk into a tree. A girl I'd gone out

with one weekend went out with another boy the next weekend and was killed when the car she was in was destroyed in a high-speed, alcohol-fueled accident. It didn't escape my notice that the car was a Corvette.

What I was certain of was that one more semester like my previous one and college would be over for me. My father declared, through the voice of my mother, that he wouldn't pay another nickel for me to "act stupid." I didn't argue.

In September, I went to every class the first week. I bought all the books and read every assignment. Prepared to recite, I raised my hand to volunteer answers. My grandfather became a bogeyman, not an omen. If there had been a "comeback student of the year award," I would have won that prize. I nearly doubled the grade point I'd received the previous semester. My lowest grade was a B I'd earned without the benefit of careful penmanship. I didn't have to be perfect; all I had to do was stop being an idiot.

"Your father won't say it," my mother said when my grades arrived, "but he's pleased."

Everclear is the most common brand name for grain alcohol. Distilled twice, it's 190 proof (95 percent pure alcohol). It's odorless, tasteless, and very potent.

When the next semester began, the bills paid for without comment by my father, my grades were even higher than they'd been during that long-ago freshman semester. Shortly after that term began, another girl I knew was killed in a car driven by a student who was drunk. I'd laughed with her a few hours earlier when I'd seen her stealing, like I once had, a glass from the cafeteria to drink beer from at a rival fraternity's keg party. On the way back to school, she died less than half a mile from campus.

I didn't even know you could buy nearly pure alcohol, but when somebody in the frat house, a week later, enlisted my help to concoct a few gallons of Purple Jesus—to celebrate, he laughed, the beginning of Lent—mixing one part grain alcohol to four parts grape juice, I refrained from drinking more than one small cup when the party started. What I learned was how stupid my friends looked to someone sober after they'd spent an hour drinking that swill. I didn't envy anyone his fun. I was still capable of bad choices, but this one seemed particularly lousy.

As the end of college was becoming more than an abstraction, Vietnam showing every sign of turning worse, I was beginning to feel something more than regret about time wasted. I felt panic, and that anxiety, paired with alcohol,

fueled anger rather than happiness when I worked through my second six-pack of the night. For months, I drank alone—with nobody else, as the old blues song goes—because I was prone to complaint and insult.

Now I made vows that I kept. Not to climb into cars driven by friends who were drinking, an easy one. Not to get drunk-sick, a bit harder, but something I didn't do for that entire school year. When my grades arrived, I opened them in broad daylight in front of both my parents. I knew how good they were going to be. Another first-rate semester and I was going to have a shot at graduate school, where I'd be a real student from the first day on if a university would have me.

That year, too, I recognized what I'd always known, but never admitted, that a few of my friends drank differently. It wasn't frequency. During my sophomore year, I could be talked into drinking on a Tuesday or Wednesday night. It was that they drank with urgency.

The friend who drank in spite of the stomach ulcer that made him throw up blood. The friend who had beer on ice in the trunk of his car in case we ran low at a keg party. The friend who brought a beer along in the car while we drove two miles to a party. The friend who bought a six-pack as we left a bar for a wedding half an hour away. As if drinking was not to be interrupted. As if it was necessity rather than entertainment. As if it was embedded in his genetic code.

I was belatedly learning one of the old chestnuts of school-run behavior classes: the difference between drinking to have a good time and drinking because daylight was fading. And at last, I encountered the first friend I'd ever seen with a beer in his hand in the morning. "Hair of the dog," he said, as if that excused him. When I noticed a second can, already empty, I felt like I'd caught him jerking off to porn. I felt like a father.

Our Hearts Keep Singing *is the title of an old album I discover in a bin marked* Nothing over $2.99. *The name of the group is the Braillettes, who are pictured on the cover, three apparently blind women who beam their best version of good attitude toward an unseen camera. According to the jacket, they've been recorded by Heart Warming Records.*

Last night I woke, saw nothing, and knew it was my Bill Nelson dream, the one where he makes change in the perpetual dark, handling each coin in his black purse until he's satisfied which ones accurately pay for his rolls. As soon as I'm awake, the dream, as it should, turns to memory—the times when I imagined Bill Nelson, the blind customer I delivered baked goods to, would cheat himself so I could pocket the extra quarters and dimes, lying to myself about the blind, how they mistake coins like I misread, in my half-vision

Night Vision

five decades later, the brief rebus of road signs, the colorful puzzle of passersby.

The air puffs between blinks confirm it's not glaucoma sucking my sight. Better, better, worse, better—these chants focus where things stand since the last time I heard diopters, thickness, and the measurements for the great curve of inadequate correction. The doctor hums the ceiling tunes, adds his strings to the ones playing "My Girl" and "Uptown Girl." "Follow the light," he croons. "Now ignore it."

I want to say "How?" half expecting him to switch it off, smiling in the dark at optometrist humor.

"Have you worried?" he'd say, the room struck black, waiting for what I'll answer, my optimistic eyes still blinking, whether or not I'll be sadly clever with compensatory, heartfelt singing.

Aldous Huxley, whose eyesight was worse than mine, learned Braille to relieve his eyes. He saved vision for writing and followed a regimen of

exercises to improve his sight. One of these was "Nose Writing," during which he fixed his eyes on the end of his nose and moved his head as if he were writing. I write nearly every morning; my head barely moves except when I turn a page.

Each time I have my lenses changed, I ask the woman who fits my glasses whether I've become the patient with the worst prescription. We play it like a joke, and to tell the truth, when I first asked fifteen years ago, I was certain there were dozens of patients, in this office alone, who were worse off. Now I am less certain, and her answer arrives less quickly. "Oh no, not the worst," she eventually says, rehearsed by now, but *nearly blind* is no longer a vague expression.

Specific enough, I know, because I've had my first anxiety attack in the optometrist's chair. An embarrassment reserved in the past for blood tests, stress tests, and the foul shield stuffed in the back of the mouth for serious dental work, I've gone clammy and faint under the gaze of so many doctors and nurses that I am the champion of medical catharsis.

Now, I've had to ask the optometrist to stop and step back; I've had to slow my breathing and take the water and forehead wipe with another terrible joke about resurrection.

When I was in first grade, before I was fitted for my first pair of glasses and could manage the blackboard from a seat halfway back the row, my parents took me to a minstrel show in our church basement.

On the stage were six men in blackface, three on either side of a patriarch of the church who was always called Major Hartman. There was an hour of foot-shuffling, fried-chicken-eating jokes. The congregation laughed and so did I, able to pick out, even from ten rows back, the enormous lips of my Uncle Ted. But what I remember most clearly now is Major Hartman, after the show, being led from the stage and down the aisle to an open space, where he stared from eyes so opaque with cataracts that he cocked his head like a bird to listen for voices.

"He can see shadows," my father said. "He sees light and dark and movement"—making the Major's world seem as if it were appropriate for the first day of Genesis. I wanted to know if the Major recognized me, but I couldn't bring myself to say anything. Instead, all I could do was walk up to him and squint at his eyes, his head swiveling toward my father, who was speaking, and then briefly, when I stepped back, peeking down toward the tap of my cleated shoes.

In the past, some people wore gold earrings, believing they sharpened eyesight. Dubious even as motive, I think, but the Sioux believed in the more likely power of bezoar stones, inorganic masses of magnesium phosphate and lime that form around foreign substances in the alimentary canals of ruminants like buffalo and deer. The dust from these stones was blown into the eyes, so direct, so irritating, those patients had reason to be hopeful.

Years ago, the optometrist explained the paradox of size and clarity, beginning by telling me that vision peaks at seventeen; and I told him mine peaked at six, or maybe sooner—how in second and third grade, I memorized the eye-chart lines that said my sight was 20/30, delaying glasses until I suddenly plummeted to 20/120 when my cheating was exposed. "Weakness in a boy was taboo, according to my father," I said, explaining, but the optometrist was already fiddling with his instruments.

"Well, now it looks as if your near vision is going," he warbled, not at all reassuring when he couldn't correct my vision with glasses and my contact lenses irritated my dry eyes.

"It's a struggle," he admitted. "You gain clarity but you lose size, so you can't quite break even at your prescription."

I nodded and thought of future conversations, how enlightening he would be about the struggle with fog and darkness. And then he told me why my decrease in night vision had superseded my nearsightedness—"We require more light to activate the retina," he said. "It's another one of those age signs."

For centuries, men and women, for a fee, have performed the Blindfold Drive, using carriages and bicycles, cars and tractors. They drive through traffic as if they were sighted; they speed and manage to survive. One of these performers did the trick with a steamship in a crowded harbor, keeping his technique a secret.

My family revels in the failed-eyesight anecdote. The day of the median strip, for instance, when I'd had the compulsion to take everyone in the family to a theater an hour away to see a movie I knew would never arrive in our small town.

I managed the open highway well enough, but it was dark and drizzling when we reached Harrisburg. I drove below the speed limit and tried to see far

enough ahead to keep from crashing into any darkened object carelessly out of place. I squinted. I pressed my glasses against the bridge of my nose to stir up the coagulated soup of my vision.

I followed a lane that was merging with a crowded highway. A strip of franchises and shopping centers glowed ahead of me, throwing the middle of the highway into obscurity. I slowed and pulled left when the headlights in the side mirror broke slightly. At once I felt the car rise on the whitecap of a median strip I'd thought was flat. My daughter, rapt inside headphones beside me, clutched at the air above her head, transformed by the sweet horror of the roller-coaster simulation.

The car dipped and then rose again, completing its small tumble into traffic. "Good job," my fifteen-year-old said from behind me.

"You can't see," my wife said. "You're blind and you won't admit it."

"It's all these lights. It's the way they saturate the road and forget about what it does to vision."

I made out what had to be the sign for the quadriplex of cinemas and slid into the left lane to look for the entrance. When I saw the full-scale median end, nothing to block my way, I was sure there had to be an entrance over in the gloom. I turned hard left and knew by the shouts from the back seat that I was in the midst of error.

No entrance to anywhere appeared. There was only a curb that was high enough to cave in the front axle, so I swerved right, facing the oncoming traffic while my wife screamed and my children, for once, sat silently. There was nothing to do but accelerate, race up the slow lane and pray for a break in the curb before the nearest headlights exploded through the windshield.

I heard my name and God's repeated twenty times in three octaves before I pulled the car left at the first open space, a drive-through bank, as it turned out. A chorus of horns faded into the Harrisburg evening. "Get out from behind there," my wife said, and there was nothing to do but agree. I stood beneath the first sign I could read—First Northern Bank, I said to myself, listening to the bells that were telling me I'd left the keys in the ignition.

Five hundred years ago, people believed in the Doctrine of Signatures, which claimed the curative values of plants could be predicted by their shapes and colors. Everything in this world had a purpose: The Chinese lantern plant is bladder-shaped, so it's good for kidney and bladder stones; the ginseng root looks like a human figure, so it's good for

longevity; the blossoms of the eyebright plant look like bloodshot eyes, so they are good for pink eye and clearing vision. There are hundreds of thousands of people, still, who subscribe. After all, the man given most credit for popularizing this theory was Paracelsus, who was a Swiss physician.

Once upon a time, I intended to be an eye doctor. I had a stack of applications; I was completing the preprofessional program in order to transfer to a school of optometry. The doctor who had prescribed and fitted my first pair of contact lenses had encouraged me. "I make a good living," he said, "and nearly all of my patients walk away smiling."

I agreed with that. I was fifteen when I received my contact lenses, and for the first time in nine years I understood what it was the rest of the world was seeing. My parents verified the expense, and I divided the number of hours he'd spent with me into the fee he charged, discovering the joyous profits of correcting eyesight. The last day I visited, getting the go-ahead to wear those lenses as many hours as I wanted, he opened his desk drawer when I handed him the final payment, and a flutter of personal checks rose and then fell magnificently to the plush, azure carpet.

The Sioux weren't the only ones who believed in magic powders. The British had a recipe, once, that instructed sufferers to burn the head of a black cat. Three times a day, for as long as it took to restore sight, someone blew that ash into the eyes of the blind, trusting that the stories of recoveries passed down to them were true.

"Do the eye gouge," roared the singer for a group called the Novas, who had a small cult hit with this song called "The Crusher" in 1964. At the time, The Crusher was the name of a professional wrestler who pinned an assortment of muscular or fat contenders each Saturday on a Pittsburgh television show. He snapped animal bones and growled in a voice so hoarse that the singer for the Novas must have suffered for his royalties.

What could be worse than the eye gouge? I didn't wince at the backbreakers and body slams; I didn't worry for the skulls of men who were tossed against the turnbuckles. But I cringed when victims reached for their gouged eyes, screaming their mock agony. It was as dangerous as the Three Stooges, but I shifted in my

chair and never laughed with my friends when Moe said, "Pick two" and fired those fingers at Curly's eyes.

The year before the Novas hit the charts, Ray Milland starred in *The Man with the X-Ray Eyes.* I watched, fascinated, as he developed miraculous, unnatural sight. He could look through objects, and he began wearing dark glasses for the sensitivity his gifts brought him.

Eventually, he crossed over into danger, seeing more than he should. He did carnival tricks; he read the top cards of the dealer during blackjack. Normalcy irretrievable, he cracked up his car when the ordinary world became unbearably muddled.

"If thine eye offend thee, pluck it out," the congregation inside an evangelist's tent is chanting when Ray Milland staggers in, and unable to deal with seeing so deeply into the world, he takes the Oedipus route. I shuddered more than I had five years before, wasting an afternoon with grade-school friends watching *The Crawling Eye,* which, complete with tentacles, slithered down the Alps to threaten a resort town full of extras. I didn't take a giant eye personally; I didn't worry about alien attacks. What I was anxious about, beginning in second grade, was going blind or having my vision tumble into the irretrievable world of disability.

My father used witch hazel for aches and pains. He slathered it on my back after I injured it playing basketball; he rubbed it into my hamstrings during track season. "Can't beat it," he said, though nobody I knew could find a bottle in their houses. A few centuries earlier and he might have poured it, minus the alcohol, into my eyes. Especially if we'd lived in New England, among the Indians, who boiled the bark of the tree into a potion that relieved the dimming of the eyes.

In 1964, besides listening to a daily dose of "The Crusher," I was busy with discovering the failure of self-discipline and the collapse of my grades in science and math, the very things that were necessary to prepare me for a career in optometry. By the end of two semesters, I had as much chance of completing that curriculum as the Novas had of going #1 on the national charts.

My chemistry professor, during the period set aside for recitation, instructed me to sit up in my chair. I slumped, sullen and incredulous, pondered the give-and-take of possible obscenities and violence. The semester had nine weeks remaining; my grade was still in flux. I pulled myself up.

I might as well have opted for the theatrics of profanity and door slamming. A month later, though still treading water in chemistry, I was irrevocably failing calculus and being advised to change majors by the man who had just returned my third F of the semester.

It was advice I didn't need. Advanced Composition and British Literature were the only classes I didn't dread attending.

"What's your major?" my chemistry teacher asked me, and I gave it to him straight. For a moment, he looked over my head as if he thought someone else had spoken. Finally, he lowered his gaze, leaned forward, and uttered, "Why?"

I mulled over the answer—money, prestige, family pressure, and the romance of working with danger. "You have a fear, you attack it head-on," my father said, and so I wanted to examine closely, completely credentialed, the hell of failing eyesights.

And then I thought how I could watch eye surgery on television instead, or write about it from experience whenever its inevitability caught up to me. Each time I popped out my contacts, the tentacles of the darkness seemed to have slithered further down the Alps of my future.

H. G. Wells wrote, "The bards were once blinded so they would not wander from the truth," and as I settled into the English major and the desire to write, I discovered the blindness of Homer and Milton and Borges. Not to worry, I thought; but the list of the nearly blind was more extensive: Thurber, Joyce, Charlotte Brontë, and the eye-exercising Aldous Huxley.

Each time I get new glasses, I take a test drive in the country—close one eye and then the other, measuring the differences in acuity. I take off the new glasses and put on the old; I put myself through ten miles of vision tests and decide I still can't be trusted driving, especially at night, when my eyes lower their power like the small AM stations near the rural town in which I live—suddenly, at sunset, reverting to static.

As a passenger, I touch the brake every time something rushes out of the fog. I take off my glasses and start getting acclimated to the way my corrected vision will be just before the light goes out forever. Moons and void. The landscape reverts to Genesis, the first day, when it was good because there was light and darkness.

In Philadelphia, on a journey with the family, I made a guesswork turn in

near daylight toward lanes marked Wrong Way in letters just large enough for me to see as I entered the double barrel of oncoming holiday traffic.

"Oh Christ," I said, swerving and jolting one tire over a safety island and back into lanes that held cars pointed in the same direction as I was. Nobody said anything that time, so I knew this mistake had been made by someone hopelessly mired in impending blindness, someone beyond criticism and ridicule.

Someone writes to a columnist whose job it is to answer common, yet tricky questions from readers. "Why is it," she says, "that when I take my glasses off and look in a mirror from six inches away, all of the reflections are still blurry?"

Years ago, I listened to a student admit her phone bill for the past month was $660. She was enrolled through a program I directed that was designed to attract students who could not afford college unless they were 100 percent aided and brought some physical, social, or academic handicap with them.

This student was blind. What's more, she was married to a man who was also blind and spoke nothing but German. When I asked her how $660 could accumulate in thirty days, she explained that her husband called home to Germany each morning after she left for school. "He's so lonely," she explained. "He doesn't have anything to do but talk."

The program paid tutors to read mail as well as textbooks to her, and earlier that day the phone bill had been itemized, thirty-dollar call by thirty-dollar call. "He doesn't call on weekends," she said, "because I'm with him all day."

I took off my glasses and she turned to fuzz. I imagined myself without corrective lenses in a foreign country, the phone nearby, but I didn't see myself picking it up. Without my glasses, I couldn't see myself at all unless I pressed my face against the glass of imagination.

In the eighteenth century, a device called the Claude glass was popular. It was constructed like a camera without film, a lightproof box with a lens in its front which produced an image reflected by an inclined mirror onto a glass screen. More often than not, the users turned their backs to the view; they retreated while they stared at the reflection of what was behind them, fascinated more by the boxed image than the unlimited, actual view.

A lifelong friend of mine, nearly thirty years ago, casually told me that he had glaucoma. He was driving us through traffic near New York City, and my first thought was to check the lanes on either side of us, trying to compensate for what I thought must be his tunnel vision. Neither of us bothered with physical examinations. We were in our early thirties; we took our small children to the doctor, not ourselves.

By that time I knew that Bill Nelson, the man to whom I carried sweet rolls, had had glaucoma and that his case had gone too long untreated. My friend, because he was changing jobs and was required to take a physical, was surprised and then devastated and then relieved to be diagnosed.

Medicine, eye drops, two surgeries—thirty years later he sees better than I do in traffic. For years, he and his wife trained seeing-eye dogs as a charitable hobby. They showed me videos of the ceremonies where the blind men and women, each of the three I saw appreciably younger than we were at the time, received their newly certified guide dogs.

I've told my father none of these stories, but one night, a month after the death of his brother, I drove him to my aunt's country home.

Late December, yet Pittsburgh was experiencing a temperature inversion, which produced fog that froze on the branches of trees and the bare lawns of lighted houses.

We had twenty miles to travel in the slightly foggy dark, and I said nothing about how little I could see. We missed a stop sign and a side-road turn. We doubled back, and my father began to announce each stop sign and curve, to detail an assortment of signals that revealed the location of turns.

Regardless, I maintained my speed. I wasn't about to shift into third gear, or worse, second. I came out of bends late, occasionally jolting through the shoulder. Even at twenty miles per hour on the unpaved road, I nosed right by my aunt's driveway, but my father said nothing while I backed up and turned.

When my aunt held up old photographs, I stepped so close to see that she mistook my gesture for love and compassion. She embraced me, the pictures dangling against my back. She handed me the pictures so I could take my time with them, and I found a seat under good light that directed itself over my left shoulder, one thing I still believe in, though the optometrist who stuffed cash and checks into his desk drawer confided the futility of that belief.

Three hours later, the fog was heavy enough for me to drive slowly without

humiliation. Passing under the faint fuzz of street lamps, I remembered the slogan of a light bulb advertisement that asks me to select a particular brand "so you can see the world the way you want to see it."

My father lapsed into silence. Because I settled into the speed of the nearly blind, he didn't need to point out the return-trip sequence of turns and signs.

A retaeus, a third-century Greek physician, found enough anecdotal evidence for the cyclical nature of dyspnea (labored breathing) to declare, "The evil is much worse in sleep."

When I read about Aretaeus and his medical colleagues, the dark settles like an unshakable superstition. I nod assent to this ancient observation of evening's threat. More than twenty years into full-blown asthma, I've suffered four or five attacks per year in daylight, one per week in the dark.

Circadian rhythms are the cycles our bodies go through over a twenty-four-hour period. We're tuned to a daily clock; we're cycled for strength and memory, for pulse and body temperature. If I were worried about heart attack and stroke, I'd be most anxious at seven A.M. I'd get out of bed with caution. Soon enough, most likely, I won't do sit-ups and push-ups ten minutes out of sleep, but right now I'm ecstatic in the morning. I'm able to take long pulls of breath, slow and deep as if memory could materialize as simple physical success.

I write in the mornings, the earlier the better. I drop into those push-ups when I'm stuck; I play golf, on the days I don't write, as early as partners are willing.

Come darkness and I'm listening to my breath for the first faint whistles. "So take care," my wife says, ignoring the obvious signals of my carelessness— alcohol, dairy products, an evening in the home of a cat owner or the comfort of an overstuffed chair. I might as well be speeding home from three hours of beat-the-clock at a distant bar, a gallon of half-priced beer shorting out the reflexes that keep us on the highway.

Last week I told her the story I'd heard about a man who suffered from shortness of breath. He blew up balloons to save an emergency supply and inflated so many he floated away holding them.

"Nice," she murmured, saying nothing about the emergencies she's witnessed first-hand.

Listed in a book of oddities and curiosities, under the heading "Names of people who became food," is Dr. J. H. Salisbury, a nineteenth-century physician who recommended

shredding all food before eating it. Hamburger was ideal, therefore, and he convinced his patients to eat, well-done, ground beef three times a day. It was a cure for asthma, he said, as long as you ate those hamburgers directly off the plate accompanied by generous portions of hot water. And, he cautioned, on the condition you followed those meals with a life full of "reasonable habits."

The consequences of bad choices:

(1) Fettuccini alfredo, created so perfectly with butter, parmesan cheese, and heavy cream, an enormous plate of it at the best Italian restaurant within a hundred miles of Selinsgrove, the town in which I live. A meal to die for, one old expression announcing itself loudly less than twenty minutes after the final swallow.

I walk around the parking lot while my family eats dessert. The October evening is extraordinary, sixty degrees and clear while the last week of daylight-saving time holds the light. Until the first killer frost, until the all-day rain or the shift of the jet stream, the pollen hangs on like the brown leaves of the pin oaks that border this plain of asphalt.

By the time I've twice followed the perimeter of the lot, I'm wheezing the steady whistle of the respiratory ward.

"You have your inhaler, don't you?" my wife asks like a teacher waiting for homework.

I'm failing this assignment. I become a passenger in an impromptu ambulance, my wife steering us toward the hospital. My children collectively fall silent. No one suggests a Led Zeppelin tape or the progressive rock station. And then, as if embarrassment were antidote, I recover before we reach the emergency room.

(2) Eggnog with beer chasers at a Christmas party. No problem, perhaps, except for the alcohol-enhanced panic that accelerates the windpipe's constriction. I rear up in the dark, knocking my glasses to the floor while I inhale the Proventil, my two-swallow dose. And then, when those seem to accomplish nothing, two more. I rush to the shower and feel myself, instead of relaxing in the mist, strangling naked and seeing the last vision of this life so blurred by steam and myopia I might as well be carrying cataracts to the grave.

The paramedics arrive. They offer pure oxygen and apply their gear to measure pulse and breath and blood pressure.

So I can see my precarious numbers. So I can plead my arms free of straps and summon the breath to curse their training.

I relax in anger. I manage the expletives of life going on as always, and my older son steps between me and the attendant who begins to preach.

"It's OK," he says. "He's all right."

The attendant tells him he's interfering with treatment. He raises his hands like the first fool facing the aliens. I think, "heat ray." I say, "Get out," as if they'd caved in my door with thrusted boots.

"You need to sign a release," he says, and for the first time I notice a gurney's been unfolded in the hallway.

"Sure," I say, my son behind me now, my wife clutching his arm. I'm ecstatic with the solidarity of my family. I'm sucking in the great gulps of primeval breath. When the ambulance leaves, I want to herd all five of us into the street so the neighbors can verify the continuation of my intact family.

Twenty-three years ago I swallowed my initial dose of theophylline. "Let's see how this goes," the doctor said. He was the same physician who had prescribed steroids two months earlier "to knock this thing out." Two weeks into that experiment, I'd poured the rest of my prescription down the sink after I'd slammed a door in my sister's face and fired an apple across the kitchen at the middle-school sneer of my son, opening a nova of splatter on the wall two inches above his head.

"Nice," he said, prequoting his mother.

J. I. Lighthall—"the great Indian medicine man"—wrote a book containing his folk-medicine advice in 1883. He recommends skunk cabbage, juice from the roots, 5 to 15 drops every two or three hours "when there is nervous irritation of the windpipe and bronchial tubes." A few pages later, he suggests red clover—tea made from its blossoms to alleviate asthma. He advises taking that tea hot, every hour or two.

Perhaps he's right, although doctor number three told me to empty my house until free breathing returned. Cats and hamsters had to go; so did my indoor evergreens. "No dust," she said, "and get some foam rubber pillows." I nodded my head until she said, "Get rid of your books," frowning when I told her I had thousands of them, that I read and wrote for a living. "They're no different than cats," she said, and then she prescribed theophylline as well, which produces circadian rhythms of its own. For fifteen years I took it twice a day, morning and late afternoon. It's time-released, so I had reason not to forget until the wheezing

began. "You'll be a bit antsy," the doctor said, and she was right about that—if ants feel like they're coming out of their skins, if ants cut their sleep by 50 percent during the second half of their natural life spans.

"I could get more done," I said during each yearly exam, "if only I wasn't so restless and distracted, so quick to paranoia when I'm awake until two A.M., when I'm alert four hours later."

"Your choice," she reminded me, "side effects or frontal assault."

I almost always know, as soon as I lie down to sleep, when I'll have trouble breathing. Premonition. Sixth sense. The lungs deliver the first, faint twinge of cramping.

Eight years ago, my doctor prescribed Singulair, which isn't caffeine-based. Now I drink coffee instead of avoiding it. I take one pill each morning and forget about asthma until a problem arises. "Use the inhaler as a preventative," she advises. She smiles the way counselors grin at clients who, they trust, will ignore advice. Like my father, I prefer self-reliance; I prefer wheezing until I can't control it with will.

I occasionally succeed, things calming inside me. I do better, at least, than the Washington Generals, those hapless straight men for the Harlem Globetrotters; but the sequence of collapse is as familiar as the routines of confetti-filled water buckets and deflated basketballs.

Not only do the bronchial tubes spasm during an asthma attack, but they're further constricted by the muscles around the airways contracting. I've read the articles and seen the diagrams, and I can vouch for another characteristic: once the lungs are damaged, they're more susceptible; one attack makes the next more likely. I don't need a clinical study to tell me that my inhaler is deceiving—the relief it supplies makes you feel better temporarily, and it's more likely you allow yourself to be exposed to things that ultimately make you worse.

It's not surprising to learn that the number of asthma cases, during the twenty-three years I've suffered, has nearly doubled in the United States. What's surprising, and unnerving, is that during those same years, despite better treatment and a choice of effective drugs, the death rate for asthma has risen 8 percent per year.

So we keep our eyes open for early warnings: A man named Bernard Jensen

developed a theory of diagnosis called iridology. He claimed flaws in the irises showed signs of the location of illnesses. It only takes a mirror and Jensen's strangely detailed chart.

At one-fifteen, in the left iris, the slight marring of the nearsightedness I share with billions. At three o'clock, in the right iris, the hairline crack of asthma, the disability which gets so little respect it's in the afternoon of our eyes, not the evening where the kidneys and heart and liver are revealing themselves—everything in Jensen's theory a sort of doomsday clock for the nuclear midnight we're moving toward, setting it forward, back, forward, back, fine-tuning the shadows that gather in our lungs.

In one of my favorite films, *The Invasion of the Body Snatchers*, circadian rhythms are important. When you fall asleep at night, when you're at your weakest, you're vulnerable enough to be replaced by the aliens, your memories and personality sucked out until, no longer human, you disintegrate into dust. In both versions of the film, special effects notwithstanding, you're reborn, but you're exactly like everybody else except for physical features. The world, within a short time, becomes exactly like the vision of heaven I was promised while I was growing up. All of us angels would equally share an enthusiasm for eternally singing God's praises; none of us would regret carrying our earthly weaknesses and deformities forward into infinity.

When I was thirteen and home from my first semiformal dance, I told my parents the girl I'd spent four hours with had used an inhaler twice. "She's allergic to dust," I said.

"You can't be allergic to dust," my father said. "It's everywhere."

My mother agreed with that deduction, and I was left considering Sharon Richardson's inability to deal with the natural world. She'd looked frail with that nozzle pressed between her lips, her midwinter pallor emphasized by the pastels of her gown.

I thought she had the beauty Edgar Allan Poe described in the poems we recited in Mr. Sutton's English class. I believed she'd grow out of it, because asthma, my father went on, was for children and sissies.

Certainly, Sharon Richardson grew out of her interest in me, but during a recent Christmas vacation, instead of attending a dinner dance or even another

eggnog party, I spent an hour cleaning the basement spare room, because I wanted to throw darts and the path to the board had been clogged with trash since my son had graduated and stored boxes of clothes and books for that day when he lived in more than a half-apartment.

I moved everything to the perimeter. I stacked boxes we'd set aside when we moved into this house years earlier. Just before I was ready to pull the darts from where they'd been stuck in rotation for more than a year, I started to wheeze.

I threw three sets of six, getting in rhythm, and then I walked upstairs, pausing three times, to search for my inhaler.

I went outside to try the remedy of cool, moist air. I said NO to panic and followed the sequences of blinking lights across my neighbor's gutter—red, white, red, white—as if they simulated regular breath.

I considered driving myself to the hospital; I considered calling for help. And then I walked slowly back and forth along our street of fourteen houses, sure I could recover as long as I wasn't in one of them by myself.

Some charms work. I crossed and recrossed the street, and thirty minutes later I felt the boots step off my chest and air silently slip into my lungs.

"A woman I work with died last summer," my wife said when I told her about the attack. "She had asthma and was cleaning her attic. They thought she had a heart attack, but she'd strangled from the dust."

In the retelling, I kept my symptoms small. I wasn't the sissy of an hour's work, but I thought of that woman wheezing and saying to herself, most likely, "Another five minutes and I'll have this done." She must have been surprised, finally, like fire victims who expect the horror of flames and succumb to the banality of smoke.

"I didn't want to tell you when it happened," my wife said at last. "I didn't want to give you something else to worry about."

The record for the longest time spent in an iron lung is thirty-seven years and fifty-eight days, set by Mrs. Laurel Nisbet, whose endurance ended with her death.

In January 1951, my aunt held my hand and guided me through a ward where iron lungs were working to keep a dozen of Pittsburgh's polio victims, all of them children, alive. Nurses paused to murmur near each disembodied head, the room a theater of whispers. My aunt, their supervisor, said nothing while

I breathed in and out through my sterile mask and thought of steam irons at the dry cleaners, our family's best clothes tagged and returned like pigeons; the smell of trichloroethylene, how it dizzied, how it followed us for a half block of storefronts.

I was five years old, and my aunt was showing me problems more serious than my upcoming tonsillectomy. She wanted me to appreciate my relative good health and trust the doctor who would operate in a few hours, but she was the same woman who told me God expected an account for every hair on our heads—that as a result, she stored cut hair and clipped nails to ensure compliance. She was going to ask my mother if she wanted to have my tonsils pickled and sent home with me, and I held my breath for as long as I could and watched those children who'd lost the means to deal with air have their lungs emptied and filled nine times before I gasped.

In Fiji, once, people were told that if they suffered from bronchitis or asthma, they were running the risk of losing their souls. There were magicians available who cast spells and did conjurings, some of their incantations effective at capturing the sick person's "butterfly" (the Fiji associative name for wavering breath) and securing it firmly to the body.

"I'm not going to make it this time," said Richard Green, the New York superintendent of schools, the night he died from an asthma attack a few days before he was supposed to receive an honorary degree during commencement at the university where I teach.

The degree that was to be presented to Richard Green was Doctor of Laws, Honoris Causa. The biographical sketch was read, and then we listened, before the graduating students filed forward, to why he wasn't there. Behind the stage, the sun seemed fixed at eye level. The president was a silhouette, and we extended our applause as if it might conjure a curtain call. Suddenly, the failed encore entered my chest, some shallow empathy for the dead. I whistled the Richard Green chorus; the gowns of the graduates turned into a flock of enormous black wings, all of them fluttering the beginnings of a symbolic howl.

"Get back, give him air," somebody always shouts on these occasions, but when asthma returns, I check back for sins—some, at least—enough to stifle breathing. In each lung cell is my mother, telling me about vengeance and God's awful fire. I wheeze under stress. Someone is paying me back and singing the

Richard Green song; someone is paying me back when my daughter wheezes in the wind and the lost Pittsburgh mills from my old neighborhood shoot soot through my lungs from their foreign steel graves. The Old Testament lives here. It's lasted nearly twenty-three banked-furnace years. Each airless dream of death that wakes me to inhaler and regret says real death is for others who wake up drowning in their sea-dark rooms.

My father's judgments have endured. Until now, I've been so readily restored, I find it difficult to mention I have asthma to others. Believing he's being generous, one friend I've told throws his cat outside when I arrive. I tell him to leave it out there for six months if he wants to be helpful, and he takes my advice as a joke.

I leave meetings early because of poor ventilation in the sealed rooms my college has constructed to support central heating and air conditioning. Dust, mold, recirculated air—if someone lit a cigarette in those rooms, he would be chucked out by the outraged. If any of those rooms hinted at stale smoke, no one would enter.

My colleagues, who placidly inhale great doses of carbon dioxide, believe the timing of my exits is directly related to the dullness of the meetings, but they don't follow me outside and listen to my whistling. They equate good air with comfortable temperature. They gather in fast-food restaurants at lunch, disdaining the hamburgers and French fries for the pleasures of the salad bars, dismissing the severe reactions and occasional deaths that sulfites—still used on occasion, despite the law, to preserve the seven praised choices of green leaves—produce. I could declare "guilty" or "not guilty" before I finish a meal, but it's more practical and much safer to give up salad bars altogether.

And red wine. And whiskey. And especially champagne and Asti Spumante and nearly everything else in the liquor store. I asked the manager of our local store, once, to show me which products did not contain sulfites. Our tour was quickly over. I'd be dead, most likely, from strangling long before my liver gave out.

Compliance with the law: Often, if you pick up the bottles of carbonated alcohol drinks, you'll find the warnings printed underneath the base. Normally, that means you'll discover the news "contains sulfites" when you invert the bottle to coax those final few drops into the crystal goblet you've pulled from the cabinet to enhance your champagne celebration. You may or may not get them swallowed before the bronchial spasms set in.

In some cultures, the breath of the dying was believed to reenter the living. The Algonquins, as a result, buried their dead children in places where tribespeople passed by frequently. So those souls might reenter future mothers.

One night my wife roused me by listening for the breath of a car engine, a closing door, or our daughter's voice three hours after the deadline for her arrival. Lost in anxiety, my wife wanted the phone to settle this. "I want to know, one way or the other," she said, meaning the result of the nightly danger of speed and carelessness and alcohol, what compounds Shannon's food allergies, the reactions in her throat and lungs.

I opened my eyes to search the double darkness of our drape-drawn room, both of us listening as if we once again expected to hear the demands of our daughter's thin breathing the first night we couldn't lift her to relief. "Hold her to the phone," the doctor had said, and we waited one whistle, then two, and pressed our ears to the receiver where Shannon, less than a year old, had wheezed the water going to vapor insistence up the narrowing pipes of her throat.

"Bring her at once," we heard, the tone of his phrase arriving through our nerves. We learned the force of sirens, each whistle pitched impossibly higher than the last until she reached the silent song of impending absence, its coda of *nevermore*, and I laid fingertips to her throat to detect the shrieks heard only by the dogs of terror.

I heard nothing but the vowels of our own anxious breathing, something that sounded as if my wife and I were reconstructing the first shared-terror evening of language. A minute more and we were with the doctor who saved her that evening and taught us caution and prevention, what worked until she became old enough to frighten us with the silence of late-night absence.

In every one of my childhood comic books, the drop-from-heights victims always did more than merely fall. They needed to have an expression of absolute terror as their arms spread wide in panic, and they were always looking up at whoever was still standing at the edge of a cliff or the roof of a skyscraper or the doorway of a helicopter in flight.

They plummeted. For two or three panels, they screamed aieeeeee! or yaaaahhhh! as they vanished into a speck I knew was blood and guts and shattered bones.

Those falls were more frightening to me than being devoured by army ants or being attacked by aliens who always had more than two arms in various shades of green or blue. I didn't cower under my blanket when creaking sounds slipped into a friend's house during a sleepover, but I began to feel unsteady when I had to climb into the tree house his father had constructed less than ten feet up among the limbs of an oak tree. I didn't worry about being alone outside after dark, but I hugged the inside wall as I climbed

Plummeting

to the second deck of Forbes Field to watch the Pirates.

My father produces a photograph of me in his arms overlooking the abyss below Niagara Falls when I was four. "See?" he says. "You weren't the way you are when you were small." I look happy with my legs tucked around his waist, high enough off the ground that if he opened his arms, I would have fallen into the spray. I remember enough about my childhood to know that by the time I was five, I was terrified of heights. Nothing terrible happened in those twelve months. As far as I can tell, I simply arrived at the age of reason.

At the Spang-Chalfant playground, built by the steel company that employed most of the residents of Etna, there were two sizes of slides. The baby slide had six steps and a high nest of metal at the top so even a three year-old could manage to sit down without tumbling into space. The "real" slide had a dozen steps, making it nearly twice as high, but the problem for me was the platform at the top—there was nothing on the sides but a low railing. Taking

on that slide meant you were graduating from security to risk, and though there were no confirmed falls from that platform, I froze at the top the summer before first grade, both hands on the end of the staircase railing, unable to make myself let go and throw one leg, and then the other, onto the ledge.

I knelt. I held onto the rims of the slide, and the boy behind me, believing I was a daredevil, shouted "Whoa!" just as I half rolled to the side and let go, sliding like a fetus until my feet caught the sides and I barely moved. The boy who'd been impressed enough to shout kicked me from behind as I neared the bottom. I had to crawl off and walk away as if I had some inexplicable injury.

The swings were no better. I'd reach somewhere around a forty-five degree angle, and I'd begin to lose my nerve. I'd learned to "pump" a swing just like my friends, but as they soared to near horizontal, I'd act disinterested, like swings were for babies, something I'd already grown out of because I'd just celebrated my sixth birthday.

Even seesaws were problematic. The sudden rise, the sense of flopping forward and up. I sought out the checker tables. I played dodge ball, where the farthest my feet got off the ground was when I jumped over a bouncing, hollow rubber ball.

It got worse. In a played-out strip mine that was left over from the soft coal decades that had ended before I was born, my father led me and a dozen other eleven- and twelve-year-olds up a trail that peaked along a narrow crest of whatever had been left behind as worthless. Suddenly, each step in the dark felt so uncertain, I allowed all the other Boy Scouts to pass me and finally knelt to grip the ground with my hands, convinced I was about to tumble into the acid pool below.

Peer pressure sometimes fails. Every boy who watched me whimper said nothing, even when my humiliated father had to lead me down like a suicide with second thoughts, taking the lengthy low route through the scrub trees until we met the troop where the scars ended. Afterwards, none of the boys made fun of me, not even the ones who taunted anyone who dropped a football pass or failed a swimming test, but once, when we were driving past that old strip mine, my father observed, "There's where you acted like a baby."

It's one of many such panics I bring to hearing about how even the veterans of height feel a hand on their backs during night storms. James Roberts, a railroad foreman, confessed he dropped down to grasp both rails and crawl, that he wished himself a snake when a train vanished crossing the single track of the

two-mile-long Tay Bridge in 1879, nothing to be done along its ninety-foot drop to water except go forward, tie by tie, until train or disaster could be verified.

A third of a mile out, he reached where the bridge had wrenched apart and split. He stopped one handhold from the brink and heard his body ask for speed. I felt, he said, I'd lost the brakes of common sense, that I'd roll forward like a train, my hands and knees crawling onto the unthinkable air. And because backwards was impossible, he pressed himself so tightly to those tracks, he thought he would tattoo his chest with their pattern when his legs, while turning, were over air.

For a moment, he said, I thought I might sail—what any of us believe, recalling thick branches carried off by wind, siding and shingles stripped from houses, our panic when, like always, we hear from survivors who remind us of what is possible.

Because of height, certain places long-ago visited reappear with clarity. Cooper's Rock, for instance, an enormous stone overhang in West Virginia. You can stare down on the Cheat River from its edge, protected from disaster by a rustic wooden fence designed to look natural, meaning it appears to have been homemade by pioneers long dead.

I'm in none of the photos taken on our family trips there when I was eight or nine or ten. All of the photos include the view. Nobody thought of taking a picture of me, because I stood a comfortable ten feet from the edge, enough space so that if I flopped forward I could land on the surface of that rock instead of the tops of trees hundreds of feet below.

And our return trip to Niagara Falls when I was twelve? I kept my distance from the railing as if a junior-high dance chaperone was preventing me from brushing against the breasts of any girl willing to dance with me.

And that fall, a year after the strip-mine fiasco, I entered junior high school, where we had gym class twice a week with Mr. Seibert, who thought he'd toughen us by having us climb thick ropes that hung from hooks bolted into the ceiling of the gym. They were knotted on the bottom, a place for your feet as you gripped the rope and swung in small arcs getting ready to ascend. By the time we began eighth grade, Mr. Seibert expected success. He held a stopwatch and clicked each time a boy began to pull himself up, using both his arms and legs in the way Mr. Seibert had taught us.

Halfway up, fear of falling overcame my fear of failure. Miserably, I hung onto the rope, gripping it so tightly the strength was rapidly draining from my skinny

thirteen-year-old arms. Mr. Seibert kept calling out the seconds by fives—twenty, twenty-five, thirty, he said—thirty-five, forty. No one, I imagined, had ever spent so much time on the ropes. And then I plummeted down, feeling the heat of the warned-against rope burns searing my hands just before my feet slammed against the thin mat that was about as protective as a cheap living room carpet.

Mr. Seibert said, "I warned you about sliding down." He held my palms up for inspection and told me to take my wounded hands to the nurse's office for treatment. "But first," he said, "take a shower," even though the only exercise I'd had for the past half hour was hanging onto the rope with my clenched hands and knotted feet at basketball-rim height.

I ran hot water over my reddened, shredded palms until I had to suck in a gulp of air. I skipped the shower and dressed as fast as I could so I'd be gone before my classmates came down. Gym bag tucked under my arm, I ran water from one shower head to be sure, if Mr. Seibert checked, that he would see the floor was wet.

Shortly thereafter, the Wallendas, the most famous high-wire act in the world, fell during their pyramid stunt. I stared at the pictures in *Life* magazine, the first of which showed the intact pyramid—four men on the wire, two on their shoulders, a girl on the chair at the top. The camera had caught the one man who wobbled and then, still frame by blurry still frame, his fall and that of two others from the bottom row, accompanied by balance poles and the chair the girl had been sitting on. The caption explained which two men had died and which one was paralyzed.

"Ich kann nicht mehr halten!" the wobbling man had shouted, the German so close to English that translation wasn't necessary for the last words he'd spoken before plummeting.

You grow up and put such things behind you, I thought, but during my freshman year in college, for eight weeks, with fifteen other guys, I suffered the indignities of pledging—running errands, doing push-ups on command, learning the Greek alphabet, and all the rituals that seemed like so much medieval play-acting. Hell week finally arrived, worse than what I expected. Thirty minutes of sleep per night, psychological intimidation, work details, and the force-feeding of concoctions designed to make all of us vomit.

The best part was running for two miles at five-thirty A.M. That morning jog meant we were finished for another night, and because I was a basketball

and tennis player for the school, I was in better shape than most of my pledge brothers. By Thursday morning, more than halfway through the week, using the playground equipment in the park where we ran seemed like an easy alternative to running an extra mile.

Seesaws. Swings. Two slides. And the monkey bars where each of us was told to climb and sing out stupid things to entertain the frat brothers, who seemed to enjoy our humiliation more than our fatigue. There were only four crossbars on that circular contraption in Packard Park, but I turned anxious with my feet on the second bar, and I panicked on the third, gripping the top bar with both hands as if I was fifty rather than five feet off the ground.

The fourth bar, another two feet higher, was impossible, even though there was a thin railing above it so children could hold on if they climbed to the top. I froze, unable to do anything but lean into the cold metal of an early May morning while shouts of ridicule began—what a pussy I was, just get up there and sing and get off. When a minute of that didn't budge me, pledges and brothers alike turned quiet. I could tell from the silence that my behavior was new and unexpected and maybe a little scary. I looked down between the bars at what appeared to be a precipitous drop. The earth packed by thousands of small feet looked hard and unforgiving.

My arms quivered. My knuckles were white. Somebody, at last, began to coax me down. "Just step back and let your feet come down to the bar," I heard, and when I didn't move, a sort of chant began. "Just step down. Just step down," as if all it took to reach the ground was the fundamental movement of a preschool child.

It took me three minutes, a long time to be glued to a playground toy. It took two pledge brothers standing on either side of me, guaranteeing I couldn't fall. And then I was down, completing the backpedaling through the air and rejoining my pledge brothers, all of whom kept their thoughts to themselves as we started to run back to cold showers, breakfast, and classes.

So something like stairs doesn't help. Sure, the ones that rise and fall routinely between floors of houses and high-rises aren't a problem. But if they are open, if I can see down through them to the air beneath my feet, anything more than a short flight of stairs becomes a challenge.

When I was twenty-five years old, the group of tourists I was with, at the end of our trip through Mammoth Cave, was told to climb out of the darkness on a damp set of open stairs that towered toward the surface. I trudged upward,

my wife behind me, while other people in our group chattered and laughed as if we were still safely on the floor of the cavern. With each step, I slowed until a gap opened up in front of me. My wife kept saying, "Don't stop" every time I paused. And though I never stopped for more than a few seconds at a time, there was a one-minute break between me and the man in front of me by the time we reached the dizzying platform at the top, where people stared anxiously at me, thinking, I was sure, that I was the youngest heart patient they'd ever seen.

Curious in the way that picking at a scab is irresistible, I've discovered that thirty feet is the cutoff point for the probability of a falling fatality. That is, above thirty feet and the chances are you will die when you hit the ground; below it, the odds for living are on your side. That's not very far, and more than enough to confirm the good sense of my fear. As soon as you get to the third story of a building, you're at the mercy of luck if you plummet.

Worse, I've studied up on terminal velocity. A person weighing 170 pounds takes about fourteen seconds to reach a maximum speed of about 120 miles per hour. After about 2,000 feet, I'd be falling as fast as I ever would. I weigh 210 pounds. The last time I was on an airplane, I flew at 31,000 feet. According to what I've learned, I'd fall a little faster than the 170-pound example, who would take about a minute to plummet the first 10,000 feet. Figure me for a little less than three minutes in the air if, as I often imagine, I somehow fell out of the plane at cruising altitude.

I was in graduate school when a professor copied a recent poem by James Dickey and passed it around the room. "Give this a read," he said, meaning it to be a supplement to our workload in the study of Southern literature. The poem was "Falling," which is based on a news item about a stewardess who, over Kansas, was sucked out of a plane's suddenly sprung-open emergency exit and fell tens of thousands of feet.

Dickey gives that stewardess several pages of falling before she slams into a farmer's field. I read the poem twice, fascinated and horrified. "Falling living beginning to be something / That no one has ever been and lived through screaming without enough air."

Dickey makes that woman plummet into extended metaphor: "She is hung high up in the overwhelming middle of things"; but that poem has made me listen for literal leaks in airplane cabins. It has made me wary of emergency

doors—the most likely place, I've decided, for the plane to open into nothing but "the overwhelming middle of things."

Being in a car doesn't mitigate fear. I use the passing lane on bridges, even though I'm driving slower than anyone in the lane closest to the edge. A few years ago, I drove so slowly up to Los Alamos that the line behind me was the kind reserved for following fully loaded cement trucks up miles-long steep grades. "Don't stop," my wife kept saying, calling up the memory of Mammoth Cave.

On an earlier trip, a colleague drove me to the summit of Pike's Peak, and when we passed the tree line, nothing between us and disaster but a narrow dirt shoulder, I leaned into the middle of the car as if I could influence our stability.

I leaned even harder when a friend drove me in his jeep up an unpaved series of switchbacks above Telluride. I could see the road becoming so narrow, there were stretches where two cars couldn't pass. Frightening enough to back up on such a road to give way, but the real terror came when there was barely enough room for a car coming down to squeeze past as we drifted to the absolute edge. Of course I looked out the side window and saw no trace of land for over a hundred feet.

I told myself he drove his small children up that road several times a year, a sign he saw the risk as minimal. I told myself we couldn't possibly be in as much danger as I imagined. Finally, as we neared the top, the drop hundreds of feet by now, my friend said, "You're not alone"—small comfort to know there had been previous terrified passengers while our tires turned inches from disaster. That Telluride side trip up the face of the mountain was the first vacation anecdote I told to my father when we next visited him.

"Who did you get that from?" he said. "Nobody acted like a scaredy-cat when you were growing up."

With an open parachute, even from thousands of feet, you land at about fourteen miles per hour. The longest fall survived without a parachute is 22,000 feet by I. M. Chisov, who landed, surely traveling at well over a hundred miles per hour, at the edge of a snow-covered ravine and rolled to the bottom. More remarkably, a man named Alan Magee dropped 20,000 feet and survived after he fell through the skylight of a train station. Compared to that, the 18,000-foot plummet of Nicholas Alkemade, who landed in trees, underbrush, and drifted snow, seems almost ordinary.

Two years ago, I took my four-year-old grandson to a nearby playground. He let me push him past a forty-five-degree angle on the swings. He happily climbed the steps of the baby slide, and while he was distracted, I climbed to the top of the regular slide and rediscovered the same fear I had as a six-year-old in Etna, Pennsylvania. I couldn't bring myself to take the extra step necessary to get seated at the top. How asinine, I thought, but I leaned forward with my elbows on the small deck and acted as if I'd climbed just to have a view. When my grandson turned his back to scamper toward the seesaws, I hurried down and followed like a grandfather who wanted to join him for a ride.

And what's the point of not being afraid fifty feet from the ground? So what if I can't be a window washer or a construction worker. So what if I miss the thrill of hot-air balloon riding. And so what if Mr. Seibert gave me a C in phys ed even though I was a three-sport junior-high athlete, lumping me with the fat boys who couldn't do a push-up and the uncoordinated who stopped the flights of footballs with their faces.

It's easy to slip into this flippant tone when I'm typing my fear onto the page. What better way to alleviate it than self-deprecation? But how false that tone becomes when height, inevitably, returns, whether on the upper deck of a stadium or along a railroad trestle spanning a gorge at a state park, a site I traveled to as first-hand research for a story.

The trestle overlooks Letchworth State Park in New York. It's a place to which families flock, and when I forced myself to take twenty steps out on it, counting each of the mincing strides as one way of measuring the validity of first-hand observation, I was still far from the center, inching sideways a few more feet until I was sure I would die if I fell. Two elementary-school-age children ran past me, their parents trailing behind, oblivious. I knew where the longest drop was by where they stopped and peered over the railing. I knew then that my character would be foolish in his fear, that he would see how little danger he was in, yet be frozen like someone panicking in chest-high water, convinced his next step would end in an unseen underwater chasm.

Here's a story for testing suspension of disbelief: In September 1999, Joan Murray's parachute failed to open after she jumped from a plane at over 14,000 feet. Her reserve opened briefly but then deflated. She landed in a mound of fire ants, whose stinging may have helped keep her heart beating. After two weeks in a coma, she awakened and returned, eventually, to skydiving.

One afternoon, I climbed a ladder to the roof of the first house I owned. I was twenty-seven years old, a father, and I'd taken on the job of painting every inch of wood, including the dormer windows that jutted out from the shingled roof.

It was a trial, of course. I kept my weight pressed toward the roof, making it awkward to paint, but I finished without a serious problem until I was unable to summon the sense to step back onto the ladder. It was just one story high where the ladder reached the gutter. There was nothing below me but the soft earth of flower beds. My wife, when she noticed, stood at the base of the ladder and called the simple directions. "You have to turn around," she said. "You can't get on facing away from the house."

I understood, but I couldn't act. It was a remake of my experience with the slide, the character a decade older. I absolutely wanted to face forward as I put my feet on the ladder, something that would propel me in a sweeping arc onto the lawn.

A half hour went by, and there was no sign I could do anything but sink deeper into panic. I felt unsteady on the roof, as if I would pitch over its edge if I did anything but lean into it like an Olympic luger.

Our neighbor stepped out of his house and crossed the lawn with a purpose that convinced me he'd been watching for longer than a few minutes. Without speaking, he climbed halfway up the ladder and began to coax, reassuring me he'd tell me when my feet were about to touch a rung. It took another two minutes, but I managed. "There's peculiar in all of us," he said. "This one belongs to you is all."

Five years later, Karl Wallenda, who had survived the pyramid fall in 1962, fell from a high wire strung between hotels in Puerto Rico. He died instantly. I have never mentioned my rooftop panic to my father.

Endings

For three weeks, each time I've called my father, no one has answered. I've allowed the phone to ring twenty times. I've counted because I want to be certain I can tell him how far I've gone to account for his near-deafness, his arthritis. How long I've waited in case he was outside trying to fumble his house key into the lock, nervous because the floodlight that illuminates the front porch and the driveway hasn't been replaced after months of being burnt out.

Altogether, I've called seven times, once each on every night of the week, staggering the attempts over the days from Thanksgiving to the middle of December. I can explain my system to him as well, that I haven't just dialed his number on three Monday evenings when he was playing dart ball in his church league. Or three Wednesday nights when he was watching television at my sister's house until the local newscast began. But with each succeeding call, I've understood I was counting the rings the way a boxer, standing in a neutral corner, might be singing along with the referee, impatient for ten.

My Father Told Me

I blame the joy of twenty on my father. For the first forty-two years of my life, either in person or on the phone, I talked with my mother. And when she died, there we were, my father and I, having to feel our way into dialogue.

My mother had managed all of the financial records, so I spent the first day I returned to help him working through the books while my father vacuumed carpets and dusted furniture. Three hours after we started, my father stopped in the spare room and asked me if I wanted lunch. "Sure," I said. "Whatever you have." He returned with an American Cheese sandwich and a cup of coffee, put them on the table, and left.

In the middle of the afternoon, he stopped by again and picked up the dishes. He paused for a moment, glancing around the room as if it had turned unfamiliar. "Well," he finally said, "we're getting along here, aren't we?"

My mother had died on New Year's Day, and I saw how Christmas had stalled at gifts opened but unpacked, how her medicine was

arranged by frequency: Crystodigin, Diaranese, Almodet (once daily); Cytomel (three times per day).

They had duties that supported her weak heart. I lifted the vial of Percocet (as needed, for severe pain, no refills), and I wondered at the gaps between the demands screamed by my mother's heart. Beside it was Nitrostat (as needed, for chest pain), those pills the ones that the foolish in movies always grope toward as they tumble one room away from their carelessly placed relief. The urgency of labels leveled to a kind of democracy, a haze of help from which nothing can emerge.

By then I'd learned my own medicine from the tablets I took, twice daily; the capsules I swallowed, as needed; and the vapor I breathed in the lapsed-lung darkness, lying back like Proust, whose life I'd learned for my job, whose asthma bedded him for years. He didn't take Theolair, Optimine, Ventolin. He insisted, finally, a huge black woman was chasing him.

So she caught him. So now my father strained to speak, trying, "Well, did you sleep good?" to unmuzzle the following morning, and I answered him, "Good enough," as if truth might trigger prescriptions, as if accidentally we might talk, as needed, swallowing to save our faulty selves, carefully speaking from the confluence of our altered blood.

My father had allowed my mother to die an old-fashioned, stay-at-home, natural death. No machinery. No hospital. No exotic drugs beyond the maintenance ones she'd taken for years. Most likely she could have lived another year; probably another two; maybe another three—all of those thousand days as an invalid he would have cared for if either one of them could have put up with even one day of her not being able to stand up or walk.

She'd managed, on the day she died, to finish the crossword puzzle in the *Pittsburgh Post-Gazette*. All the way to having the patience to look up "orison," a six-letter word for "prayer," and "alim," which turned out to be "a Turkish standard." Or maybe she simply knew that stumper from having worked ten thousand crosswords. No matter, I'd thought, when I found the folded *Post-Gazette* beside the couch on the day before the funeral. It was the kind of definition a lousy puzzle maker would resort to when he'd worked his way out of English words. What remained was the evidence that she'd solved it, that there was no chance she'd filled in the toughest six spaces by checking the solution in the next morning's paper.

On the last afternoon of her life, my mother wrote and mailed her weekly news to me. After the funeral, after traveling home, I received her two-page note from the neighbor who'd held our mail. That letter kept me in a chair for half an hour before I opened it. Her handwriting was as perfect as it had always been. There was a return address affixed in the envelope's top left corner as it's supposed to be, insurance against loss.

Every December, as the year runs down, I play my *Phil Spector Christmas Album* and reread the January issues of *Life* that I've collected. The year-in-review specials mix well with the Crystals singing "Santa Claus Is Coming to Town." The fads and the recent dead sparkle when Darlene Love is belting out "Winter Wonderland."

This year I start with the January 1984 issue, the one I purchased on Christmas Eve in Hollywood, Florida. I was wearing shorts and loading up on expensive delicatessen food to take back to the condominium my family was living in for the holidays. The Hitler Diaries. Wacky Wallwalkers. Boy George posing with his mother. I end up reading a page of quotations, stopping at one attributed to William Fears, telephone lineman of Mill Valley, CA: "There's nothing in space—Believe me, I'm positive of that. My father told me."

I think about Bill Fears, whether or not he'd followed the space probe Voyager to Neptune, the trip featured in the January 1990 issue. And I remember that I'd woken up on Christmas morning, 1983, to the worst Florida cold wave in fifty years. I'd driven my family down to the Keys, thinking it would be warmer and recalling my father's anger at our not coming to his house for Christmas. "There's nothing in Florida," he'd told me. "You'll see." My family spent the afternoon shivering in the bleak 50-degree sunlight of a Northeast March.

On my stereo, as I reminisce, Bob B. Soxx and the Blue Jeans finish "Here Comes Santa Claus," and they're replaced by the voice of Phil Spector himself, the Wall-of-Sound producer delivering his early-1960s, end-of-the-album soliloquy over a wash of "Silent Night." "It is so difficult at this time to say words that would express my feelings about the album to which you've just listened," Phil begins.

"Sure, Phil," one of my sons, visiting for the holidays, says from the kitchen. I look up from the pictures of Buster Crabbe and Arthur Godfrey, two people who died in 1983.

"Of course, the biggest thanks goes to you," Phil insists, and my son, standing in the doorway now, says, "Sure it does, Phil," as "Silent Night" swells louder. "What a cheesy record," he adds, though since it's over anyway, I'm not going to

argue with him. Neither of us says a word about where Phil Spector has arrived, accused of murder in California.

On the second day at my father's, I went into the basement to see what needed to be packed and kept, packed and given away, or packed and dumped at the end of the driveway for the trash collector. "You decide," my father said. "I won't argue."

I saved pictures, books, and souvenirs—anything somehow symbolic. I charity-boxed used clothes and the appliances that appeared to be most recently moved to the basement. And then, listening to my lungs for the first sign of wheezing, I hauled two dozen cartons of carpet remnants, wrapping-paper scraps, ribbon pieces, and a hundred thousand labels from products that had promoted some sort of refund offer.

Maybe five hundred General Mills cereal coupons. At least as many Betty Crocker box tops and Planters' Peanuts vacuum-jar seals. An old RCA color-television boxful of miscellaneous wrappers. A Sears washing-machine box crammed with sorted, rubber-banded coupons. I didn't check to see what my father might receive if he mailed all of them in or lugged bundles to each of the three nearest grocery stores. Whatever it was, he'd never miss it. There were expiration dates from the 1970s, thousands of *must redeem by*'s from the 1980s. I didn't want to tell my father to spend the rest of his life searching for "9's" among the decade digits.

"Just you wait," my mother would say, "you never know." There were two broken hot-water tanks and three nonfunctioning upright vacuum cleaners. She'd shelved four ancient toasters and six radios, stored three televisions tuned to clouds. As if that personal landfill would follow her soul, junk as faith, gathering like a Pharaoh, believing she'd sort it out later, when she had time, when there was an eternity of leisure to order and classify what filled her cellar.

In the first year after my mother died, my father called twice. Neither time was I home. He called after twelve, and my wife answered, thinking it was the police inviting her to the morgue to identify our son, who was less than a year into driving. Perhaps my father was living strange hours now. Maybe he believed the rates were lower after midnight. Each time he simply said, "Tell him his father called."

On the third day I stayed with my father, after breakfast, I went back to the basement, entering the root cellar, where there was a tub full of potatoes that had sprouted into what looked like a mass of thick-bodied, tentacled insects. On one shelf were cans of vegetables, fruit, and potted meats—some of the cans looking so ancient with rust, I imagined them being there when I was a child.

Above them were more than a hundred jars of home-canned vegetables and fruit. I wondered about how they were arranged, whether my father could tell which were recently prepared and which might be approaching some sort of unwritten expiration date, canned five years before or even ten. Something about the beets and the near-soup of tomatoes made me consider the possibility of botulism. Already my father had regressed to eating sandwiches and hot dogs as if there was nothing to meals except removing hunger. These things would be here years longer, sitting in the dark until he happened on them one day and opened one jar on a whim.

Or they might stay there forever untouched, like the thirty jars of apple butter my friend Paul Kress and I had discovered one winter afternoon in a long-abandoned house we were exploring.

It was as if the surviving members of that family hated their mother's specialty, taking beans and peaches, but leaving the apple butter behind. The boy who'd driven Paul Kress and me there was six years older, strong enough to throw those jars accurately through the upstairs windows while mine and Paul's lobbed against the side of the house ten feet below, making a satisfying splatter.

The older boy fired his next jar against the wall, shattering glass, spraying apple butter in a glorious, huge splat that began to ooze down the wooden slats. It was ten minutes work, that wreckage, followed by ten minutes of pitching hard-packed snowballs at windows until every one was broken.

And then, when we were back in the car, ready to leave, the tires spun in the softened snow, sinking. Within seconds we were halfway up the hubcaps with no chance of moving.

I was young enough to begin thinking God had seen to it that the car would get stuck, that judgment had been made and we'd been found wanting. My friend and I were nearly useless for pushing. I was ten, all skin and bone, and he was eleven, even skinnier, but at least he had some idea of how to drive a car, giving gas and letting out the clutch.

I pushed anyway. I slipped and slid beside the sixteen-year-old who'd taken

us there in the old rattletrap he'd bought with money saved from a summer job. I took splatters of slush because to do otherwise was to announce my worthlessness.

The broken windows leered at us. The hilarious stains of apple butter began to talk among themselves about the stupidity of vandalism. It took a set of chains dragged from the trunk and applied to the rear tires, wooden planks salvaged from the house, rocks jammed into the deep grooves in the slick, soft snow, but finally we were out before anyone stopped to help and noticed what we'd been doing.

That scene followed me the rest of the morning. My mother had spent days canning the hundreds of jars of peaches, pears, green beans, beets, and tomatoes that remained, the kitchen fogged by steam, the counter littered with stems and peels. She'd stood, evening after evening, to slice and chop. I thought of those jars being there years from now, the house falling to ruin and entered by boys from some other neighborhood who knew nothing about the people who'd lived here. I was turning so sentimental with guilt that I wanted to find someone to whom I could apologize.

After lunch, my father said, "I want to show you something."

"What?"

"In the garage."

There was no point in saying "What?" again. It was maybe twenty degrees outside, maybe thirty in the garage, and I buttoned up my coat while waiting for him to choose from the floor-to-ceiling junk that surrounded us.

It had been five years, at least, since he'd squeezed a car in there. And finally, when he'd given it up, the room had narrowed rapidly to the width of a lawn mower. I felt, for a moment, like somebody whose job it was to rescue earthquake victims, reach among twisted metal and broken concrete for quivering or lifeless hands.

I was watching my breath while he moved a barrel that for all I knew held a million Cheese-Puff labels. "Here," he said. "Look."

It was a safe. For sure, I hadn't been expecting a safe. "You need to know the combination so you can get in here some day." He had me stumped. I didn't know what my father could have been hoarding that needed a combination lock to protect it.

"OK," I agreed.

"Pay this some mind now."

"OK," I repeated with brilliance.

"Right four times to forty; left three times to thirty; right two times to twenty; left once to ten; right to zero and bingo."

I thought he was kidding. I thought he was making certain I wasn't daydreaming about cutting the lawn with one of the three hand mowers jammed against the back wall under a set of bedsprings.

"You got it?"

"No problem."

He gave the dial a spin. "Go ahead."

I decided to play it out, call his bluff. When I got back to zero, I tugged the door as if I believed in my father's infallibility, and the thing opened. "Good," he said. For a brief moment I saw a few small boxes stacked inside. He pushed the door shut with his foot and respun the dial. "Now you know."

Outside it was snowing so heavily I decided to stay another day. The forecaster promised the snow would end by mid-afternoon. A warm front was approaching. In January, that meant the temperature would approach forty degrees the following day. The Pennsylvania Turnpike would be cleared, and neither my father nor I would have to worry about my driving into impassable conditions.

A month later, when I returned, the snow that was falling when I arrived was nothing but an hour's cover. When we walked across my father's yard, the grass reappeared where our shoes pressed.

After dinner my father led me back outside. "There's my sky," he said, and not knowing what he expected, I answered, standing in his driveway, "It's turned clear, all right."

I thought my father was planning to tell me the ancient names for the stars or the tales they inspired about people who suffered and changed and ascended while somebody left behind handed their stories down to another generation. The two dippers and Orion were all I remembered, and I waited for him to show me where he believed my mother was, how one cluster of stars had reformed, at least for him, to suggest hope in the future.

The two of us stood with the night in our lungs. We breathed a sentence of silence until he said, "Venus and Jupiter," directed me low in the sky where there were so many lights I could nod, certain they were among them.

Phil Spector over with, I turn on the radio, an oldies station, and pick up *Life*, January 1989, the issue I bought one year to the day I returned home from my mother's funeral three days after her death on New Year's Day, 1988.

Pictures of Roy Orbison, John Houseman, Billy Carter, Louise Nevelson—

they'd died, for sure, after my mother—even Roy Orbison, who, as I remember, died just in time to make this issue.

Despite his failing memory for things that have happened or been said less than an hour before, my father astounds me with remembering more than the trivia of annual deaths. For instance, he can recite the thirty-one lines of my poem about my mother's death. The elegy is in calligraphy, framed, on his living room wall, a birthday gift from my sister, who says she's followed along as he speaks, checking for accuracy.

"That's not the way it happened," my mother would say if she read it for herself. The last time she visited, we watched the videotape I rented of *Gunga Din*, replaying the scene where Rudyard Kipling has a cameo part in the film based on his story. I told her that's Kipling himself writing near the end, that here he appears again alongside the colonel, who, lost for words, borrows the poem Kipling's character has been composing.

"They've changed it," she said. "They've added something." And I told her she was right, that the studio erased Kipling from the theater version, that the movie she's watched ten times on television shows only Kipling's ghost, the colonel oddly off-center to make room for the vague emptiness beside him.

"So it's not the real *Gunga Din*," she said, and I gave it up to rewinding.

On the radio, just after a commercial, the announcer says, "Hello, Solid Gold Saturday Night—Who's this?"

"This is Bill," the caller answers, sounding eerily like my father.

"Where you calling from, Bill?"

"Pittsburgh," the caller replies, and I'm sitting up, listening, because so far it's a match of voice, name, and city.

"That's triple-W, S, right?"

"Right," Bill from Pittsburgh says, "WWSW." The call letters sound as if they're being spoken by a man in his eighties, somebody who would never call a syndicated rock-and-roll show.

"And what can we play for you, Bill?"

"'The Hippy, Hippy Shake.'"

"I can't stand still . . ." The Swinging Bluejeans begin, and I imagine my father listening to the recording of his call, thinking somehow the odds were excellent that I was simultaneously tuned in hundreds of miles away. Wasn't this my music? Hadn't I been glued to the radio all of the time when I was in high school?

Though of course there are thousands of Bills in Pittsburgh, dozens of them who would sound like my father on the radio. And one of them loved "The Hippy, Hippy Shake." And that particular Bill was holding a beer and dancing by himself in his living room, shouting through the house to his wife, saying, "Listen to that, would you? Isn't it great?"

One evening, when I was eleven years old, my mother wrote down everything I said, smiling as my sentences, spoken faster and faster, sped into a stutter of stupid phrases I machine-gunned out to keep her from recording every word. Minutes later, those fast-talk fragments made me sound like an idiot when she read each one exactly back from her perfect shorthand.

She handed me her soft-bound notebook to examine. On the two pages she'd filled was nothing but curves and loops and squiggles. Those marks looked like something you'd write if you slept in a crib. It seemed to me that she'd doodled while somehow memorizing everything I'd said.

After that, frustrated, I opened the family Bible, the King James Version, and speed-read each verse of one of the longest psalms, sitting back as I finished, triumphant with pronunciation and endurance. A moment went by, and then I listened while she recited from those scribbles as if she were cued by the whispered voice of God.

The Piecework of Writing

I'm thinking of my mother's shorthand, what she learned and then never forgot, because the news, tonight, carries the story of a woman who can't stop writing. She lives an hour's drive from my house, according to the reporter who pauses to mention a list of history's cases, people who moved, like the normal, from words to sentences to paragraphs, and then, like almost no one else, to pages and pages and pages.

For privacy, the woman says, she built an addition to her house in which to write. This room is filled with notebooks. She keeps it locked.

The reporter, who's done his own homework, relates the story of William Harvey, the British physician who, because he found darkness stimulating, dug secret spaces under his house in which

to think—discovering, in spite or because of his eccentricities, the functions of the heart and the circulation of blood.

Often, in the bad light of those private caves, Harvey wrote compulsively. Not as much as the woman on the news, but he left evidence of his mania by not only spelling pig with three g's, but by tripling the last letters of *hearttt* and *blooddd* and hundreds of other words, developing a sort of shorthand for his own desire to nonstop write. I watch the reporter finish. I watch the woman looking impatient to return, I imagine, to her writing. And I think of Harvey holding his breath, placing his free hand to his chest, keeping his pen hand ready as he listens to his heart.

The woman on the news shuffles back a step, more and more anxious to get back to work on the serial book of her life, but she reaches behind her and then holds up a bound sheaf of pages to the camera. Months, she says, it's taken to work a week into the long story of the difficult act of perpetual art.

"Look here," she murmurs, opening the volume, and the reporter softly reads: "I began to write. I kept writing. The light changes. I write. I write. I write. I write," sounding out a pulse, the words swirling, then reswirling, like blood.

I understand. On average, I've filled seven-and-a-half spiral notebooks per year with cursive writing. For the past twenty-seven years, at least—so that's 202.5 notebooks × 120 sheets × 2 sides. Which equals 48,600 pages. At about 200 words per page, the total comes to almost ten million words I've recorded.

Of course, not every back of a page is filled, I would be quick to say, but my father would approve of my diligence, especially if I told him I write directly on the computer screen when I construct my newspaper columns and magazine articles, that all of my essays and stories and poems inevitably get longer in the drafts I lift from those notebooks, placing them on the hard drive, then saving those that seem worth it to disk—or these days, onto the miracle of a nail-clipper-sized 256MB Travel Drive.

It's fair to say I've doubled those ten million words through these means, that I'm at just about 100,000 pages. And then there are all those revisions (some saved, some blinked off forever from the hard drive), ranging from the occasional magic of a single one to the struggles of seven, eight, twelve, sixteen while nobody sauntered over to suggest I slow down on this work of the self. On the contrary, I have to pause and pursue the business of selling my words to others.

It's the piecework of writing. Certainly, I'm evaluated by my work rather

than the time I've put in. "What do you think you're proving?" my father would say every time he disapproved of my behavior. He meant that I was showing weakness or bad judgment. He meant that I needed to take a closer look at myself, the kind of look God might be giving me right about then.

Once, a man named Robert Shields recorded his life in a diary divided into five-minute intervals. He wrote for the piecework of words, so often and so long talking through his fingers, sleep was anxiety for the pages unwritten. He woke to the joy of "I rose and then reached for my pen." He worked the minutes into shape until twenty-four years had inched into eighty-one boxes full of five-minute diaries. When he brushed his teeth, he detailed it. While he shaved, he wrote. Everything he ate was recorded in the lines of the last few minutes.

Some mornings, Robert Shields made the resolution of conclusion: *Write*, he said to himself, *This is the last line*, and then he recorded the next secrets—breakfast, the shades of light in the kitchen, how many steps he took leaving and returning to the room where the diary offered itself like pornography. Until 11:20, settling into bed, pulling up blankets. Until 11:25, turning off the light, writing in the dark. Until 11:30, writing, still writing, still writing.

Recently, a woman at a reading I'd given at a university said, "You're so prolific."

"There's an urgency," I tried to explain. "I didn't write anything until I was nearly thirty."

"Nineteen books is a lot."

I want to say no, it isn't, that there are seven more books I've completed that remain unpublished—two novels, a book of essays, two collections of stories, two collections of poems. Those don't include the drawers full of published but discarded work, the boxes full of failed work, my own private museum to the piecework of writing. Keep those numbers a secret, I've learned, because prolific is a synonym for carelessness and lack of ambition.

My father, when I visit, insists on reciting the Gettysburg Address from memory. He has me read along to check his accuracy, and he gets every word right. A minute later, he doesn't remember any of the news I'd told him about my children ten minutes before he recited. "How are those kids of yours doing?" he says. "Tell me all about them."

By myself, late in the summer, I walk to the cemetery nearest my house, and for a moment, because I've traveled two miles into the country and I approach on foot, I look over my shoulder like an amateur vandal come to spray-paint the monuments.

The single-lane cemetery road winds up a small rise toward the beginning of a thick patch of oak and maple. Near the edge of the woods, I choose the grave with the brightest cut flowers, cross ten steps of perfectly mown grass, and pay attention to last week's date below the name of a woman I recognize. Her husband came here yesterday or the day before, I decide, and he must have looked at his dates 1915–200_, giving himself less than two more years to make good the accuracy of pre-need engraving.

I think of my life-span equivalent, a stone that ends with what still sounds like the impossible 203_. I think of how I would live with that sense of surety, and then I think of how I have been with my father when he stood, just outside of Pittsburgh, on the grass of the Lakewood Memorial Cemetery and said, "You'll always be able to find me here." He gestured and meant me to think of some nearby plot as mine, but for that morning, at least, I acted as if cemetery space was something middle-aged men like me had no need for.

Cemeteries

To discourage him from asking me directly, I kept walking and found whole families, like ours, together for over a hundred years, settled in from Europe and likely never moving again, never thinking of moving—not far, at least. Years ago my sister announced she was never leaving Pittsburgh, her house five miles from my father's, and asked when I was coming home just after she said she had purchased space near my father's still-unused plot, which so far leaves me out, kicking the earth hundreds of miles away, picking up the one stone I've seen in all of this grass and sailing it into the trees, where it rattles and falls into silence.

My father always enjoys the tours of Etna I take him on, driving to places I want him to identify or elaborate on. This one pauses at

his early childhood home, twice remodeled; a shoe repair shop, long closed; the shell of a failed butcher shop. I loop up to where his old school is on High Street. Unlike the other buildings he's shown me, from the outside it looks exactly the same as it did when I was a preschooler. Inside, I know, it's been converted to senior citizen apartments.

I keep driving up the hill, where the street slopes so steeply it makes me uneasy. Without asking a question, I turn into a small cemetery that is in poor repair—tombstones on precarious slants, the driveway cracked so badly we can't miss brushing against large clumps of last year's weeds. At least, at this time of year, the thistle and milkweed and small sumac are pressed down from months of snow, and I can have access to whatever tombstones I choose to approach and read.

"I'm not getting out," my father says, reminding me of his knees, the irregular, side-of-the-hill pitch of the land here.

"No problem."

"You can see everything from here all the way to Pittsburgh. It's a good place for a cemetery, but they let it go to pot."

I open the door and hesitate. All along, I'd been waiting for him to automatically give me directions, and now, with my hand propping open the door against the pull of gravity, he lapses into a silence that makes me swing my legs out and walk away uninformed, set on locating my grandfather's grave without asking for his help.

The first thing I find in the high, matted grass is a small plaque that has lifted far enough from the ground to snatch my foot. I barely catch myself, cursing, and I suddenly feel as if I will surely trip and tumble, unable to stop myself from rolling down this hill. I force myself not to look around to assess my father's watchful stare from the car.

Minutes later I see that one grave, incredibly, is new. It reads January, just two months ago. The plot beside it has a tombstone dated in the 1980s, and though I've examined less than half of the gravesites, I'm sure it's the second newest in the cemetery. These headstones remember the Horning sisters, Maude and Anna, the names of old women who attended, I recall, my father's church. Maude, the older one, is in the new grave; by two months, she made it to one hundred years old.

When I push on, there's no sign of my grandfather, dead in 1972, but the cemetery has the look of a place where people would be buried without markers,

or with something so impermanent it would deteriorate and disappear, leaving the site unmarked. My grandfather could be anywhere.

Back at the car, I slide in, but prop the door open with one foot to let my father know I'm not finished yet.

"What are we doing here?" he says. "What's to look at but a mess?"

"I wanted to see my grandfather's grave."

My father stares through the windshield as if a cortege were approaching. "It's miles away," he says. "Why did you think he was up here?"

I let the door swing shut and look at him. "I don't know. I just thought because it's so close to the old house, or you said he was here once, or something."

"You don't remember right."

"What cemetery is he in?"

"Oh, I don't know the name. Over across the river. He had people out that way."

With nothing to add, I mention Maude Horning, how her name sounds familiar, and he tells me she owned the only unused plot in the cemetery, that nobody kept track for years and they had to scrape off snow to search for the marker with her sister's name on it. "It was some weather that day," he says. "The hearse got stuck and they had to take her out and put her in the back of a pickup truck."

I imagine the hearse skidding up the steep slope. I imagine it slipping sideways and spinning its wheels, but I can't conjure a pickup truck in the funeral party. It strikes me that Maude Horning was so old and the weather so bad that the line of cars behind that hearse would have been short and without trucks. The funeral director would have had to flag down a passing driver.

In the cemetery in a neighboring town, a display of Christmas lights has gone up, and cars pay a toll to see Santas and elves, snowmen, angels, cartoon figures unfocused by the fog from a winter warmth as irrational as the priest in South Africa who, I read recently, is suing his surgeon for erasing his soul during three hours of heart surgery.

Belief, he said in the article, is like an ancient cave drawing that disappears when exposed to light, making as much sense as Disney among the headstones until my friend, listening to me repeat this analogy, tells me that priest must be referring to Abbé Henri Breuil, who, for sixty years, copied cave drawings and studied them, predicting the growth of art would be chronological, from the simple and crude to the complex—how man progresses, he assumed, toward God.

And what work it was, my friend says. Although some of those drawings could be traced on paper laid over them on cave walls, he found pigments so miraculously moist they came off on contact, forcing him to lie on his back, under the caves' ceilings, where he sketched those fragile renderings because photography wouldn't work in the weak light he could carry.

Soon after dusk, the cars will nose forward from the gate where they pay ten dollars, but now, at noon, I drive through for free. Who spent November draping these frames with colored lights? Maude Martz, whose headstone says she died last week—did she dream herself rising to take the tour, beginning with the six steps from her grave to the snowman couple?

I think of my father hobbling across Lakewood Memorial to lay his annual Christmas wreath on my mother's grave in a cemetery where he believes Christ is present. I imagine him trusting his soul to the light. What assurances do we need from the afterlife? My friend, riding with me through this cartoon cemetery, says his years-dead wife, buried here, explains to him how loneliness will rub off as easily as cave art. And then he says that science has dated those drawings differently than the abbé declared, the oldest most sophisticated, as if we required less from art after we built the miracle of faith.

My father, each time we visit the cemetery where my mother is buried, hits golf balls over her grave.

A dozen of them. The marred and the cut. The discolored. The ones fished from water hazards. He has a private set of range balls that he stores in a burlap sack he keeps in the trunk of his car, more than a hundred of them shifting with the motion of driving. I've seen him toss them into that sack the way I throw pennies in a jar, promising myself some day I'll arrange them into rolls of fifty.

He uses a pitching wedge, arranging those balls along the soft shoulder of the narrow cemetery road. He carries broken tees with him to minimize divots. He presses a dozen into the earth and picks up each one when he's finished. And though his knees are painful enough that now he uses a cane when he leaves the house, he has enough of a swing left to manage the fifty yards it takes to have those balls land in the woods that begin twenty steps from her gravesite, those balls at their peak or just beginning to descend when they arc over her headstone.

He says nothing while he swings, and I imagine him finding, though my mother never played even one hole of golf, some sort of comfort in the heights of those parabolas. She never, as far as I know, even accompanied him to one of

the courses he played on, but every time I visited and played a round with my father, she would ask, when we got back, "How did it go?"

My answer was always a short "Good" or "Not so good," but my father, ordinarily so reticent, would launch into an extended narrative that covered every sequence of solid shots either he or I had managed. When he finished, she would take the scorecard from him and file it with all of his others in chronological order.

And when, on occasion, he fails to loft one of those balls into the woods, he hobbles to wherever it lies and underhands that ball into the trees. He never strikes a ball twice, not even if he chunks one less than halfway to the grave. And we never stand at the gravesite until every ball is cleared. And though I've expected it, no one has ever approached us when I've been with him.

After that, I hand him the flowers we've brought and watch as he replaces the wilted ones from an earlier visit. He makes his own arrangements from the flowers in season in his yard. In December he weaves pine boughs into a wreath that lasts until March, when daffodils renew the cycle.

On average, I visit this cemetery with him twice a year; he visits alone, he's told me, about ten times a year. That's likely, then, about 150 golf balls a year.

My mother has been dead nineteen years, but he didn't begin this ritual until six years ago, so a good estimate is he's hit or thrown nearly 900 golf balls into those woods, driving home to silence.

So I know, without asking, there are people who must have given him ruined golf balls, that it's almost a certainty that the course he plays as regularly as his knees will allow has donated the worst of its range balls.

Or else he spent those first thirteen years, when his knees still worked, stalking the edges of golf courses until he'd accumulated more than a thousand balls—enough, he probably thought, to last him, because he was more than eighty years old when he began to loft those wedges.

He hardly ever plays now. This is likely the last year he will venture onto a course. So many fewer balls in that bag when I accompanied him this year, I think of how many are left now, whether or not he's bothering to gather replacements. If he visits this cemetery three more times, he'll run out of balls.

What I can't bring myself to do:

Criticize him for the disrespect those lofted balls might signify to others.

Help him track down the balls he increasingly leaves short.

Ask him if he'll gather a new supply before summer sets in, whether the dwindling number of balls in that sack are a kind of calendar. Whether each shot is like an X crossed over a day.

When my uncle, a son of The Prince, discovered I was writing about my grandfather, he sent me a long, handwritten letter that detailed "the good" in his father. "Unfortunately," he wrote, "your contact with Gottlob was in the later years of his life."

He listed the jobs The Prince had held, including foreman at the Steel Spring Company ("a position of responsibility"), saying nothing, like my other uncle, about having to do his later janitorial work for years. "He cut our hair," my uncle went on. "He soled our shoes and remodeled the house. He did all the carpentry, plumbing, electrical wiring, and cement work involved."

And then, among a longer list of positive qualities, my uncle arrived at "the turning point," the time when the Steel Spring Company moved to Ohio and wanted my grandfather to move there. "Mother Lang," he wrote, "refused to move, leaving him stuck with four brothers-in-law, a father-in-law, and his own five children in one house."

Looking Again: An Epilogue

"When he was drinking" is how every downbeat story begins in my uncle's letter. "When he was sober" is how the good times return.

A cautionary tale. His older brother, when I asked, repeated nearly every story, even using the same prefaces. My father, when I asked, shook his head. "I know what I saw," he said. "The drink makes a fool out of people." By then he'd seen his own brothers drink at family gatherings. By then he knew they had restrained themselves until their father had died because he so adamantly disapproved. He sat silent, holding his ginger ale, as he had at every family function. His expression was so judgmental that I'd drink the beer I was happy to accept in other rooms. Of all the relatives, aunts and uncles alike, only my father didn't change his public behavior after his father died.

My father has never seen me have more than three beers at one time. I know he would be appalled at the tens of thousands of beers I've swallowed in the past forty-five years, but in truth, according to most standards, I'm simply a social drinker.

But there's been work in coming at that name, a discipline about drinking that I follow: I don't bring hard liquor into the house, having long ago learned that nearly every bad alcohol-related episode was directly connected to it.

And some of the discipline comes from my own body: I have an allergy to sulfites. Red wine and champagne and its knockoffs send me into fits of wheezing.

Even more of my discipline comes from tastes: It's easy to be social with white wine because I'm indifferent to the professed pleasures of it, sipping my second glass and seldom pouring a third, because no matter how much it costs or how extraordinary it's claimed to be, it all, as my father would claim, "tastes the same."

That leaves beer and the empty-stomach joy of fast drinking toward the buzz that relaxes me into candor, which, in turn, blows off steam. My father would not want to see me on these occasions, but he might take comfort in their infrequency. Such drinking, for me, requires a partner whom I consider a real friend. Those are few, and they know who they are.

Still, my father's fear doesn't leave. I watch my sons when they drink. I evaluate their speed and numbers. I count their empty cans. In short, I judge—and their excess, when it occurs, slows my own drinking to a crawl.

And my own cautionary stories? I use them frequently. For instance, the night, twenty years old, I passed out in a friend's driveway and woke to find myself under a car, one of its rear tires beside my face, someone standing over me saying, "What the fuck are you doing there?"

He and the driver of that car had backed up over my prone body, and because it was foggy at five A.M., he'd opened the passenger door to see better and noticed me. The rear tires had missed me, but I wasn't exactly parallel to their direction. One of the front tires was about to do me irreparable harm. Forty-three years later, I've never again allowed myself that sort of foolishness. As the saying goes, I can put the bottle down.

And so I don't equate the stories about The Prince with alcoholism. The Prince may have, as my father puts it, simply "liked his drink." There are very few direct observers left alive; all of them are nondrinkers, hardly qualified to accurately evaluate.

My uncle, in that letter he sent, let me know, in no uncertain terms, that family business was, indeed, just that. The outside world doesn't need to know these

things, he said. He meant me to understand these stories not only were private, but also needed to be earned by having lived through them.

Fair enough. For the record, everyone agrees that The Prince kept things shipshape in his own house, while all of the other men who lived there showed no signs of fixing even the simplest of household problems. But no one denied, not even my uncle, that The Prince abused himself, and his family suffered from something like fallout.

It was about weakness. Excessive drinking wasn't a disease. Nobody "caught it." It was a weakness that required strength of character to correct. It was, in fact, a sin. A failure of discipline. A physical shortcoming like lust and greed and sloth. What followed was guilt. I knew that sequence of what passed for proof from first grade on, an expectation of perfection instilled so early and so often that every flaw and failure swarmed around my head like the clouds of gnats that rise from the river valley in which I live to ruin summer's late afternoons.

So now, at the end of writing this, I learn a handful of additional details:

When my mother married my father, her brother gave her away; there is no mention of my grandfather in the newspaper account of the wedding. My sister confirms that we weren't told that The Prince was our grandfather, that I haven't conjured this up from half-remembered childhood events.

No, it's more than what I thought. She tells me The Prince visited the upstairs rooms we lived in until I was seven. *He came to our apartment.* What did my mother call him? Dad? Pop? She couldn't have. She called him nothing at all, just opened the door and let him in and talked and accepted his gifts of vegetables, most often potatoes, from the farm where he lived and worked.

My sister and I said, "Hello" and went about the business of being small children. I had a set of what would be called action figures today. Cowboys and Indians and cavalry in various poses of shooting rifles and pistols and bows and arrows. I arranged them and chose favorites who were accurate and brave. I toppled others over on their sides, pronouncing them dead. My sister had dolls, all of which said "Ma-ma" when they were tipped. She had books she could read, and she was busy teaching me the words so that by the time I reached first grade there was nothing to do but read her third-grade books in order to avoid boredom.

He gave my sister and me money each time he visited. As much as twenty dollars each, according to my sister, since I don't remember any of that money.

Each week I had exactly one nickel to spend on candy, the extent of extravagance in my family. My mother saved it for us. She bought savings bonds.

And the crocheted circular throw rug my sister had in her bedroom through junior and senior high school? The Prince had constructed it from rags. The one I remember standing on in my bare feet to feel its ripples and grooves while I stared at dozens of different colors woven together because they were available.

One more item—there were times The Prince gave each of us a Golden Delicious apple. "His favorite," my sister tells me.

This year, when I drive my father to the cemetery to visit my mother's grave, there's no mention of hitting golf balls. He uses a cane, and even that doesn't seem adequate on the uneven ground.

I park where I always do and take his free hand, letting him lead while I balance a small water bottle and the daffodils he's cut in the crook of my other arm. It's a long time covering the distance down the slight grade, but when he stops, I can see that the marker doesn't bear my mother's name.

He studies the lettering, and I let his hand drop, giving him time. I drift to the right, doing what I can to examine nearby markers without announcing that I know he's confused.

He hobbles to the left, taking in the names one by one. I look back up at the car, gauging the distance and direction against my memory of infrequent visits. "Something's not right," he finally says, and I nod in order not to agree out loud.

"Oh hell," he says, using his strongest oath.

We search for another two minutes before he loops back toward me from farther down the hillside. "Here," he says then, pointing with the cane, and I relax, bringing him the flowers.

He gives me directions, starting with removing the pine boughs and tossing them among the nearby trees. There's an order to all this—pouring the water halfway up the vase, inserting the daffodil stems, spreading them until he says "yes." After that, he grips my hand, and we stand together for a minute.

Neither of us mention the search for the grave. Not then, and not on the drive to his house.

Later, my father tells me he's had one of his assisted-living caregivers haul the old picture of the *Titanic* sinking from the basement. He's dusted it off and offered it

to my sister, who's refused it. My guess is that the painting was popular once. I know someone whose parents own it as well. Disembodied faces look up from the water. It doesn't look anything like fine art, something an expert on *Antiques Roadshow* would appraise for thousands of dollars.

Before he can offer it to me, I tell him to put his coat on so I can show him something.

Years after I showed Greismere Street to my wife when I learned the cliffside would be blasted down to widen the highway, that the entire side of the street across from where my father's bakery stood would be leveled and reconstructed as additional lanes for traffic, I drive her and my father up into the old neighborhood because, after years of delays, the work has begun.

My father, eighty-eight now and so forgetful he has notes tacked up around his house to remind himself what to do each day, names the families who lived in each house on the street. He gazes up at the third floor, where he shared a bedroom in the attic with his three brothers. We work our way to where the street turns sharply to the right and steeply upward, and here is where the hillside has been blasted back to. Right up to the pavement. Always three or four feet to the left, that sheer drop to where Route 8 is being widened follows the curve of the one-lane street. Above his old house, the telephone pole where my cousin and I shot a basketball for hours still leans slightly over the broken asphalt. The reshaping of the cliff confirms my eleven-year-old guess—an air ball now could take one hop and plummet more than a hundred feet straight down to bring astonishment and damage to a passing driver.

The narrow street turns even thinner and steeper. My wife, from the back seat, begins to question my judgment. Snow flurries swirl around us. The steep down slope has picked up a thin glaze. I concentrate on not riding the brake as we slide down, turn right, miss every parked car that narrows the street even further, and get back to Kittanning Street, "the real road" back down to Etna.

We have to pull out—the turn I remember with anxiety because it's at the base of a curve on Kittanning, only a few feet from being totally blind. There's a mirror on the telephone pole across from us that wasn't there when we visited as I was growing up. I stare at the reflection longer than I need to, not trusting the image. Finally, my father says, "It's clear," and I take two breaths, then a third, to allow enough time to go by so that I'm not following his directions. I look again and pull out.

"In the old days, you had to be careful there," he says.

We drive up Dewey Street so he can show us the house where he lived as a

child. I try to imagine five children in what looks to be a four-room house, and the only arrangement is all of them sleeping together in one bedroom until necessity drove the family to Greismere Street, which must have seemed palatial with its five large rooms and an attic divided into two makeshift bedrooms.

"Red Dog lived there," he says, pointing to the house next door.

"Red Dog?" The name sounds like a pirate's.

"He was something. Always drunk," my father says. He doesn't elaborate.

We drive to where we lived in those upstairs rooms, and now things look so shabby, I wonder if my father notices. As soon as we turn, the side street is so pocked and rutted, it threatens to lurch us into the cars jammed bumper to bumper on both sides. We drive at continuous speed-bump pace, maybe ten miles per hour. When we turn at the end of Angle Alley, there is barely enough room to squeeze past untended, overgrown shrubbery and a decaying cement wall.

I feel the word "escape" surface. There are hundreds of worse neighborhoods, I tell myself, and yet the houses and the streets themselves could only be called "awful," as in "Who, by choice, would live here?"

We leave Etna again by Route 8, the weeks-old sheer cliff towering up to where we stood fifteen minutes ago. A half mile passes before my father says, without prompting, "There's what's left of the house where I was born."

I slow and look to my right, but there's nothing but vacant lots. He points, and I follow his finger to six concrete steps set into the hill that rises from the widened shoulder to the plateau of milkweed and sumac and wild berry tangled and brown from last summer. "Right there where the steps go."

The enormous machinery of road construction sits a hundred yards away. Before too long, most likely within days, those steps will be gone as well, but right now they nearly shimmer with presence. Another quarter mile and we turn up Middle Road toward his house. Every place he ever lived is within three miles of each other.

It reminds me that he walked to get where he wanted to be until he was thirty-one years old and bought a pickup truck—that until then, when I was nearly five, I walked everywhere as well.

"You two kids never asked for anything," he says, including my sister as if she's in the car. It's what he repeats about once each hour that I visit. His version of a compliment. If I told him that I still don't, that not asking for help has stuck all these years, he'd be pleased. "You made do with what you had," he adds, and I'm certain he's being accurate.

When I talk to my sister an hour later, she tells me our grandmother's house has just been sold, at a sheriff's sale, for five thousand dollars.

"Five thousand dollars?" I say. "That can't be right." It's been less than two years since my wife and I examined that house the day we visited the DOH. The figure is absurd. The price of one enormous, flat-screen television.

"It must have been neglected," she says.

Neglected sounds like a euphemism for "fallen to the ground." The lot the house stood on would be worth more than five thousand dollars.

Unless the buyer knew he'd be spending thousands of dollars to level the house and start over.

Unless the neighborhood had fallen apart as well.

I think of Greismere Street and Angle Alley, the third-world condition of their surfaces and the shabbiness of the houses that border them. I think of Butler Street obliterated by highway construction, the bakery carried in memory only by people more than fifty years old.

I think of the only businesses that remain open on Butler Street, the bars where men and women still sit inside until two A.M. sends them home, though none of them live on Butler Street anymore, though all of them have to head out in another direction.

And I think of the story my father has told me four times this day, the one about how my sister, put down for a nap when she was three, climbed out the window onto the porch roof.

My sister, because she was barely three at the time, doesn't remember being on that roof, but he tells the story exactly the same each time, the words so identical he might have memorized them the way he has the Gettysburg Address, or the words to that poem about my mother's death that hangs on his living room wall. A neighbor across the street noticed my sister on the roof, and because we didn't have a phone, she called a closer neighbor, who ran upstairs and told my mother, who woke my father.

"There she was," he says each time, "walking in the gutter. I told her to just stand there and wait for me to come get her, and she did."

I remember how high that porch roof was on the side above Angle Alley. A child falling there would likely die. "It's amazing it all worked out," I say each time he finishes, and he says, "A miracle," as if the word is an exclamation point.

And each time he begins that story again, I wonder if there is a tale about me that precedes my memory that he repeats to my sister. Is it a story about his boy in danger? Does he rescue me?

Acknowledgments

The Ass-End of Everything	*Shenandoah*
The Plagues	*Tampa Review*
Home Remedies	*The Cresset*
The Canals of Mars	*Shenandoah*
Look Both Ways	*International Quarterly*
The Theory of Dog Shit	*Sonora Review / Blue Mesa Review*
God of Our Fathers	*Under the Sun*
The Faces of Christ	*Southern Humanities Review / The Cresset*
Say It	*Pleiades*
The Technology of Paradise	*North Dakota Quarterly / The Cresset*
Clemente Stuff	*Pittsburgh News-Tribune*
The Handmade Court	*Ecotone*
In the Bakery	*Passages North / Central PA Magazine*
Union Grades	*Under the Sun*
Useful Things	*Central PA Magazine / The Cresset*
Going Inside	*Pennsylvania English / The Cresset*
Subsidence, Mine Fire, Golf	*Southern Humanities Review / The Cresset*
Night Vision	*Southern Humanities Review*
Labored Breathing	*Southern Humanities Review*
Plummeting	*Under the Sun*
My Father Told Me	*Lake Effect / The Cresset*
The Piecework of Writing	*Tampa Review*
Cemeteries	*Weber Studies / The Cresset*

Some of these essays were published individually in very different forms.

"The Canals of Mars" was reprinted in *The Pushcart Prize, XXV* and subsequently reprinted again in *The Pushcart Book of Essays: The Best Nonfiction from the First Twenty-Five Years of the Pushcart Prize.* The following essays were cited as Notable Essays of the Year in *Best American Essays:* "The Ass-End of Everything," "Night Vision," "Labored Breathing," "Subsidence, Mine Fire, Golf," "God of Our Fathers," and "The Handmade Court."

"My Father Told Me," in a markedly different version, appeared in *For Keepsies*, a collection of short stories published in 1994 by Coffee House Press.

"Cemeteries" was awarded the 2007 O. Marvin Lewis Prize for nonfiction.

the
canals
of
mars